"A Peculiar People"

"A Peculiar People"

Anti-Mormonism and the Making of
Religion in Nineteenth-Century America

J. SPENCER FLUHMAN

The University of North Carolina Press
Chapel Hill

Frontispiece: Eber D. Howe, *Mormonism Unvailed . . .* (1834), frontispiece (L. Tom Perry Special Collections, Harold B. Lee Library, Brigham Young University, Provo). This woodcut from Howe's anti-Mormon tome marks the first visual representation of Mormonism. It depicts a fanciful tale of the Book of Mormon's origins, allegedly related by the Joseph Smith family themselves. According to Howe, the Smiths told how the Mormon founder was kicked while running from Satan with the famed record. The image received new life when it was reprinted in Origen Bacheler's *Mormonism Exposed* (1838).

The paper in this book meets the guidelines for permanence and durability of the Committee on Production Guidelines for Book Longevity of the Council on Library Resources. The University of North Carolina Press has been a member of the Green Press Initiative since 2003.

Library of Congress Cataloging-in-Publication Data
Fluhman, J. Spencer.
A peculiar people : anti-Mormonism and the making of religion in
nineteenth-century America / J. Spencer Fluhman.
p. cm.
Includes bibliographical references (p.) and index.
ISBN 978-0-8078-3571-5 (cloth : alk. paper)
1. Church of Jesus Christ of Latter-Day Saints—Controversial literature. 2. Mormon Church—Controversial literature. 3. Church of Jesus Christ of Latter-Day Saints—History. 4. Mormon Church—History. 5. United States—Church history—19th century. I. Title.
BX8645.F58 2012
289.309′034—dc23
2012004089

Portions of this work have appeared earlier, in somewhat different form, as "An 'American Mahomet': Joseph Smith, Muhammad, and the Problem of Prophets in Antebellum America," *Journal of Mormon History* 34, no. 3 (Summer 2008): 23–45; "Anti-Mormonism and the Question of Religious Authenticity in Antebellum America," *Journal of Religion and Society* 7 (2005); and "The Joseph Smith Revelations and the Crisis of Early American Spirituality," in *The Doctrine and Covenants: Revelations in Context*, ed. Andrew H. Hedges and Alonzo L. Gaskill, with J. Spencer Fluhman, contributing ed., 66–89 (Provo and Salt Lake City: Religious Study Center, Brigham Young University and Deseret Book Company, 2008), and are reprinted here with permission.

16 15 14 13 12   5 4 3 2 1

For

John Dunne,

Ashley Marino,

Sarah Taylor,

& Mark Turco,

who have found a better way

CONTENTS

ILLUSTRATIONS

On Familiarity and Contempt

Preaching to a Mormon audience in 1855, Joseph Young marked Mormon identity with biblical language: "I am aware that we are a peculiar people."[1] Speaking in a similar venue decades later, church president Wilford Woodruff softened the reference. "The Latter-day Saints are somewhat peculiar from other religious denominations," he told a congregation in 1892.[2] Interviewed on CBS's *60 Minutes* in 1996, church president Gordon B. Hinckley further shrank the distance between Mormons and other Americans. "We're not a weird people," he told host Mike Wallace.[3] In another meeting with the press, Hinckley emphasized Mormon Christianness while preserving some distinction. "We are a part of the great community of Christians," he explained to the Religion Newswriters Association in 1997, "and yet we are a peculiar people. . . . We are somewhat peculiar in our doctrine."[4] Just as anti-Mormon constructions of Mormon peculiarity transformed across the years, Latter-day Saints (LDS) have positioned themselves in various ways over time. Certainly the two discursive processes have not developed independently. Though the Mormon-produced *Encyclopedia of Mormonism* maintains that the church has "largely ignored" anti-Mormonism through the years, it will become clear to readers of this volume that LDS identity has been crafted in dynamic tension with its critical appraisals.[5] This study offers an account of the early criticisms of Mormonism and links them with broader ideas about religion in America. It argues that Mormonism has been central in significant transitions in the nation's thinking about religion, both as a window on the history of religion's conceptualization and as a force in the shaping of that history. The book outlines the intellectual dilemmas faced by those who attempted to explain or categorize a controversial but vibrant new faith.

This prologue reminds readers that Mormon/non-Mormon engagement

"The Great Sin of the Century," *Daily Graphic*, 21 November 1883 (L. Tom Perry Special Collections, Harold B. Lee Library, Brigham Young University, Provo)

is still haunted by this history. Indeed, the classification of Mormonism continues to be divisive and confounding. Modern evangelicals bristle at recent Mormon claims to the label of Christianity. When Southern Baptist leader Richard Land offers his most "charitable" characterization, he places Mormons among the "Abrahamic" faiths. Debates over Mormonism's Christian credentials multiply in religious and scholarly presses.[6] Latter-day Saints routinely ignore Catholic and Protestant history and tend to define themselves as Christians apart from either branch, though some recent writers and leaders argue that the Protestant Reformation was a prerequisite for the restoration of true Christianity through Joseph Smith. Latter-day Saints resist most ecumenical movements; they are wary of being just another

Christian church. Conservative Protestants still use the word "cult," and Mormons position themselves somewhere between the "restored Christian church" and "the Kingdom of God on earth." Some scholars, especially given the church's growth and international presence, have characterized Mormonism as a fourth major division within Christianity.[7] While such a perspective respects contemporary Mormon self-identification, it remains to be seen if the characterization will win lasting appeal.[8] Scholarly opinion seems similarly conflicted as to Mormonism's rumored graduation to world religion status. Sociologist Rodney Stark described Mormonism as the first world religion since Islam, but some scholars have rejected his perspective.[9] British scholar Douglas Davies doubts its capacity to constitute a true world religion because mainstream Mormonism has hitherto failed to transcend its originating culture, to interact with world cultures creatively, or to exhibit substantive regional diversity.[10]

Mormonism remains entangled with American Protestantism, as Mormons have wrestled mightily with their Protestant beginnings. What haunts Mormon and non-Mormon engagement is the fact that constructions of similarity and difference are both true and false. The discursive gulf between Mormons and Protestants is unquestionably dynamic, going through periods or even moments of affinity and renunciation. Furthermore, both communities have consistently used the other as the awkward cousin against which normative identity can take shape. Modern Mormons routinely resist suggestions of any theological connection to Protestantism, sometimes preferring affinity with Judaism.[11] But historically speaking, Mormon/Protestant relations tell much of Mormonism's American story. The Latter-day Saints, like many religious groups, tend to view their beliefs and practices as timeless. Yet the historylessness of religious identity-making projects has had negative consequences in the Mormon/Protestant story. Past strife has left Mormons in particular with oddly paradoxical historical instincts. For people so connected to ancestors and their founding narrative, Mormons steadfastly resist historicizing their faith. The reasons for this bipolarity are complex, but part of the tension springs from the ways Latter-day Saints both drew on and repudiated their Protestant heritage. As a result, the Mormon/Protestant discursive dance has taken destructive and creative turns.

American Protestants have been important partners in the making of Mormonism. Early LDS theology and practice can seem either conventional or radically new, depending on one's angle of vision. A new scripture and a new prophet, yes, but scholars have located Joseph Smith in an age of seers and have described the Book of Mormon as conventionally Christian scripture.[12] Smith's revelations and sermons, which grew increasingly less conventional over time, often invoked Protestant positions to nudge Mormons into new understandings. In one of the more fascinating examples, the revelation now appearing in Mormon scripture as Doctrine and Covenants, section 10, strikes modern Mormons as odd until they grasp their early faith's Protestant context. The 1828 revelation cautioned Smith's followers against viewing the LDS movement as an utter break with the Christian past—a point that seems discordant given subsequent LDS rhetoric. The revelation promised: "If this generation harden not their hearts, I will establish my Church among them. now [*sic*] I do not say this to destroy my Church, but I say this to build up my Church."[13] What makes sense of the language, of course, is a spiritualized sense of "church" that would have been comprehensible to most 1830s Protestants. Protestants, especially the Puritan generations from which Joseph Smith descended, had called the two churches "visible" and "invisible." The "restored" Mormon church, as of this 1828 revelation, was to be less a clean-slate, ex nihilo creation than the refurbishing of an existing edifice. The revelation's language and the categories it invoked depended on Protestant understandings. And so it went with subsequent Mormon discourse. Renowned Methodist itinerant Peter Cartwright, for instance, recorded a memorable exchange with the Mormon prophet. "[Joseph Smith] believed that among all the Churches in the world the Methodist was the nearest right," Cartwright recalled. "But they had stopped short by not claiming the gift of tongues, of prophecy, and of miracles, and then quoted a batch of Scripture to prove his positions correct." Cartwright remembered Smith concluding: "We Latter-day Saints are Methodists, as far as they have gone, only we have advanced further."[14]

Mormons emerged from the 1840s with an enhanced sacramentalism, a robust theological materialism, polygamy, and emphasis on human perfection and divine anthropomorphism. These combined with intermittent anti-Mormon violence and rhetoric to produce an escalating sense of alienation from traditional Christianity. By midcentury, it was clear to Mormons that Mormonism was something other than Protestant. As the century wore on, Mormons and Protestants found less and less to agree on, especially when polygamy became the symbolic wedge for both sides. This trend forged strong Mormon communal solidarity but it also had downsides. For one, Mormons struggled to hold together their early revelations' emphasis on grace and redemption with the bold Nauvoo utterances relating to polygamy and divinization. As a telling indicator of this strain, the Book of Mormon figured less in the nineteenth century than one might expect.[15] With Mormons and Protestants rushing to defend or decry Mormon singularities, both sides settled into a protracted squabble over polygamy's biblical and legal status. By the late twentieth century, Latter-day Saints crafted a public presentation that veered sharply toward the Christocentric emphases of the 1830s, but so much attention had fixed on polygamy that an alarming number of Americans to this day have trouble articulating what makes a Mormon a Mormon beyond that single practice.

As a faculty member in Brigham Young University's religion department for a half-dozen years, I witnessed frontline identity formation of a fascinating sort. As one called upon to represent Mormon history and thought to visiting evangelical scholars and student groups, I enjoyed an exceptional view of anti-Mormonism's reverberations. Modern Mormons are offended by the suggestion that they are not Christians, but they are often unprepared to respond to the charge. They still hold to some of what one might call the Nauvoo theology, of course, but they are hard pressed to explain where much of it comes from. Young Latter-day Saints have a hazy sense that God the Father was once a man, but an overwhelming majority of my students admitted to never having read the famed "King Follett" address where Smith propounded the idea. They tell Protestant questioners that in the afterlife they will create their own worlds as gods, but they are unsure where that idea comes from. In terms of what modern Mormons actually read, the Nauvoo theology presents some glaring problems for interreligious communication. Young evangelicals intrigued (or disgusted) by Mormonism often have had more exposure to the nineteenth-century themes than their Mormon counterparts.

The reemphasis of Mormon Christianness forces Mormons and Protestants to redefine what separates their communities.[16] Though some traditionalists bemoan the more orthodox versions of Mormonism issuing from popular LDS writers, church president Ezra Taft Benson did more to awaken modern Mormons to grace than any popular writer ever could. In several 1980s sermons, Benson called Latter-day Saints back to emphasis on the Book of Mormon and, though such a move might seem like retrenchment or a reemphasis of Mormon peculiarity, the opposite has proved true.[17] Immersion in the Book of Mormon and revelations of the 1830s has brought Mormons unavoidably to Christocentric salvation. One dramatic effect of the complicated neo-orthodox turn in Mormonism is a decade-long dialogue between Mormon and evangelical scholars. Conservatives on both sides charge the LDS contingent with cozying up to evangelicals to avoid ridicule. Seen historically, however, such conversations can as easily be viewed as the natural consequence of a call to hear the Book of Mormon's soteriological bottom line. For detractors of the Mormon recovery of its Christocentric beginnings, be they Mormon or Protestant, the response is typically to trumpet the now deemphasized nineteenth-century theological themes (though mainstream Mormon apologists tend to avoid polygamy's historical and theological complications). It remains to be seen if Latter-day Saints can fuse those parts of their tradition that resonate with conventional Christianity and those that mark them as a distinctive faith community. So far, the Saints seem to be able to play but one note at a time. Mormons attempted to be "peculiar people," though, to do so, they had to overlook much of the content of the Book of Mormon, their early revelations, and their connections to traditional Christianity.[18] Mainstream Mormons sometimes now seem bent on not being weird, as Hinckley put it, but many of what their ancestors took to be Mormonism's most satisfying elements risk being tossed aside in the process.

Contemporary Mormons often ignore their faith's distinctive nineteenth-century elements in official talk but acknowledge them in popular discourse. Even so, the theological world of the 1840s is increasingly foreign to modern Mormons. Their historical consciousness has a gaping hole, beginning somewhere in the 1840s and stretching to somewhere in the 1970s. As with many faiths, the dissonance between memory and the denominational archives has spawned anti-intellectual tension and a selective, uneven master narrative. The modern story line picks up the supernaturalism of Joseph Smith's autobiography, the emergence of the Book of Mormon, the persecution of early Mormons, the heroism of the western trek, and late twentieth-century international growth. The blank spot in the middle of the chronology contains elements that fit awkwardly with Mormons' current emphasis on public relations. The ironies emerging from such a fraught relationship with the past would take a second volume to document. Two general examples are poignant enough. When Mormons leapt into the fray over California's 2008 gay marriage controversy, some activists spoke publicly as if their tradition had always sided with defenders of traditional monogamous civilization. Less conspicuous is the fact that many Mormons know a great deal about Joseph Smith's biography but nothing of his polygamy. So while portrayals of polygamy in popular culture annoy mainstream Mormons, there are more fundamental problems afoot for Mormon identity. Put simply, academic history's ongoing fascination with Mormon cultural deviance runs against the strategic forgetting apparent in the modern LDS collective memory.[19] Ordinary Mormons and professional historians alike gravitate to the nineteenth century's dramas, be they in hagiographical or exoticized shades. Both groups seem bored with Mormonism's twentieth-century historical trajectory.

Another telling echo of the nineteenth-century story is a contemporary public-sphere strategy that observers have discerned in LDS discourse. Mormons, so the arguments go, have developed one language for outsiders and another for those within the fold. The gaps or contradictions between the outsider and insider talk can be cast as the inevitable by-product of communal identity, a strategy for self-preservation, or a spotty record on candor, depending on one's perspective. Critics see continuity in Joseph Smith's carefully worded denials of polygamy, Joseph F. Smith's strategic downplay of the role of prophetic revelation during the Reed Smoot Senate hearings, and Mormon equivocation on theological or historical questions in the contemporary media.[20] Sympathetic observers note the precariousness of early Mormonism or its continued misrepresentation in the present. In any case, Mormons struggle to fuse the remnants of their nineteenth-century protectionism with the aggressive optimism of their modern corporatism. While it would go too far to say that Latter-day Saints crave opposition or that LDS success depends on persecution, it must be acknowledged that tension with the broader society is woven so tightly into Mormon consciousness that, when entering into public discourse, many Saints expect to be misunderstood or misrepresented.[21]

In this still-charged atmosphere, Mormons often lack the space or the will to articulate Mormonism's varied themes. When prominent Mormons in politics or popular culture tilt the spotlight toward the faith, a sound-bite media age offers little room for complexities. Modern presidential candidates need only one-sentence caricatures of Mormon teachings to call up unspoken discomforts and to construct easy distance. When, before a national audience in 2007, Mike Huckabee "asked" if Mormons believe Jesus and Satan are brothers, the awkward silence stood as a profound legacy to Mormons of their sojourn in America.[22] The cultural power displayed in the question's asking and the inability of Mormons to effectively answer it remain as survivals from the bitter story told in the following pages. Stranded between the technical accuracy of Huckabee's quip and their inability to manage perceived peculiarity, twenty-first century Mormons face a profound set of choices. Unequivocal absorption into the broader Christian community would come at a high cost for most Mormons. Full-blown communitarianism or quietistic withdrawal would be equally unpalatable. The former amounts to a painful bridge already crossed; Mormons have worked too hard for their respectability to fade into insignificance. The negotiations between familiarity and contempt that Mormons and their detractors might yet track will continue to strain against the deep ruts of their shared history. That history, as offered in this book, rides primarily on the voices of skeptical Americans who were in turns fascinated and repulsed by a singular religious creation. What they originally understood as a fraudulent approximation of true religion became—by the mid-nineteenth century—a "foreign" faith. At the turn of the twentieth century, Mormons moved (and were moved) from the discursive margins of American society, though Mormonism was only partially accepted as an American religion. In the process, anti-Mormons not only helped recast Mormonism through representation and transform it as a social reality, they helped shape the meaning of religion in America.

Religious Liberty as an American Problem

In the newly disestablished United States, not all religious claims were created equal. The young nation had a host of them to survey as new theologies, new rituals, and new charismatic leaders glutted the public sphere. In this cacophony, anti-Mormonism supplied a focused social enemy for a public divided by sectarianism and wracked by economic and political instability. Long before Mormon polygamy or Deseret theocracy boggled Americans, early national anti-Mormonism constituted an implicit concern that disestablishment had left too much room for religious expression. The landscape was littered with counterfeiters, frauds, and confidence men, and the people just might choose amiss. The ostensibly "free market" of churches included unintended consequences that someone—or some discourse—needed to police.[1]

This book charts how Mormonism was defamed and defined as a nineteenth-century American religion. It argues that through public condemnation of what Mormonism was, Protestants defined just what American religion could be. The mutability of anti-Mormon rhetoric adds intrigue to the sheer volume of its invective. While various approaches to Mormonism appeared intermittently across the century, immersion in the anti-Mormon documentary cache has shaped a developmental periodization for this study. Put in admittedly oversimplified terms, critics first found Mormonism to be a fake religion, then an alien or foreign religion, and finally a merely false one. The first two chapters examine the complicated charges of religious fraudulence. The third and fourth chapters trace the ways polygamy and ascendant notions of religion, civilization, and race coded Mormonism as alien. The fifth chapter documents the postpolygamy rapprochement that left Mormonism a heresy, dangling somewhere between acceptance and rejection as an American faith. Mormonism's

HE THINKS HIS SHELL WILL PROTECT HIM.

"He Thinks His Shell Will Protect Him," *Harper's Weekly*, 9 January 1886 (L. Tom Perry Special Collections, Harold B. Lee Library, Brigham Young University, Provo)

long, slow march to heresy illustrates both the centrality and the instability of religion in nineteenth-century negotiations of American identity. This was a fight over authenticity conducted in the popular press in service to an evolving American public sphere. This study is thus less a history of the Latter-day Saints than it is a history of the idea of religion in nineteenth-century America. The tale of Mormonism and its detractors offers an unmatched view of the underlying problem haunting American religious liberty: Who decides what is religious in a disestablished polity?

Though some historians have taken the epithets hurled by anti-Mormons at face value or as more or less accurate descriptions of Mormon deviance, these interpretations fail to explain the virulence of anti-Mormonism. A better explanation emerges when one uncovers the tacit assumptions grounding anti-Mormon arguments, which typically lingered just beyond claims that Joseph Smith was a charlatan, that Mormon religious practice was little more than delirium or occult magic, that Mormon theology amounted to a thinly veiled moneymaking scheme, or that Mormon community building was a menacing empire-in-the-making. Mormonism, in short, blurred lines between the real and the counterfeit, magic and religion, and faith and politics, challenging the definition of Christianity in the new nation.

Given the attachments Americans felt to a Christian (or Protestant) republic, Mormonism's allegedly fraudulent Christianity crossed too many cultural and religious norms for comfort. Whereas Roman Catholicism vexed nineteenth-century Protestants as a corrupted Christianity, Mormonism was first represented as a fake religion, another cheating mountebank on the American frontier. Typical among the documents of this diagnosis was a work by evangelical apologist Origen Bacheler, a veteran of religious controversy. Bacheler's *Mormonism Exposed, Internally and Externally* (1838) offered perhaps the most succinct articulation of early anti-Mormonism's inner logic and corresponding tensions. "I respect the rights of *conscience*," he wrote, "I am opposed to persecution for *opinion's* sake." But, Bacheler warned, it would be a grave mistake to extend the same "forbearance and compassion" due the "*dupes* of the Mormon imposture" to the "*lying knaves* who *dupe* them."[2] Bacheler's invective acknowledged religious liberty as a positive good in American society but also points to the destabilizing question of religious authenticity. This study of anti-Mormonism (its propaganda, its court cases, its role in Mormonism's trudge westward, its presence in late-century intellectual life) offers a profile in the changing image of religious authenticity and authority in an expanding republican empire.

Anti-Mormonism developed against a backdrop of varied Mormon engagement strategies and responses. Though the spectrum of Mormon engagement receives mostly passing notice in the pages that follow, it is significant for this study that Mormons mostly rejected quietism as a plan for social interaction. Though flight dominated their strategies before 1847, Mormons could also aggressively press their case, defend their priorities, and order their communities before and after their famed exodus to the Great Basin. Authoritarianism also figured prominently in nineteenth-century Mormon thinking. Ultimately, strong forms of Mormon religious authority challenged—and threatened to expose—ostensibly weaker forms of ecclesiastical authority lurking behind the forming Protestant "moral establishment," a coercive set of social, political, and legal goals that has been elegantly described by David Sehat.[3]

Anti-Mormons derided LDS authoritarianism as the threat around which they might forge or strengthen various kinds of social or legal hegemony. Mormons provided substantial grist for these discursive mills, since they contested the Protestant moral establishment in myriad ways. Mormons routinely engaged, rather than withdrew from, partisan politics as a means of counteracting what they regarded as infringements on their religious liberty. Joseph Smith himself ran for the U.S. presidency in 1844. Brigham Young firmly grasped the mechanisms of territorial politics as territorial governor. LDS leaders presided over a church and a political party before (and, some would argue, after) Utah gained statehood in 1896. Moreover, the political and ecclesiastical visions of Latter-day Saints bled together in the heated contests of the nineteenth century. Theocratic ideals formed, mixed with strands of American political thought, and were then dismantled before Mormons could implement a coherent political vision in the Utah Territory. All the while, polygamy's inherent inequities conspicuously divided Mormons among themselves as readily as they separated Saints from non-Mormon "gentiles." At the far end of the spectrum of Mormon responses, the grisly 1857 murder of approximately 120 non-Mormon emigrants at Mountain Meadows, in southern Utah, at the hands of Mormon militiamen gave antagonists their bloody example of theocracy's threat. Tellingly indicative of the tortured place of "religion" in narrations of American violence, modern retellings of the horrifying act have to a considerable extent localized on the question of whether high Mormon leaders—Brigham Young in particular—ordered the attack. Implicit in the bitter historiographical volleys is the question of whether or not Mormonism itself stands implicated in the atrocity, a clear carryover from the knotty questions posed by nineteenth-century anti-Mormons.[4] Because of the richness and comprehensiveness of modern accounts of Mormon theocracy, polygamy, and the Mountain Meadows massacre, this book makes no attempt to replow those fields. Suffice it to say that these aggressive forms of Mormon power provided antagonists a foil that enabled their various forms of control. Much as "republican motherhood" could simultaneously valorize women's place in the republic and discursively buttress patriarchy, anti-Mormons could reenshrine the myth of antiestablishmentarian religious freedom alongside bold calls to marshal state power in the suppression of minority religious practice.[5]

This is a story as much about patterns of religious classification as it is about the realities of a religious tradition and its critics. Religions had been appraised and condemned for generations. Indeed, the intellectual frameworks employed against early Mormonism were in place before Joseph Smith stepped onto history's stage. What makes the tale of anti-

Mormonism significant rests, in part, in the ways it surpassed other vitriolic rebuttals to new religious movements. Mormonism seemed to inspire previously unseen levels of organized opposition in the United States. Without an established ancient history or significant demographic bulk, Mormons experienced gubernatorial extermination orders, federal military "invasion," and systematic disenfranchisement. While little would be gained intellectually in somehow ranking religious groups by the severity of their persecution, the fact that police powers of the state were marshaled with unique force against Mormonism hints at the peculiar political consequences of anti-Mormonism and the climax of a discursive thread in the rise of new religions.[6]

This account tracks antipolygamy as a phase in a longer process of religious classification and cultural imagination. Preexisting histories of Mormonism and anti-Mormonism tend to emphasize polygamy as Mormonism's central offense, despite the fact that Mormons themselves were scarcely aware of the practice until the mid-1840s and official recognition came only in 1852. Significantly, anti-Mormonism's bloodiest phase preceded widespread knowledge of the Saints' controversial marriage doctrine.[7] Acknowledging that shrill cries of Mormon un-Americanness could be heard before critics learned of polygamy, the third, fourth, and fifth chapters of this study map a paradoxical relationship for anti-Mormonism's pre- and post-announcement (of polygamy) phases. "Celestial marriage" moved Mormonism further from the discursive middle, but the new antagonisms' aggressive exoticism ultimately hijacked anti-Mormonism. Most postbellum critics esteemed polygamy as the undeniable marker of Mormonism's fakery or Oriental foreignness. What real religion could recommend something so utterly outside nineteenth-century norms? In a supreme irony, however, polygamy was also the element that seemed to offer Mormonism its sole claim to particularity. After the early 1850s announcement, polygamy grabbed the headlines, but it also subsumed and obscured other criticisms of the movement. Even when critics cited theocracy or some other perceived evil as outstripping polygamy's menace, all were forced to reckon with the undeniable fact that polygamy not only provided the most effective entrée for addressing other anti-Mormon concerns, it also drew foot soldiers to the anti-Mormon standard in droves.

This study terminates in the mid-1890s, around the time of polygamy's official discontinuance and Utah's statehood, not because the existence of a Mormon state caused anti-Mormonism to fade into insignificance, but because a seemingly monogamous Mormon people were deemed just innocuous enough for a seat at the national table. Congregationalist A. S. Bailey voiced resistance to just such a reconciliation in 1888 when he charged that Mormonism "is not a church; it is not religion according to the American idea and the United States Constitution."[8] Many agreed, making the late 1890s all the more remarkable for the ways that national leaders were willing to countenance a host of perceived Mormon errors so long as polygamy was not numbered among them. Because so much animosity had localized on polygamy, in some ways it abetted Mormonism's conflicted acceptance within American culture.

Situating antipolygamy in the longer history of anti-Mormon agitation helps to clarify how Mormonism itself presented a dilemma of religious classification. "Religion" as a category of human experience had a lively history before America's founding. Throughout its complicated history, religion had always served as a "highly charged marker of difference." Its ancient Greco-Roman etymological beginnings marked a distinction between authenticity and superstitious illegitimacy, the latter typically described as being rooted in ignorance or fraud.[9] As the concept developed in late antiquity, religion came to pertain primarily to elements of Christian practice such as ritual obligation or monastic duty. These practice-heavy conceptualizations transformed during the Protestant Reformation, however. Ulrich Zwingli and John Calvin tended to equate religion with piety rather than ritual; by the mid-eighteenth century, many Western intellectual and religious circles tilted religion toward virtue, reverence, or the knowledge of God.[10] Religion's role in demarcating the authentic only increased with the West's repeated discovery of non-Christian religion.[11] Early-modern European colonials in North America thus found themselves caught between a view that identified religion as essentially Christianity as revealed in the Bible and practiced in European churches and one that regarded it as "a ubiquitous human phenomenon" observable in non-Christian cultures. The related synonymousness of "faiths" and "religions" marked the confluence of an older, theological category (religion as Christianity) with a newer, comparative one (religion as any tradition deemed religious).[12] Enlightenment debates did much to press the question of the relationship of the religions and a broader, generic religion. Eighteenth-century efforts to observe human societies and construct taxonomies that would rationalize observably diverse but ostensibly religious ideas and practices presented problems still considered urgent by nineteenth-century thinkers. For nineteenth-century theorists, religion could be "several, one and only, or countless."[13] An often-awkward classification system along lines roughly framed by "ours" and "theirs" persisted throughout the century, and an array of identifiers (from "heathenism" and "paganism" to "idolatry" and "magic") ranked and organized ideas and practices in self-referential ways.[14]

In both intellectual and popular circles, then, religion came to mean more than the practice or dogmas of Christianity. Knowledge of non-Christian religions scarcely went beyond superficial understandings, but Americans knew that different faiths existed and fell far short of Protestantism's perceived superiority. Protestantism organized the fictive spectrum that Americans constructed. The further a religion strayed from Trinitarian Protestantism, the further down the scale it fell. Americans proved erratic, though, in their charges of religious deviance, unsure how to delimit perceived radicalisms of ecclesiastical form, theological content, and religious experience. This comparative framework carried tremendous cultural weight and tended to mark Mormonism as non-Christian more by a process of historical analogy than by theological categorization, at least initially. What Jonathan Z. Smith wrote of the category "sacred" might well have been written of "religion" in American culture: "There is nothing that is inherently sacred or profane. These are not substantive categories, but rather situational or relational categories, mobile boundaries which shift according to the map being employed."[15] Normative conceptions of religious liberty were complicated by the parochialisms inherent in such a discursive spectrum. Whereas Revolutionary rhetoric had sometimes soared toward a more universalizing language—perhaps most forcefully issued from Thomas Jefferson's pen—practical understandings in the nineteenth century more often sought what or who might be authentically religious. And, as the fifth chapter of this volume documents, universalizing discourses came with complications and compromises of their own.

This unstable comingling of the theological and comparative (eventually, "anthropological") senses of religion clearly formatted hostile reactions. Anti-Mormonism, in turn, played no small part in the construction of religion and religious liberty. Torn between rejecting Mormon claims and crediting religious features within Mormonism, antagonists situated Mormonism on a continuum that ran from the religiously "false" to the "real" but was mired in multiple ambiguities. Ann Taves has carefully plotted an Anglo-American setting where something could be either religious and "true" or religious and "false," but anti-Mormonism calls attention to a critical third understanding: the merely seemingly religious.[16] Launched in a setting where a great deal was at stake in determining the difference between the true, the false, and the ostensibly religious, it is no wonder that

Mormonism drew comparisons to Islam, Hinduism, and Buddhism more often than it did with the Disciples of Christ, Hicksite Quakers, Universalists, Millerites, Methodists, or Shakers, groups that modern historians tend to lump with the early Mormons.[17] Anti-Mormons found they could exploit the complexity lurking within nineteenth-century religion. Daniel Kidder wrote that Mormonism's "spread" could be "accounted for on natural principles," adding that "our only opposition to Mormonism is on the ground of its being a religious imposture."[18] Given these assumptions, antagonists could dismiss observable religious externalities by claiming that Mormonism was both "religious and false" or merely imposing on the category religion.

Seen in this way, the Mormon story helps map the construction and failings of an uneasy fin-de-siècle compromise over religion, a nominal consensus forged as liberal Protestants presided over rituals of pan-religious appreciation in the 1890s.[19] The apparent renunciation of polygamy coupled with the rise of a powerful religious discourse with roots in modern science opened up new possibilities for Mormonism. In both a universalizing academic understanding of religion's scope and a secular set of cultural standards for gauging the success of American faiths, Mormonism reasonably expected a move toward respectability. Though such developments made it possible for national commentators to imagine space for a defanged Mormonism, the following pages offer no happy endings. As torn as ever over what counts as religion, Americans still expressed skepticism about Mormonism and only partially embraced it as an American faith.

Scholars long ago shed the popular perception that religious liberty was achieved definitively in a Revolutionary past, yet some depictions of disestablishment continue to portray it as a happy fact of American history. Historians narrate the LDS Church in ways that reinforce long-held assumptions about religion and the new nation, citing Mormonism's emergence as an example of America's gleeful plurality. Though some have implied that religious diversity and creativity facilitated toleration, anti-Mormonism shows that this was not always the case.[20] This study calls into question the depiction of Mormonism as essentially American, not because of Mormons' real or imagined religious eccentricity or political heterodoxy, but because, first, such a characterization obscures the depth of anti-Mormon animosity and, second, because historians' accounts of Mormonism's Americanness often explicitly or implicitly equate it with democratic populism or various evangelical themes.[21] With the meaning of both religion and American identity so hotly contested in the period covered here, Mormonism's Americanness cannot be conclusively decided without an implicit commitment to some particular view of each. While early national revivalism may have fit some religious groups for political democracy and given rise to populist movements like Mormonism, it also created the tensions that helped draw others to authoritarian religion or fanned the flames of oppositional movements like the one described here. Mormonism was profoundly American but perhaps in counterintuitive ways. I concur with Jon Butler, who criticizes historians for interpretive models that assume laicization, evangelicalism, and antiauthoritarianism. Wondering if a "Catholic" model might better suit narratives of American religion, Butler finds Mormonism to be "quintessentially American" in its authoritarian spirit, its emphasis on institutional coherence, and its craving for sacred space—hardly traditional themes in American religious history.[22] Mormonism assumed a counterimage to American Protestantism by both enacting its more "Catholic" themes and partaking of its evangelical ethos while simultaneously repudiating it. This point was clear enough to nineteenth-century Roman Catholics. Writing for the Italian journal *La Civiltà Cattolica*, Cardinal Archbishop Karl August von Reisach argued that Mormonism was the "natural consequence of North American Protestantism," a profane effort to correct its "fundamental errors."[23] Accounts that respect nineteenth-century diversity but blunt its religious invectives may miss the centrality of religion as an interpretive and social problem. What follows underscores how scholarship on Mormonism must recognize that it was not merely another in a long line of democratizing religious movements, but also a feature of a society newly acclimating to the very idea of diversity.

This study begs similar questions of existing scholarship on American religious liberty. First, it complicates Philip Hamburger's work on church/state relationships. Whereas Hamburger wants anti-Catholicism to be the lodestar for understanding modern separationist conceptions, my work shows this to be only partially the case. Instead, as Sarah Barringer Gordon also argues, I observe that it was in their conflict with Mormonism that Americans discovered that church/state separation was a critical element of their republicanism. Complementing Gordon's emphasis on the ways antipolygamy "remade legal history and constitutional law," my study charts the discursive traditions that placed Mormon polygamy and other controversial elements outside the purview of religion in American minds.[24]

Stressing religion's categorical instability, I also provide fine-grained historical texture for theorists' recent interpretations of American religious liberty. Eric Mazur contends that religious freedom is so enmeshed with Euro-American norms that the more a tradition varies from those understandings, the less likely it is to benefit from religious freedom. Though Mazur cites Mormonism as a prime example, he may have underestimated the problem it posed historically. Hardly an imported religion, Mormonism staked the limits of homegrown religious creativity.[25] Mormonism might stand as signal evidence of what Winnifred Sullivan calls religious liberty's "impossibility." Since the U.S. Constitution does not define religion, courts (and publics) are inevitably mired in the question of what is and is not protected.[26] Whereas courts historically have been reticent to decide what religion is, nineteenth-century Americans were confident that Mormons embodied what religion was *not*.

Finally, this book contributes to recent efforts linking Mormon history to mainstream historical narratives. It attempts to build on excellent recent work on anti-Mormonism by pulling the piecemeal strands together and relating them to the construction of modern understandings of religion itself.[27] Prominent among the episodic studies treating anti-Mormonism, Kenneth Winn's treatment untangled some of the early issues while documenting versions of republicanism at play in Mormon/anti-Mormon battles; however, his analysis not only curiously pushes religion to the margins, it covers less than twenty years of the conflict.[28] Sarah Barringer Gordon has lent her considerable legal expertise to the antipolygamy story, and Kathleen Flake has offered a superb analysis of national anti-Mormonism's denouement amid the Reed Smoot Senate hearings. Patrick Mason documents anti-Mormon violence in the American South, and Megan Sanborn Jones examines anti-Mormon representations on the nineteenth-century American stage.[29] Terryl Givens's study of anti-Mormon depictions in American fiction brilliantly analyzes anti-Mormon literary tropes, underlining the critical space occupied by religiously themed literature in the nineteenth century. In this historian's complement to a good friend's literary analysis, historicism intends to highlight anti-Mormonism's variability and to stress its ideological heft. Anti-Mormon assertions often amounted to more than strategic veneers cloaking an aggressive orthodoxy that lacked the political environment to assault Mormon "heresy" on theological grounds.[30] Heresy was in fact a hard-earned achievement for nineteenth-century Mormons. For three-quarters of a century, anti-Mormons concerned themselves with the nature and meaning of religion itself; accordingly, their charges plumb (and obscure) pressing ideological problems. Mormons would have to wait until the twentieth century to enjoy the station of heretics.

This study cannot boast of comprehensiveness, despite its exertions to survey anti-Mormon discourse in all its nineteenth-century variety. With each passing year, it became clearer that no single volume could account for the massive flow of material. I gathered published material and courageously intended to offer some quantitative analyses and observations, but in the end was forced into a rather unscientific methodology. Based on several years' worth of reading published anti-Mormon material (harvested from the archives at Brigham Young University and the historical department of the Church of Jesus Christ of Latter-day Saints) and guided by excellent bibliographic work, I opted to highlight those texts that I sensed either memorably voiced a particular discursive trend, seemed especially influential, or appeared to signal a significant change in direction.[31] My use of "sensed," "seemed," and "appeared" might provoke concern. I can only say that I have crafted an account that represents substantial experience in the genre and a good-faith effort to contextualize and comprehend that genre's significance. I consciously excluded British materials after an early flirtation with the transatlantic flow of polemics.[32] I leave to others the much-needed examination of twentieth-century anti-Mormonism.[33] While I am aware that the terms "Mormon" and "anti-Mormon" were themselves historically constructed, I tabled those discussions for another time and perhaps another book. For the purposes of this text, "anti-Mormon" remains an admittedly amorphous and generalized term, catching practically any negative appraisal of Joseph Smith's (then Brigham Young's) movement in its conceptual web. The time for richer comparative work with anti-Catholicism, anti-Shakerism, or anti-Spiritualism never materialized, either. There are glancing nods to other polemical genres, but my most pressing questions kept me focused squarely on the complexities of anti-Mormon rhetoric. For the most part, I chose to lightly treat specific Mormon countercharges or the fascinating rounds of interreligious sparring. In doing so, I did not intend to strip Mormons of historical agency. Rather, in focusing primarily on the complications of the antagonism offered against them, I acknowledge the realities of cultural power in the nineteenth century. I sensed that placing Mormon push-back on par with anti-Mormon attacks or assuming that Mormon growth demonstrates anti-Mormonism's failure was to misunderstand that power. Mormonism was refashioned in the crucible of national opprobrium, and while Mormons survived to thrive in the twentieth century, it was hardly on their own terms. Seen in this way, Mormon conceptions of religion or their responses to critics were far less significant in American culture than the considerable indirect influence Mormons exerted, an influence that existed primarily in the form of the questions their lives begged of nonbelievers.

CHAPTER 1

"Impostor"

The Mormon Prophet

For New Yorker David Reese, antebellum physician and self-appointed social critic, too much in American culture amounted to a mere counterfeit. His 1838 tirade against a host of "humbugs" warned that the "unsophisticated" and "weak sisters" were dangerously prone to deception. Deceivers deserved most of the blame, but Reese thought it unflattering that so many Americans had already been led astray. Though his humbugs ranged from animal magnetism to phrenology, he reserved special venom for religious frauds. With prophets, societies, and sects proliferating, Reese found the nation's religious scene unsettled by charlatans. The fleeting success of Matthias (Robert Matthews), the New York prophet whose controversial career had sparked a penny press uproar, struck him as a telling indicator of popular gullibility. But even the infamous Matthias was not the age's paramount religious fraud. For Reese, the "most shocking humbug" was the "*Mormon oracle*" Joseph Smith. Dismayed by the expansion of Smith's church, Reese played prophet himself, predicting that Mormonism would not "cease to spread, until like the kindred enormities of Matthias, some high-handed and out-breaking iniquity shall wind up its history in pollution, infamy, and blood."[1]

This chapter seeks to account for the momentous shift in the American public perception of religion's potential for danger. Traditionally, religion had been threatening because of its association with government. Religion in the young nation became dangerous because it was unmoored. In this riotous new social setting, Mormonism functioned for many as it had for David Reese: as a foil against which commentators might imagine a less turbulent legacy for religious liberty. Caught between universal celebration of religious freedom and its destabilizing aftereffects, writers by the

Pomeroy Tucker,
*Origin, Rise,
and Progress of
Mormonism . . .*
(1867), frontispiece
(L. Tom Perry
Special Collections,
Harold B. Lee
Library, Brigham
Young University,
Provo)

SMITH'S ACCOUNT OF TAKING THE "GOLDEN BIBLE" FROM MORMON HILL.

droves decried Mormonism as a fake religion but found themselves faking tolerance in the process. In worrying about the country's future, observers looked back for examples of the trouble that might infect societies that forsook true religion. Viewing Christianity's rivals as counterfeits of real religion, anti-Mormons set about "exposing," "unveiling," or "unmasking" Mormonism in ways that portrayed it as both new and old. They viewed it as an extraordinary and unprecedented threat, but one in a long history of religious "impostures."[2] As a result of this dependence on distinctively Protestant versions of history, a major strain of early anti-Mormon

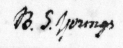

MORMONISM UNVAILED :

OR,

A FAITHFUL ACCOUNT OF THAT SINGULAR IMPOSITION AND

DELUSION,

FROM ITS RISE TO THE PRESENT TIME.

WITH SKETCHES OF THE CHARACTERS OF ITS

PROPAGATORS,

AND A FULL DETAIL OF THE MANNER IN WHICH THE FAMOUS

GOLDEN BIBLE

WAS BROUGHT BEFORE THE WORLD.

TO WHICH ARE ADDED,

INQUIRIES INTO THE PROBABILITY THAT THE HISTORICAL PART

OF THE SAID BIBLE WAS WRITTEN BY ONE

SOLOMON SPALDING,

MORE THAN TWENTY YEARS AGO, AND BY HIM INTENDED TO HAVE

BEEN PUBLISHED AS A ROMANCE.

. . . .

BY E. D. HOWE.

. . . .

PAINESVILLE :

PRINTED AND PUBLISHED BY THE AUTHOR.

1834.

Eber D. Howe, *Mormonism Unvailed . . .* (1834), title page (L. Tom Perry Special Collections, Harold B. Lee Library, Brigham Young University, Provo)

polemics localized on Joseph Smith himself and his claims to new revelation and prophetic authority. "Anti-Smithism," in fact, dominated anti-Mormonism during its first two decades.[3] Tracing the stories of religious impostors in early American writing provides clues to the intellectual and cultural environment from which Mormonism sprang and helps make sense of anti-Mormonism's scope and ferocity.

Pervasive sensitivity to illusion and deception in the new nation exacerbated Protestant misgivings about religious innovation and the uncertainty facing American churches. Smith's claims to prophetic authority, additional scripture, and ecclesiastical superiority seemed to resolve the problems of diversity for some Americans, but far more took the movement as pluralism's cautionary tale. The very conditions, in other words, that gave rise to movements like Smith's also engendered the uncertainties that, in turn, shaped critiques of it. Anti-Mormons dismissed the charge of religious persecution because they typically did not consider Mormonism a religion. At the same time, they found themselves participating in a more extended conversation about religious authenticity, the nature of religious authority, and the place of religion in the republic. In the end, works like *Mohametanism Unveiled* (1829), *Mormonism Unvailed* (1834), *Noyesism Unveiled* (1849), and *Spiritualism Unveiled* (1866) shared more than similar titles.[4] They each betrayed the admission that religious claims were complicated and that, if left to themselves, people might just choose amiss. In a religiously disestablished United States, the new free market in churches entailed unintended and unwanted consequences.

Authenticity and Disestablishment

Early Americans' preoccupation with deception is easily detected but not as easily explained. Add complicated and unprecedented religious circumstances to the formidable political, social, and economic upheavals that marked early national culture and the anxiety or befuddlement become comprehensible. In the fluid social world of early national culture, "confidence men" seemed to lurk on every corner.[5] Revolution had doomed churches to varying degrees of upheaval and often-significant declines in membership. In the early republic, membership surged but disestablishment—gradual but complete by the mid-1830s, at least in terms of state funding for churches—meant that traditionally dominant churches could no longer combine with the state to fence out religious upstarts.[6] Joseph Smith and the Book of Mormon provoked claims that these new arrangements allowed too much room for religious expression.

Traditionalists had warned against such a circumstance during the disestablishment debates, but the specters of unwieldy diversity and an uncertain future had haunted both pro- and anti-establishment arguments. Those attacking the colonial establishments had wondered about a future where Roman Catholics or non-Christians might come to dominate a particular locale. Would they be permitted to legally establish Catholicism or Islam? Proponents of religious establishment also worried about the future. What beyond established Christianity would suffice if non-Christians came in numbers sufficient to imperil a Christian republic? The practical questions of how to legally establish Christianity were complicated enough to give antiestablishment statesmen and Protestant dissenters the day, and Christian churches, ostensibly unhinged from the state, came to exist on a theoretically even playing field.[7] Evangelical churches, especially those that adapted to the new setting, fared phenomenally well. But because they could less predictably count on state support, the traditional means for suppressing false religion, American Protestants were left with fewer options in dealing with troublesome religious figures.[8]

The pitfalls of religious freedom and the exponential growth in religious variety were by no means resolved when Joseph Smith added his voice to the cacophony in 1830. The boisterousness of the early republic's religious scene sent writers in search of a way to manage what Leigh Schmidt has characterized as the nation's modern religious predicament: a spiritual abundance that had as much to do with "God's loquacity as God's hush."[9] Counterfeit detection assumed added urgency with the nation's religious efflorescence. As mobile and fecund Americans pushed ever west and crowded into cities of strangers, writers patrolled the boundaries of religious authenticity tenaciously.[10] That prominent commentators experienced early national religious liberty and diversity as a profound, if somewhat subterranean, tension is most evident in their efforts to organize American religion into a comprehensive narrative and to situate Protestantism in the context of other religious traditions.[11]

Many of these writers saw their work as a vital step in realizing a denominational détente. Hannah Adams, whose *Dictionary of All Religions* (1817) was published in several editions in the United States and England, avoided passing "judgment on the sentiments" of various Christian groups and even terms such as "Heretics, Schismatics, Enthusiasts, [and] Fanatics." Her concern for fair representation, however, did not extend to the "heathen nations," whose ceremonies appeared "obscene and ridiculous." Nor did it apply to the Anabaptists, the French Prophets, or the Shakers. Islam, she maintained, was the result of Muhammad's "pretensions to a divine mission" and strategic deployment of "poligamy and concubinage to make his creed palatable to the most depraved of mankind."[12] Adams's Unitarian-leaning account had an influential evangelical counterpart in Charles Buck's *Theological Dictionary* (1807), which promised an "Impartial Account of all the Principal Denominations." But only two pages later Buck turned defensive. "Perhaps it may be said, the Work is tinctured too much with my own sentiments," he predicted. He thought it a "false liberality" to treat all ideas as equally legitimate or to "trifle with error." Even so, he expected his own theological and ecclesiastical preferences to tread lightly in the massive two-volume reference: "I trust the features of bigotry are not easily discernible in this Work."[13] With American churches competing for members and influence among themselves and, at least in the abstract, with non-Christian religious traditions, other writers were forced to admit the same. Their task was not simply to describe different faiths objectively, but to compare, to weigh, and to assign value. They intended to "educate" in the Protestant sense of the term.

As reference writers took on the interpretive problem of Mormonism, they routinely deployed the fraud motif to stitch together these seemingly contradictory commitments to impartial description and theological judgment. J. Newton Brown's massive *Encyclopedia of Religious Knowledge* (1835) featured an entry for "bigotry" that linked Christian and national progress with free inquiry, tolerance, and religious liberty.[14] His entries for "heretic" and "orthodoxy" complicated matters, however. He granted that "heretic" was often used as a term of reproach but went on to define it as one who transgressed "what is made the standard of orthodoxy." His passive construction obscured the dilemma: Who, in a disestablished America, decided who or what was orthodox? Brown's litmus tests for Christian orthodoxy—"the fall of man, regeneration, atonement, repentance, justification by free grace"—provided sufficient space for early Mormonism. But Mormons, despite adhering wholeheartedly to each item (albeit ambiguously in the case of the last), remained unorthodox in Brown's estimation.[15] He pitied Joseph Smith's "misguided followers" for believing in a book Smith "pretended to interpret" and felt it his duty to make "the facts" of Mormonism "known . . . which show the real foundation of the imposture."[16] By invoking the imposture thesis, Brown avoided the question of theology altogether and, instead, occupied himself with turning Mormonism's founding narrative against Mormons.

This rhetorical strategy points to an important paradox in early-century formulations of religion. Theology, it turns out, could either trump history or be trumped by it depending on the author's needs. Theology held considerable sway in various early American imaginings of religion; most Protestants considered it the essence of true religion. As a result, movements where theology operated in a comparatively muted way, as in the case of early Mormonism, could be construed as false or fake.[17] More typically, though, Mormon theology was dismissed as a smokescreen. History could also be invoked to dismiss theology, in other words, argumentative circularity notwithstanding. When Protestants read their own histories of religious imposture in tandem with early Mormon history, they found resonances between the two that rendered Mormonism's self-account a shabby veneer.[18] Such a framework for understanding fraudulent religions in the past thus provided unintended but perhaps not unwanted consequences when attached to contemporary movements. Mormons could emerge as pseudo-Christian or non-Christian more by a process of historical association than theological taxonomy.

Throughout the literature, antebellum Americans agreed that the propagation of true religion was critical for maintaining American strength. They also agreed, at least in principle, to the denominational theory that versions of the truth might reside (and should coexist peacefully) among the various Protestant churches. Even so, the catalogs of faith amounted to more than lists because not all movements claiming to be religious were accepted as valid. Disquieted by fears of deception, antebellum Protestants found the old grounds for determining heterodoxy to be problematic and, as a result, routinely collapsed their interreligious comparisons into the simplistic framework of fraud. The seeming contradiction between the authors' stated aims of objectivity and their treatment of non-Christian and unpopular Christian groups is made comprehensible if viewed with a particular set of assumptions and a corresponding logic. True religion, which was vital to the republic's health, should be tolerated and encouraged in all its variety. On the other hand, what appeared to be religion in other cultures—or unpopular movements at home—was not real religion at all and therefore worthless or harmful. The question of tolerating these groups was correspondingly muddled.

Seen in this light, imposture was an indispensable conceptual category. It ostensibly resolved the danger lurking in the term "religion" because it granted that fake religion could mimic the "form of godliness" even if it lacked the power. Religion thus claimed two meanings in period writing: one leaning toward "religion in general" and the other meaning "true" religion. Since writers rarely formally distinguished the two, religion often emerged paradoxically in the narratives. This is no surprise given the notion's tangled roots. The imposture thesis, after all, had been wielded by Enlightenment skeptics against religion generally and by Protestant polemicists against Catholicism. Its use as an explanatory device during the century or so preceding Mormonism's advent was so jumbled that one scholar concluded: "It is difficult to mark where the Protestant's polemic ends and the rationalist's begins."[19] Mormons and anti-Mormons, then, found ready-made tools when they plunged headlong into their tussle over religious legitimacy.[20]

Attuned to imposture's menace, anti-Mormons did not detect a blatantly false message at first. Smith initially seemed close enough to the Protestant theologies of his day, and many of the early movement's teachings seemed conventional. The restoration of ancient Christianity was sought by a host of antebellum reformers; one of Smith's most committed opponents (Alexander Campbell) and one of his most articulate defenders (Sidney Rigdon) had been onetime allies in just such a restorationist project.[21] Smith's emphasis on immediate revelation, millenarianism, spiritual giftedness, dispensationalism, and prophetic authoritarianism had analogs in other movements as well. And, while some have pointed to the Book of Mormon as a radical departure, Jared Farmer reminds that it bore resemblance to no text more than the Bible itself.[22] Characterizing what exactly was wrong with early Mormon doctrine challenged early anti-Mormons and later historians alike, the latter seemingly unsure how to reconcile the apparent Americanness of early Mormonism with its thoroughgoing nineteenth-century rejection.[23]

Other unpopular religious groups might have been sympathetic to Mormon woes, given their shared occupation of the religio-cultural periphery, but they were among the most critical.[24] Devoted anti-Mormons Alexander Campbell (a founder of the Disciples of Christ) and Joshua V. Himes (eventually an Adventist), various Shakers, Universalists, and Catholics concurred with conventional Protestants' assessments. After being visited by Mormon missionaries outside of Cleveland, a Shaker concluded that they were "very ignorant of Christ or his work." One of them was no more than a "Filthy Beast" trying in vain to "imitate a man of God."[25] The Universalist *Evangelical Magazine and Gospel Advocate* could only despair: "'Good Lord deliver us' from such accessions to our ranks as the Mormonites."[26] After visiting Mormon Nauvoo, Illinois, in 1843, Catholic priest Samuel Mazzuchelli wondered how Americans, so astute in business and so fond of reading, could "believe all the errors invented by artfulness and religious fanaticism."[27] Mormons' insistence that theirs was the "only true & living Church" no doubt helped erode any nascent ecumenism along the non-Protestant religious fringe. Even similarly marginalized Americans, then, found little in Mormonism to commend.[28] For every contemporary textbook celebrating religious liberty, there were a host of documents underscoring the widespread bitterness of denominational rivalries.[29]

Hostility from these quarters compounds the problem of relying on

Mormon theological deviance alone to explain anti-Mormon sensibilities. With Mormonism providing considerable fodder for the imposture charge, anti-Mormons were initially less concerned with LDS theology than with its prophet.[30] The early attacks thus focused more on Mormonism as form than as content. And, given American attachment to religious freedom, especially in a setting where religion was routinely defined in terms of one's sentiments, countering any particular tradition's theology was problematic. Mormon theology became important for anti-Mormons, but long after they had concluded that Joseph Smith was a mere, if somewhat talented, charlatan. Hiram Mattison's *A Scriptural Defence of the Doctrine of the Trinity* (1846), which castigated Mormons and others as purveyors of modern Arianism, reads like a different kind of attack because it was.[31] Mattison's work, in taking up Mormonism as a theology (albeit a fatally flawed one), signaled a certain maturity in both Mormonism and anti-Mormon thinking. The earliest critiques of Mormonism could not credit it with theology because none were prepared to credit Smith with anything but imposture.

Interlopers in the Protestant Historical Pantheon

When anti-Mormons explained Joseph Smith by situating him in a history of religious impostors, they included a set of usual suspects. Abner Cole, Smith's New York neighbor and part-time newspaper editor, was among the first to publish his objections to Mormonism.[32] The "*spindle shanked* ignoramus" Smith, he wrote, was hardly a prophet. Rather, he was best understood in the context of ancient impostors like Muhammad and more recent frauds like Jemima Wilkinson and Joanna Southcote.[33] Others offered more extended lists but kept with the main contours of the narrative. Alexander Campbell, whose *Delusions: An Analysis of the Book of Mormon* (1832) was the first extended response to Smith's scripture, began his list in Jewish antiquity.[34] He found similarities between Smith and the would-be messiah Shabbatai Tsvi and continued on through history to include the sixteenth-century Anabaptists, Shaker Ann Lee, and finally the "Barkers, Jumpers, and Mutterers" among Campbell's revivalistic contemporaries.[35] Showing surprisingly little variation, anti-Mormon writers found ready precedents for Smith and his followers among history's religious upstarts and controversial innovators. With all the regularity of the lists, anti-Mormon writers settled on two figures in particular as archetypal metaphors for Smith's religious deception. One, the prophet Matthias, drew comparison with Smith in part because of their shared proximity in time and place. The other, Muhammad, served for many as history's arch impostor. Interestingly, observers found that Matthias's failures had exposed him as a fraud, while success had done the same for Muhammad. This distinction helps to explain why Muhammad eventually became the preferred explanatory device for Smith. Whereas Smith's presumed imminent failure drew short-lived comparisons with Matthias, Muhammad ultimately helped anti-Mormons cope with Smith's seemingly inexplicable success.

Anti-Mormons found similarities between Joseph Smith and Matthias that were almost too good to be true. Matthias created a stir in the mid-1830s with his outlandish dress, long beard, religious commune, and, especially, rumors of sexual shenanigans and the controversial death of one of his followers.[36] His brief rise to infamy did nothing to help Smith, but many—anti-Mormons, historians, and apparently Matthias himself—have drawn parallels between the two.[37] Not surprisingly, those seeking to expose Matthias did so in conventional ways; he was associated with all the figures populating the accounts of religious fraud and with Joseph Smith in particular.[38] Some writers embedded both prophets in the same narrative of deception. New York polemicist Origen Bacheler published blistering critiques of each. He first introduced and edited the account of Margaret Matthews, Matthias's estranged wife, who detailed her unfortunate marriage to the would-be prophet. In it, Bacheler contrasted what Matthias "attempted to pass off as religion" with "real Christianity."[39] Later, after a spirited public debate with Mormon preacher Parley Pratt, Bacheler again took up his pen. His *Mormonism Exposed* (1838) recounted his debate with Pratt, excerpted several prominent anti-Mormon works, and concluded that Mormons were "ten thousand times worse than gypsies."[40] Having cut his anti-Mormon teeth on Pratt, Bacheler capped off his career in anti-Mormonism by going on the lecture circuit with ex-Mormon renegade John C. Bennett in the mid-1840s.[41]

Others agreed that Smith and Matthias were two of a kind. Missouri anti-Mormon Samuel Lucas linked alleged Mormon fanaticism with the "success of the impostor Matthias, whose long beard and white wand led astray rich, well-educated people." James M'Chesney used Matthias as something of a shorthand slur, noting only that the "famous Matthias, the prophet, appears like a child compared to" Smith. E. G. Lee maintained that Matthias, like Smith, had succeeded because of a widespread "love of the marvellous." Similarities between the two prophets' careers prompted Illinois college professor Jonathan B. Turner to formulate a typology of false prophethood, with similarities ranging from dogmatic certainty to a tendency toward scriptural literalism. Edwin DeLeon declared that frauds like Smith and Matthias were almost always "coarse, illiterate and vulgar impostors, whose ignorance is only equaled by their villainy."[42] As testimony to both Matthias's notoriety and the lack of debate about either prophet's legitimacy, most writers comparing the two New York seers did little more than mention Matthias's name. *Christian Palladium* editor Joseph Badger could only bemoan the fact that both men had progressed as far as they had by 1834. With the "*fanaticism* of the *Mormons* in the West . . . and of *Matthias* in New York," he huffed, "we are astonished that such false systems should have any adherents."[43] The *Palladium*'s masthead banner—"Religion Without Bigotry—Zeal Without Fanaticism—Liberty Without Licentiousness"—not only encapsulated Badger's vision for the republic but also hinted at the paradoxical nature of its application in an antebellum context. As the prophets' religious visions transgressed theological, social, political, and sexual convention, most concluded that religious liberty was a glaring American problem.

Whereas Matthias's abrupt exit from public gaze presented commentators with a relatively easy example of fraud, Islam's prophet provided a different but increasingly useful simile. Historians have long noted the comparisons made by nineteenth-century writers between the Mormon and Islamic prophets, but few have sought to explain them in their early American cultural context.[44] Anti-Mormons, after all, associated Joseph Smith with Muhammad long before Smith was charged with inappropriately mingling church and state, and years before polygamy or removal to the great Western desert made the analogy irresistible. The specter of Islam, while hardly the leading menace for antebellum Americans, loomed large in their thinking about religious difference, history, and the relationship between Christianity and civilization.[45]

Antebellum Americans knew more about some facets of early Islamic history than one might expect. Though their knowledge of Islam was informed by exposure to African Muslims through either the slave trade or naval conflict off the North African coast, many Americans were versed in Protestant versions of Islamic history through religious reference works or popular biographies of Muhammad.[46] The biographies written before the Civil War almost never take up the question of Joseph Smith, but they ponder the same problems anti-Mormons wrestled with. Biographers, writing as Christians for a Christian audience, had more to do than narrate Muhammad's life. They had to provide an alternate provenance for the

Qur'an, explain the attraction of a religion that Americans found rather unappealing, and account for Islam's success, which, they were forced to admit, seemed only to be increasing with time.[47] While most biographers used Muhammad to detail "the true nature of imposture," as one author put it, a survey of the major narratives available to Americans reveals considerable ambivalence about the lessons his life and legacy held for American Christians.

British writers, who penned the earliest biographies of Muhammad available to English speakers, found an eager audience in America. Humphrey Prideaux's *The True Nature of Imposture, Fully Displayed in the Life of Mahomet*, composed in the late seventeenth century, was still popular enough for American printings in the 1790s.[48] Tellingly, Prideaux had intended to write a history of the fall of Constantinople but was persuaded by the religious indifference of young people to write the story of Muhammad's life as a warning against spiritual apathy. Prideaux's Muhammad used religion as a shroud for his political ambitions. Having observed the divided state of Arabia, Prideaux reasoned, the prophet "concluded, that nothing would be more likely to gain a party firm to him . . . than the making of a new religion." Muhammad then mingled Judaism, Christianity, and an ample dose of sensuality to delude an unsuspecting Arab populace.[49] The notion that Islam was something of a cheap rip-off of other religious traditions, repeated time and again throughout the genre, became thoroughly self-serving for Christians. Not only was Muhammad denied the credit of original thought, but also anything praiseworthy in Islam could be dismissed as a mere borrowing from real religion.[50] As many later authors, Prideaux found in Muhammad's life a cautionary tale against Catholicism, noting with delight that the prophet's rise roughly corresponded with the bishop of Rome's claims of supremacy. Both prophet and pope "conspired to found themselves an empire in imposture" and used "the same methods . . . those of fire and sword" to trample upon Christ's church.[51]

Like Prideaux, an anonymous *Life of Mahomet* (1802) found parallels between Islam and Catholicism too important to ignore.[52] Its author credited Muhammad with giving Catholics the idea of "forcing men to believe," wryly adding that they had "faithfully improved it."[53] With Islam as the narrative backdrop, the author laid out a defense of certain governmental "restraints" on Catholics. State regulation of Catholicism was not designed to make Catholics "believe any thing"; it was intended to simply "prevent that moral, and especially that political mischief" that unavoidably followed Catholicism. To the objection that such measures constituted persecution, the biographer responded that "to keep men from doing mischief" was not persecution but wisdom.[54] So, while Muslims or Catholics served as rhetorical foils to English or American liberty, opponents of Islam, Catholicism, or Mormonism sought to decry religio-political authoritarianism by providing a rationale whereby arbitrarily defined religious extravagances could be controlled.

Though American biographers of Muhammad added variations to the English themes, they were no less ambivalent about faith, power, and coercion. Edward Gibbon's *Life of Mahomet* (1805) credited the prophet with genius yet made his life a story of duplicity and intrigue. While concluding that ambition was the prophet's ruling passion, Gibbon maintained that such was the case only during his later years. Unlike Prideaux, who had seen unholy ambition from the start, Gibbon charted a progression from youthful enthusiasm to the full flowering of fraud once the prophet found a willing audience. For Gibbon, then, Muhammad was consecutively deceived and deceiving. Originally carried away in flights of religious fancy, Muhammad's character "must have been gradually stained" by repeated acts of injustice and violence. Gibbon's concomitant moralizing about the relationship between enthusiasm and imposture was perhaps intended as something of a middle ground: "From enthusiasm to imposture, the step is perilous and slippery: the daemon of Socrates affords a memorable instance, how a wise man may deceive himself, how a good man may deceive others, how the conscience may slumber in a mixed and middle state between self-illusion and voluntary fraud." Gibbon could thus grant good intentions to Muhammad, at least early on; in the end, however, such an association not only repudiated the prophet's career, it also served as a cautionary tale of enthusiastic religion generally.[55]

New York University professor George Bush's *Life of Mohammed* (1832) incorporated many of these conventions, but his attempt to find theological meaning in the broader contours of Islamic history was novel. No doubt he surprised readers by aiming to "exhibit the Arabian prophet as a signal instrument in the hands of Providence."[56] Bush concluded that the "pseudoprophet" forged a religion, really a Christian heresy, that functioned as a "scourge upon the apostate churches in the East" and other parts of Christendom. Finding a dearth of "sufficient human causes to account" for such a phenomenon as Islam, Bush was left with God as the prime mover behind it, awkward though it was to have the Christian deity using (inspiring?) unwitting Muslim impostors and dupes to work his wrathful will on errant Christians.[57] Such an interpretive turn enabled Bush to trace "innumerable points of resemblance" between Islam and Judaism and Christianity without conceding any inspiration to Muhammad and, more importantly for his purposes, to explain away the observable successes of Islam in world history.[58]

Added to the biographies was a notable attempt to narrate Muhammad's life for the stage. George Miles's *Mohammed, the Arabian Prophet* (1850) spoke to the concerns of an antebellum audience by tapping the prophet's career for lessons about human weakness and the dangers of false religion.[59] The play portrayed a Muhammad whose career ran from the sincere to the diabolical, which in turn established Miles's primary point: "the inability of the greatest man, starting with the purest motives, to counterfeit a mission from God, without becoming the slave of hell."[60] In the first act, Muhammad bemoans the idolatry of his fellow Arabs and hopes to redeem them from superstition. Thus, while his goals are pure at the start, his turn to deceit to accomplish those ends dooms him to employ his doctrine as a pretense.[61] Early on, Muhammad soothes his conscience by reasoning with God:

> If I have falsely worn the Prophet's mantle,
> And falsely sworn to be thy messenger, —
> 'T is to reclaim the erring soul of man
> . . .
> . . . if I bring
> A nation to adore thee, shall I not
> Deserve the splendid title I usurp,
> And *be* the Prophet I *pretend* to be?

Audiences no doubt identified with various characters who at first were skeptical of Muhammad's claims. One of them urges the prophet to "drop [his] sacrilegious mask." Another sums up the impostor as a "vile composite Jew and Christian." The unwise Omer reckons that if "he be mad, 'tis manliness to spare him; If sane, we should reflect before condemning."[62] His tolerance ultimately provided the play's cautionary lesson. In hesitating to expose Muhammad for what he was, his initially wary hearers unwittingly functioned as accessories to his crimes. For audiences agitated by waves of religious trouble ranging from Shakers to Catholics to Mormons, the message was unmistakable.

As anti-Mormons made Muhammad the signal metaphor for Joseph Smith, they incorporated ready-made conventions but also inherited the biographies' interpretive dilemmas.[63] If little creativity was needed to narrate Smith's later career as a tale of lust for political power and women, anti-Mormons first had to decide what narrators had vacillated over in Muhammad's case—namely, Was he an impostor or an enthusiast?[64] The question was apparently less complicated with Smith, as few critics found him to be anything but a crafty deceiver. As one anti-Mormon had it, "The scheme of Mormonism is too deep ever to admit the supposition that he [Smith] is the dupe of his own imposture. His claims are such that they must be admitted as true, or he must be branded as a consummate knave—for his works plainly show that he is neither a fool, nor a fanatic, but a deliberate designer, who intends the whole scheme which he has set in operation, for the gratification of his own vanity and selfishness."[65] With general consensus that Smith was more a deceiver than deceived, anti-Mormons were next faced with the Book of Mormon and its limited but growing appeal. Again, they found a handy set of arguments in Christian descriptions of the Qur'an.[66] Finally, Mormonism's early history demanded that writers reckon with an admittedly successful Joseph Smith.

The first two dilemmas—the nature of Smith's charlatanry and the origins of the Book of Mormon—were inherently linked. In contrast to Mormons, who regarded the Book of Mormon as evidence of Smith's prophetic call, anti-Mormons found it to be the glaring marker of his deception.[67] Anti-Mormons, most of whom were wedded to a decidedly Biblicist understanding of Christianity, often rejected the Book of Mormon out of hand.[68] The editor of the *Wayne Sentinel* could thus confidently guess at the nature of the text and invoke the imposture thesis months before it was published: "It is generally known and spoken of as the 'Golden Bible.' Most people entertain an idea that the whole matter is the result of a gross imposition, and a grosser superstition."[69] Indeed, some critics saw no pressing need to read it. The *Boston Recorder*, for example, noted: "Of the book, it [is] only necessary to say that it is a ridiculous imitation of the manner of the Holy Scriptures." Yet the paper went on to add, "We have never seen the 'Book of Mormon.'"[70] The Book of Mormon not only struck many as a counterfeit Bible, it drew the Smith-Muhammad comparisons in the first place. James G. Bennett, one of the young nation's journalistic giants, had connected false prophet and false scripture on an 1831 tour of upstate New York. Traveling with Martin Van Buren and publishing reports in his *Morning Courier and New York Enquirer*, Bennett described Martin Harris, an early Mormon notable, as "the Ali of the Ontario Mahomet." Bennett would conclude that "Mormonism is the latest device of roguery," but he hardly needed to explain the point given his audience's likely negative appraisals of Islam's prophet.[71] Similarly, New York anti-Mormon James M'Chesney needed little more than the Book of Mormon to make up his mind about Smith. "Here we have both the book of Mormon," he wrote in 1838, "and the Alcoran before us. They both breathe the same spirit—are both in the same style—twins were never more alike."[72]

As in the case of Christian writers and the Qur'an, anti-Mormons had to decide if the Book of Mormon was completely inane or if it evinced a mixture of tedium and intelligence. Christians rejected the Qur'an as scripture but disagreed about the text in important ways. To some it was gibberish, testament to the meanness of Muhammad's mind or to Arab ignorance generally. Moderate observers found something to commend, though those admissions could easily buttress claims that Muhammad had borrowed his ideas.[73] Washington Irving, who thought some passages in the Qur'an verged on sublimity, considered its key insights lifted from Judaism.[74] Not surprisingly, conclusions about the Qur'an helped shape various assessments of the prophet and vice versa. One's view of the Qur'an helped determine whether one regarded Muhammad as an evil genius or merely a swindler lucky enough to be surrounded by idiots.

Anti-Mormons rehashed these arguments and were similarly hard pressed for a unified conclusion about Smith and the text. Explanations can be grouped into two broad perspectives or some combination of them. One set found the Book of Mormon so preposterous or dull as to necessarily have been the creation of an unlearned, backwoods impostor.[75] Others claimed that Smith had merely pilfered the text, a grudging admission that some aspects of the work seemed beyond Smith as they understood him. The editor of the *Boston Daily Advertiser* seemed relieved to receive word of the Book of Mormon's alleged original author (i.e., Solomon Spaulding), because it had been "difficult to imagine how a work containing so many indications of being the production of a cultivated mind" should be connected with Joseph Smith.[76] Various explanations creatively straddled the two claims, but, whatever their position, anti-Mormon writers found Smith culpable for deception and for borrowing material from other sources, whether from his own culture, the Bible, or another author.

Given the sheer size, internal complexity, and appeal (albeit limited) of the Book of Mormon, anti-Mormons, as Richard Bushman put it, "had some explaining of their own to do." Palmyra, New York, editor Abner Cole was sure Smith borrowed the idea of a book treating Native American origins from a "vagabond fortune-teller," but the allegation hardly resolved the problem of the text itself. Some Palmyra residents surmised that Smith, perhaps aided by others, simply borrowed language from the Bible. Large passages from Isaiah and other biblical books were obvious, but such a perspective left too many unanswered questions and as a result lacked explanatory staying power.[77] Alexander Campbell, an early but conflicted proponent of the "environmental" origins of the Book of Mormon, cataloged evidence that Smith was the work's sole author.[78] He found the book's account of pre–New Testament Christianity, non-Levitical Israelite priests, and ancient temples outside Jerusalem inconsistent with the Bible. Even more telling for Campbell was the book's attempt to resolve "all the great controversies" of Smith's own religious culture. Adding to these various anachronisms, inconsistencies, contemporary references, grammatical problems, an apparent quotation from Shakespeare, and various backcountry "Smithisms," Campbell reasoned, left one with "the meanest book in the English language." Given what he saw as the book's "uniformity of style," Campbell found no reason to think that it was anything but the half-baked concoction of Joseph Smith.[79]

Campbell later dropped his environmental hypothesis in favor of what became the dominant nineteenth-century theory of Book of Mormon origins.[80] Presented by the team of newsman E. D. Howe and ex-Mormon Philastus Hurlbut (or Hurlburt), the theory rested on the unspoken assumption that such a work, deficient as it was, was too literate for Smith to have pulled off alone. Hoping to uncover material that might damage his former church, Hurlbut came across several Ohioans who remembered similarities between the Mormon scripture and a novel penned by a former neighbor, Solomon Spaulding.[81] After purchasing Hurlbut's investigative source materials, including the Spaulding manuscript, Howe postulated that former Campbellite Sidney Rigdon might be the link between the manuscript and the Mormon founder.[82] Indeed, the learned preacher Rigdon worked better in some respects as the source for such a literary production (Howe credited him with being "the *Iago*, the prime mover, of the whole conspiracy"). Where Alexander Campbell had initially seen stylistic uniformity, John Clark saw the text's multivocality as evidence of Smith's deception: "I am more than ever convinced that there were several hands employed in its preparation. There are certainly striking marks of genius and literary skill displayed in the management of the main story—while in some of the details and hortatory parts there are no less unequivocal marks or bungling and botch work."[83] The Spaulding theory was rehashed for decades, until its flaws (especially evident once the manuscript, missing for years, turned up in 1884) led critics to search for another source of Smith's ideas.[84] Most

Americans, then, saw as much to commend in the Book of Mormon as they did in the Qur'an. Historian Gordon Wood called attention to what he regarded as the relatively brief window for the Book of Mormon in American culture, writing that its timing seemed "providential." While Mormons have enthusiastically agreed, albeit for different reasons, the volume and ferocity of early-century critiques make it clear that there has never been a good time to approach American Protestants with extrabiblical scripture.[85]

Ranging beyond the Book of Mormon/Qur'an connection, anti-Mormons exulted in the ways that Mormonism seemed to emulate Islam. Critics discerned Islamic tendencies in LDS arguments for the Book of Mormon, including emphasis on Smith's lack of schooling, which, they countered, was also claimed by Muslims for Muhammad.[86] Others saw in the Mormon gathering to Missouri an echo of Muslim pilgrims journeying "to the tomb of Mahomet."[87] James M'Chesney warned that, given what he viewed as elements of "*war and bloodshed*" in the Mormon revelations, Americans should beware lest they fall prey to a Mormon/Indian alliance and a violent grab for power. Worried that readers would "laugh at such an idea," M'Chesney cautioned that others scoffed "at Mahomet, no doubt, till his system filled the East, scourged that side of our earth, and has held dominion for twelve hundred years."[88] In the wake of the 1838 "Mormon War" in Missouri, reports of Mormon militarism sparked an anti-Mormon field day. In a characteristic example, William Swartzell roared that Mormonism, "like the religion of Mahomet . . . carries in one hand the sword of vengeance and rapine, and in the other the *pretended* revelations of the Most High."[89] In Mormon Nauvoo, where Smith found himself at the head of his church, city government, and the local militia, detractors discovered that their predictions verged on reality. William Harris fumed that though the "idea of a second Mahomet arising in the nineteenth century, may excite a smile," the Mormons' concentration of numbers and sizable city militia placed Smith within reach of "scenes unheard of since the days of Feudalism."[90] As anti-Mormons took up the question of Mormonism's Americanness in earnest in the 1840s, Islam figured more prominently than ever as the archetypal example of political tyranny cloaking its designs behind a veneer of religious piety.[91]

The Smith-Muhammad comparison thus proved elastic and durable. After Smith's death and the Mormon removal to the Great Basin, the analogy was reinvigorated and eventually, with the rise of the pictorial magazine, was given a visual element complete with exotically dressed Mormon harem girls and camels.[92] Looking back on Mormonism's first decades, writers in the 1850s evinced a mixture of disdain and disbelief at what had transpired, yet Islam helped make sense of it all. "Since the introduction of Christianity," observed Charles Peterson, "the world has seen two great religious impostures—remarkable for the absurdity of their pretensions, not less than for their astonishing success." Mormonism, like Islam, defied understanding: "In spite of ridicule, in spite of the vices of its founder, in spite of positive proof of its being an imposture, it has not only steadily increased, but increased faster than any Christian sect in the same period of time."[93] Similarly, the editor of *Harper's New Monthly Magazine* knew a remarkable story when he saw it. Anticipating—by some 133 years—sociologist Rodney Stark, who famously dubbed Mormonism the first new world religion since Islam, the editor marveled that Mormonism had both appropriated earlier traditions and constituted something new and enduring. The history of Mormonism, he wrote, troubling though it may be, marked the "rise of a new religion, and of a distinctly new religious people."[94] Whatever utility exists in comparing the careers of Muhammad and Smith, it must be understood that there were historically specific reasons for the comparison in the first place.[95] In a religious scene vexed by disestablishment and a dizzying array of spiritual voices, Americans made sense of their new religious environment by using what interpretive tools they had available. In the end, Muhammad served American Protestants as a metaphor to explain the unexplainable, to dismiss what would not go away on its own, and to rhetorically place on the margins what seemed an all-too-immediate threat.

Counterfeiters of Faith and Currency

If the Book of Mormon served anti-Mormons as the quintessential sign of Smith's fraud, other aspects of his life provided supporting evidence. Prominent among these were his "money digging" and the "magical" practices associated with it, the cooperative economics of his communitarian vision, and the political implications of his communal "gathering." Importantly, each of these controversial elements pressed on indeterminate cultural boundaries and, in arguing against the authenticity of Mormon religion in each case, anti-Mormons constructed an image against which Christian piety and religious expression could be defined.

No aspect of Smith's life has been so accentuated by anti-Mormons and so deemphasized by Mormons as his involvement with treasure hunting and the folk supernaturalism associated with it. Smith frankly acknowledged his involvement in money digging but dismissed it as a harmless youthful activity, noting "it was never a very profitable job."[96] Though no document exists in which early Mormons offered anything but unqualified condemnation of magic, anti-Mormons and contemporary historians alike have found occult supernaturalism and folk magic to be the very keys to understanding early Mormonism.[97] The controversy over Smith's magic reveals much about the categorical instability of religion and magic and offers clues as to why he was such a polarizing figure. By blurring lines between religion and magic and transgressing normative understandings regarding the natural world and modern life, Smith became an unsurprising target of opprobrium. He weathered charges of being an American trickster even as he worked to reconcile a robust supernaturalism with patterns of piety rooted in the Mormons' own Protestant pasts.

The details of Smith's magical beginnings can be summarized as follows. His contemporaries, some acquainted with his use of seer stones and struck by his claims of hidden golden plates, assumed that he had simply taken his trickery to new heights by covering up his antics with a religious gloss. Presbyterian Abram Benton, whom Smith later identified as a chief antagonist in New York, summed up Smith's career in a characteristic way. Benton knew Smith had been a "glass-looker" before his foray into religion making; he had earned a living by "pretending, by means of a certain stone, or glass, which he put in a hat, to be able to discover lost goods, hidden treasures, mines of gold and silver, &c." Townsfolk tired of his "base imposition," and he was eventually charged with being a "disorderly person." Released without punishment and emboldened, Smith then "formed the blasphemous design of forging a new revelation." For Benton, Smith's claims of translating the Book of Mormon with the aid of two stones proved that it "was brought to light by the same magic power by which he pretended to tell fortunes."[98] Benton's account, charting as it did Smith's rise from village con artist to religious fraud, did not fall out of fashion—one need only count the times Smith is described as a "trickster" in a standard synthesis of Jacksonian America to realize the power of such characterizations over time.[99]

Benton's communiqué reveals only part of a complicated culture, one in which reactions to stone gazing ranged across a spectrum. For enlightened Christians like Benton, the seer stones and divining practices of superstitious neighbors served as pitiable indicators of popular gullibility. They regarded Smith's supernaturalism as idle trickery; a common descriptor of such alleged trickery was "juggling" or "jugglery."[100] Others were curious or sympathetic. In Smith's 1826 trial, Methodist Peter G. Bridgman accused Smith of defrauding Josiah Stowell, Bridgman's uncle, with his seeric claims. Ironically, Stowell was a witness for the defense.[101] Other former Palmyra neighbors of Smith were ambivalent. When Philastus Hurlbut interviewed some of them in hopes of discrediting Smith, he found a helpful informant in Willard Chase.[102] In 1822, when Chase had employed Joseph Smith and his brother Hyrum to dig a well, he was surprised when the Smiths claimed to have found a seer stone amid the rubble. Chase insisted that he had found the stone and, though thinking it of "no particular worth," admitted that he had tried to reclaim it.[103] William Stafford, who for a time lived within two miles of the Smiths, told a similar tale. After having been invited on several Smith digs, he finally acquiesced. "Prompted by curiosity," he claimed, Stafford participated often enough to describe the brothers' methods in extraordinary detail. His admission that he offered a "large, fat, black" sheep for a sacrificial digging rite merely to "gratify . . . curiosity" seems downright disingenuous.[104] Whatever their feelings about the Smiths, many contemporaries were evidently less troubled by vernacular magic than the more cultured critics.[105]

Smith's dabbling in "the arts of necromancy" functioned in another, subtler way in anti-Mormon literature. In E. D. Howe's account, folk magic provided a training ground where Smith could hone skills of deception. Since his hunting expeditions were shams, Smith was forced time and again to soothe frustrated fellow treasure hunters by tapping "his inventive and fertile genius" to "contrive a story to satisfy them." In so doing, Howe charged, Smith forged "a natural genius, strong inventive powers of mind," and an almost uncanny ability to exploit human credulity.[106] Like the magician's audience, anti-Mormons could be assured Smith's prophethood was a hoax but at the same time remain uneasy because much was obscured from view. The magic charges, then, both exposed the prophet and added to the sense of alarm. Ezra Booth, a Methodist preacher and eventual Mormon defector, described the magic allegations' twin functions memorably. He explained that the "magic charm of delusion" had "so wrapped its sable mantle around me, as to . . . secure me a devoted slave." Mormonism had "haunted" him "like a ghost" until he found himself "hurried . . . by a kind of necessity, into the vortex of delusion." For Booth, magic soothed his embarrassment at having been duped, but it also endowed Mormonism with fearsome power.[107]

Complicating the question of Mormon magic was the fact that while Smith would distance himself from money-digging associates, he apparently saw no contradiction between biblical Christianity and the use of seer stones and other implements of spiritual power. Consider, for instance, the complicated process of scriptural "translation," which Abram Benton had viewed as a simple matter of deceptive magic. Smith maintained that translation was aided by "two stones in silver bows" (associates would also remember his using a single stone placed in a hat). He came to call the implements "Urim and Thummim," providing, as Terryl Givens has noted, an explicitly biblical framework for their use.[108] The Book of Mormon itself celebrated seer stones, giving them an honored place in God's dealings with humans. That text equated the use of material "interpreters" with the vocation of "seer" and designated the latter the greatest of God's gifts. By such "means," the text concluded, God had provided that "mighty miracles" could be wrought through faith.[109] Such passages might have provided a rich tradition of Mormon stone gazing were it not for the combination of opprobrium from without and challenges to Smith's authority from within. (An early convert's rival revelations through a stone prompted Smith to secure exclusive seeric prerogatives after considerable controversy.)[110] Most Mormons eventually followed Smith's lead. They downplayed his youthful dalliance with treasure hunting, interpreted his seeric stone gazing in light of biblical and Book of Mormon passages, viewed seeric work as his alone, and came to view seership quite apart from stone gazing.[111]

That Smith fused material implements, seeric power, and Christian faith is dramatically illustrated in a failed attempt at spiritual translation by an early associate. Oliver Cowdery, awed by Smith's dictation of the Book of Mormon, sought the same abilities. Smith supplied a revelatory response in which God instructed Cowdery that "the Holy Ghost" would provide the text's translation. In addition to the promised "Spirit of revelation," Cowdery was reminded that he had received another gift, a "gift of working with the rod" which had "told [him] things."[112] After Cowdery failed to translate, another revelation cited his lack of faith as the culprit. He had asked God to reveal the text, it was true, but he had not studied the translation out in his "mind" and he had "feared." The process of translation, then, was for Smith and Cowdery a curious combination of tangible "interpreters," intellectual effort (the "spirit of revelation," so the revelation went, pertained to both "heart" and "mind"), and faith in God.[113] If "magical practice of any sort" consists in "an effort to manipulate the spiritual, invisible world," as John L. Brooke has argued, then Smith and Cowdery were no more magicians than they were orthodox Christians, because they practiced their magic in very supplicative, religious ways.[114]

The point here is not merely that Smith and Cowdery both conformed to and transgressed traditional understandings of magical practice. Rather, it is to call attention to the ways that magic, as a construct, shaped reactions to Smith's Mormonism for contemporaries and modern historians alike. In a related vein, the accounts underscore the polemics' discursive function. In decrying Mormon magic, antagonists patrolled modern understandings of religion that deferred to Protestant sensibilities. Simply put, traditional approaches to magic, like the designation of religion as supplicative and magic as manipulative, are untenable as meaningful definitional distinctions.[115] Increasingly, scholars of religion have become cognizant of the ways that magic's descriptions have implicitly reified post-Reformation understandings of religion. Throughout the nineteenth century and through much of the twentieth, magic functioned as religion's ill-defined foil. These reflexive discursive tendencies coded the magical as antimodern, coercive, antisocial, and impious—the very inversion of Protestant piety. Enlightenment theorists posited a universal, generic "religion" but abetted the denigration of ritual, practice, and other outward manifestations of religion as effectively as Protestant polemicists. Both groups preferred the moral, the submissive, and the intellectual as religion's highest expressions. What emerged, then, from the early modern engagement with magic was a widespread desacralization of nature and a notion of religion that became, in Randall Styers words, spiritualized and "localized within the private intellect"—at least among Euro-American intellectual elites.[116] On all counts, early Mormonism represented a holdover from earlier conceptualizations of religion and the natural world.

These complexities notwithstanding, the charge of magic making stung Joseph Smith and the early Mormons. Indeed, the discussion of Cowdery's divining rod in Smith's *Book of Commandments* (1833) was modified in the *Doctrine and Covenants* (1835), where the "rod" references were replaced by more ambiguous language. In the earliest extant copy of the revelation, the original wording was "sprout." So, from "sprout," to "rod," and eventually to "gift of Aaron," the passage not only grew increasingly obscure, it eventually substituted a biblical motif for what had originally been a pedestrian reference to divining rodsmanship. This textual history virtually parallels Smith's use of "interpreters" and eventually "Urim and Thummim" for the seer stones mentioned above.[117] While some might surmise that the modifications represent Smith's effort to distance himself from an early fascination with vernacular magic, it should be noted that he steadfastly insisted that God would endow natural objects with power when coupled with sufficient faith. Though Smith's dependency on seeric implements tailed off precipitously, many accounts affirm that he continued to use seer stones and other material implements sporadically throughout his life.[118] In each case, Mormon supernaturalism was defined and articulated through a biblical lens and not in terms of occult or hermetic practice, a seemingly half-conscious redefinition of such practices—or, in Mormon parlance, a "restoration" of such practices to their proper place of esteem. Seen in this context, Smith was not simply divesting his new religion of magical elements when he obscured the "rod" talk for the 1835 revelation collection. More likely, given his socioreligious context and experience, he had not anticipated the critiques levied by anti-Mormons in the years between the publication of *A Book of Commandments* (1833) and the *Doctrine and Covenants* (1835). After all, Howe's *Mormonism Unvailed* (1834) had pushed discussion of magic to the forefront, and Smith, clearly less committed to a sharp distinction between the natural and the supernatural, was apparently caught unawares. He edited the portion of the revelation most clearly associated with magic, but not out of some new accommodation to Protestant sensitivities regarding the improper place of material objects in religion.[119]

As evident in anti-Mormon preoccupation with Smith's seer stones, the boundary between religion and magic in the early nineteenth century was integral to Protestant identity. That identity, forged as it was against Roman Catholic theology and practice, had not only traditionally evinced considerable concern with the inappropriate mingling of the seen and unseen (especially in its Calvinist and Zwinglian threads), it appears that uneasiness was increasing across the years preceding the advent of Mormonism.[120] Indeed, many practices dubbed magical by antebellum Protestants had been orthodox Christian ones in the centuries before. The antimiracle stance of the Protestant reformers was constructed in part to counter Catholic "superstition" but had only partly toppled traditional understandings by the 1830s. Stephen Fleming rightly concludes that the thrust of early American religious development had less to do with "Christianization" than with "Protestantization."[121] Engagement with Enlightenment thinking during the eighteenth century further "drained Christianity of its belief in the miraculous, except for Bible miracles," but if antebellum anti-Mormon and anti-Catholic writings are any indication, Protestants were as vigilant as ever to keep true religion unsullied.[122] What Jenny Franchot has written about antebellum accounts of Catholic practice could with little variation have been written of discomfort with Smith's seer stones: "The magic emanated from Catholicism's allegedly impure mixtures of human and divine. . . . It was less the specific content of Catholic doctrine than the mingling of sacred and profane that explained popery's power to many antebellum Americans. . . . This dangerous 'association' in Catholic worship, the mingling of what should remain disparate, threatened not only the emotional boundaries of the Protestant observer but his or her class boundaries as well."[123] In fact, antebellum Protestants intuitively connected Mormon magic with Roman Catholic ritual practice and transubstantiation.[124]

Superstition and magic were invoked not only to describe observable differences in content or form, but also to demarcate the authentic from the illegitimate. Any modern account that misses the critical historical role such language has played in cultural boundary maintenance risks perpetuating comparable marginalization.[125] In the end, concerns over the delimitation of the supernatural involved far more than theology. Rather, because the burgeoning scientific/capitalist order hinged on assumptions relating to nature's predictability and orderliness, a vibrant supernaturalism ran against powerful, secularizing cultural currents.[126] Over the nineteenth century, Mormons continued to make overt supernaturalism a core component of their message, but they increasingly preferred subjective internal experience to material implements in their practice and narration of such things. Even so, as the next chapter demonstrates, biblical warrant and emphasis on experiential internality hardly rendered the Mormon yearning for spiritual power uncontroversial.

A second, related mark of Smith's presumed imposture involved a similarly contested cultural boundary. Many anti-Mormons hypothesized that the Book of Mormon was a money-making scheme; in Smith's cooperative "Law of Consecration" they found the smoking gun behind his entire religious venture.[127] Newspaperman James G. Bennett, for instance, speculated that Smith had formulated a "religious plot" to get "money and a good living"; on hearing reports of Mormon property sharing in Ohio, Bennett was sure that he had guessed right. Smith apparently "had not dug for money in vain" because the Ohio Mormons had "adopted some of the worldly views of the Shakers and have formed a sort of community system where everything is in common." Bennett assumed that Smith and other Mormon leaders were the primary beneficiaries of such a system.[128] Mormonism hardly made Smith rich, but the redistribution of property and the support such an arrangement provided church leaders offered damning evidence in anti-Mormon critiques.

Even so, Mormon cooperative systems never materialized enough to suit Smith; rather, they remained an abstract ideal or a mechanism for episodic church fund-raising. Accordingly, the topic was oft-mentioned but largely undeveloped in anti-Mormon literature. Shorthand equation of the Latter-day Saints with the Shakers abounded early on, though skeptics were hard pressed for examples or anecdotes. By and large they had to be contented with assumptions about Smith's personal exploitation of Mormon cooperation.[129] In a culture racked with economic reversals, multiple and sometimes confusing currency systems, and much to-do over banking, charges of Mormon counterfeiting at once confirmed what anti-Mormons considered Smith's real motives and gave the Mormon menace an economic component. For anti-Mormon E. G. Lee, religious counterfeiters did not have far to fall to become currency bogus makers. He found Mormon duplicity over scriptural matters to be a fitting metaphor for their economic dealings. According to Lee, Mormons had come to "rely now altogether upon the Christian's Bible, whose style they have attempted to *counterfeit*, and from whence these 'false prophets' now labour to draw doctrines to cloak their iniquity, and mislead and deceive." "Well may the Mormons be ashamed," he continued, "of their COUNTERFEIT BIBLE, which by their own testimony is shown to be as gross a trick as are their COUNTERFEIT BANK NOTES."[130] Thus, the 1837 failure of the Mormon bank in Ohio and rumors of counterfeiting in Illinois functioned in anti-Mormon writing to expose Smith's hypocrisy, as well as a metaphor for his religion generally.[131]

What went unrealized in all of the talk of Smith's luxurious living was the traditional association between magic and counterfeiting. Though anti-Mormons failed to connect the two meaningfully, the association had a venerable history. By the late Renaissance, a second manifestation of magic had developed in concert with the witchcraft and conjuring work of the illiterate masses; among the intellectual classes, practitioners of "high magic" dabbled in various forms of alchemy, astrology, and hermetic divination. In the transformations of the eighteenth century, the alchemical fascinations of "natural magic" practitioners became the polemical target of "true" scientists.[132] By the nineteenth century, what had been regarded as disparate strands of magical practice—each with their own moral and religious implications—came to be viewed as one and the same profanation of real religion (or science). Whereas medieval and early modern witchcraft had been coded as demonic and therefore essentially sinful, in the decades preceding Mormonism's advent, magic was reimagined as "a new form of aberrational behavior, a disorder or delusion contravening appropriately rationalist, and post-Reformation, piety." In that newer view, magic re-emerged fundamentally as "a counterfeit, a deceptive and fraudulent imitation." Though not fully formed in anti-Mormon literature, perceptions of Mormon magic and counterfeiting were inherently linked historically and emerged from related concerns in the post–Reformation West.[133]

As combustible as the glass-looking, counterfeiting, or profiteering charges were, nothing riled non-Mormons more than Smith's involvement in politics. Once anti-Mormons became convinced that Smith posed a viable political threat, opposition to his movement turned deadly. Americans generally reacted with horror to reports from several Mormon defectors that Smith promised to be "a second Mahomet" if his enemies did not "let [him] alone," and those convinced he might make the attempt gunned him down in 1844.[134] So important were these questions regarding the relationship of religion and politics for Mormon/non-Mormon relations that they are taken up in detail in the third chapter of this study.

THE UNCERTAINTIES THAT characterized the new nation gave rise to Mormonism and colored the ways antagonists critiqued it. The project of exposing religious impostures, which Susan Juster describes as an already "overwrought and overdetermined discourse of authenticity" by the turn of the nineteenth century, was well under way before Smith's time. It predictably found its way to him and dominated the early period of anti-Mormon thinking.[135] Notions of religious imposture denied authentic religion to various prophets and, as a result, understood them in terms of the political, the economic, or the social. Narratives of false religion, in other words, turned to everything but religion, and history's false prophets necessarily became charlatans and crooks because Americans had few other frameworks at hand for comprehending a figure whose religious claims they rejected. Anti-Mormon anxieties about the relationship between faith, civic power, and social order converged around the figure of Joseph Smith; as a result, historians have found anti-Mormonism difficult to characterize. Given the interrelatedness of Protestant understandings of religious imposture, authority, and history, efforts to establish whether anti-Mormon reactions to Smith were religiously, economically, or politically motivated will in the end prove unhelpful. In actuality, anti-Mormons could defame Smith, thwart his movement, and seek his demise while at the same time claiming quite sincerely that they had no argument with Mormon religion whatever. Thomas Ford, governor of Illinois during the Mormons' controversial stay at Nauvoo, could thus maintain that he held no personal prejudice against Mormonism but lament that he felt "degraded by the reflection, that the humble governor of an obscure State, who would otherwise be forgotten in a few years, stands a fair chance . . . of being dragged down to posterity with an immortal name, hitched on to the memory of a miserable impostor."[136] Such logic doomed the Mormon prophet to a protracted struggle against charges of imposture that ultimately cost him his life.

CHAPTER 2

"Delusion"

Early Mormon Religiosity

Pascal Smith's religious views caused him considerable trouble. In a legal complaint, his wife declared that Smith had rendered "implicit obedience" to a "Mormon Prophet" armed with "mesmeric clairvoyance." Harriet Smith explained that her husband had been "laboring under a religious delusion" and had been duped into donating a large part of his property to the prophet. She feared additional revelations might reduce them to poverty. A judge ordered the local sheriff to bring Smith in and impanelled a jury of five freeholders to hear the case.[1] Once in court, Smith declared that his marriage was unhappy and he thought it prudent to separate from his wife. Witnesses testified that it was widely believed Smith was insane, but that on nonreligious subjects "he appeared sane enough." A physician, one Dr. Mussey, based on what he had heard at the trial, asserted that Smith suffered from "*monomania*." Under cross-examination, the doctor was pressed on how he had come to that diagnosis. When asked if belief in spiritual communications constituted insanity, Mussey said that while such things did not necessarily constitute madness, if one claimed to actually hear communications from beyond, especially if those communications concerned one's property, he would think that the person's mind "had lost its balance." He gave a similar response to the question of mental visions. Belief in them did not constitute insanity, but if one "were to be governed in his acts by them, or by those of another," then, yes, he would regard those behaviors as indications of insanity. To the next question, "If a man expressed a belief that other books were inspired besides the bible, would you pronounce him insane?" Mussey replied: If his "belief was concerning some books I could name, I should think there was something wrong about his head or heart."[2] Smith's attorney pounced on Mussey's statements. "Mr. Smith is crazy, they say . . . crazy upon the subject of religion,"

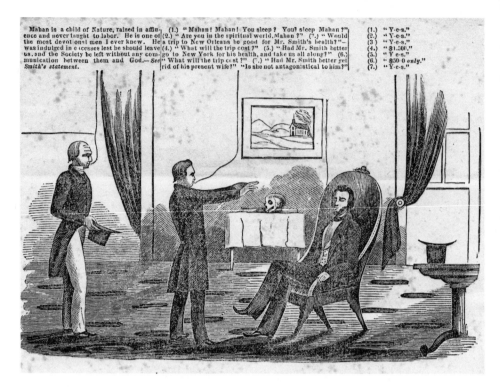

Mahan is a child of Nature, raised in affluence and never taught to labor. He is one of the most devotional men I ever knew. He was indulged in e ccesses lest he should leave us, and the Society be left without any communication between them and God.— *See Smith's statement.*

(1.) "Mahan! Mahan! You sleep? You! sleep Mahan?", (2.) " Are you in the spiritual world, Mahan?" (3.) " Would a trip to New Orleans be good for Mr. Smith's health?"— (4.) " What will the trip cost?" (5.) " Had Mr. Smith better go to New York for his health, and take us all along?" (6.) " What will the trip cost?" (7.) " Had Mr. Smith better get rid of his present wife?" "Is she not antagonistical to him?"

(1.) " Y-e-s."
(2.) " Y-e-s."
(3.) " Y-e-s."
(4.) " $1,500."
(5.) " Y e-s."
(6.) " $50-0 *only*."
(7.) " Y-e-s."

A Law Case Exhibiting the Most Extraordinary Developments . . . (1848), frontispiece
(Abraham Lincoln Presidential Library and Museum, Springfield, Ill.)

he shot back, "because forsooth, he believes in spiritual existences. Well, does this prove the man crazy?—then all Christendom is crazy, for they believe in spiritual existences."[3]

After the arguments had been heard, the jurors decided against Pascal Smith. They found that his mind had become "alienated," though it was only in the "mildest sense of the term, he is now insane." Nevertheless, they found him incapable of managing his finances.[4] The unhappy result for Smith illustrates not only the fear that religion-gone-amuck struck in early American hearts but also the influence of quasi-scientific explanations in shaping popular perceptions of religion. While Mormonism appeared in various formulations of that relationship, critics struggled to articulate exactly how it might differ from other dangerous "isms" and deemed it, as in the Pascal Smith case, a perceived instigator of popular delusion. In a setting where demonstrating Christianity's reasonableness amounted to what one historian has termed the most pressing theological task, the spread of Mormonism occasioned considerable alarm.[5]

If imposture, the subject of the first chapter, served as the framework for skeptical elucidations of the Mormon prophet, delusion answered the more perplexing explanatory problem of popular Mormon faith. The delusion epithet was repeated so often, in fact, that it took little time for Mormons to tire of it. John Whitmer, appointed church historian in 1831, moaned in his official account that Mormon missionaries typically enjoyed success until rival "priests would cry delusion! delusion!!"[6] Early anti-Mormons were baffled that anyone would follow Joseph Smith; though acknowledging that even the upstanding could be taken in, they were hard pressed to explain why. In some ways, explaining Smith or Brigham Young was easy, since their motives were with little creativity cast as lust for power, wealth, or women. Their followers, however, posed an interpretive challenge. Critics believed that ordinary Latter-day Saints had been duped, but they disagreed about how such hoodwinking could be perpetrated on such a wide scale. In their explanations of Mormon religiosity, anti-Mormons unfolded an array of questions about religious experience, biblical interpretation, the relationship of reason and faith. The lack of unified or lasting explanations of Mormon behavior highlights the irony that ordinary, largely forgotten Latter-day Saints posed perhaps the greatest riddle for skeptics.

For all their talk of Joseph Smith's trickery, anti-Mormons spent comparatively little time detailing exactly how he was able to deceive so many. More often critics turned to the reasons some Americans were predisposed, as it were, to being deceived. Charles Peterson wrote that Smith's great talent, if he had one, was his "intuitive faculty of discovering" dupes. Because Smith "was credulous himself respecting the supernatural," Peterson reasoned, he understood that "others might be equally weak" and took advantage where he could.[7] In turning to various religious, hermeneutical, evidentiary, or even medical reasons for Mormon behavior, though, antagonists were most often struck by strands of religiosity that had troubled orthodox Christians for centuries. So, while their controversial practices alienated Mormons from traditional Christians, theirs seem to have been curiously *standard* forms of Christian deviance. Thomas Kirk astutely encapsulated both Mormonism and anti-Mormonism when he defined Smith's movement in terms of the Latter-day Saints' notorious spirituality: "The distinguishing feature of Mormon Faith . . . is, that its devotees profess to be in possession of a certain *power of the spirit*, which places them in direct communication with God and his angels, endowing them with the gifts of revelation and prophecy, healing and tongues, &c."[8] Whereas the greatest opposition to Mormonism might be expected to involve distinctive doctrines, much that was aimed at rank-and-file Saints pertained to intra-Christian wrangles over experience that had been fomenting for some time. Viewed in this light, early Mormonism seems to have been less exotic than portrayed by some historians.[9]

Delusion was as ubiquitous a word in early anti-Mormon writing as any, yet it did not command a universal definition. The term proved flexible, marking a range of related understandings rather than a specific diagnosis of Mormon errors.[10] At one end of the spectrum is found a narrower, almost clinical sense of the word. Indeed, as the following pages describe a burgeoning antebellum medical field's quandary over religious experience, delusion could involve outright insanity. "I sincerely believe," wrote one critic in a characteristic formulation, "the Mormons are in a perfect hallucination of mind."[11] But more often "delusion" marked a less formal set of meanings ranging from "enthusiastic" or "emotionally overwrought" to "superstitious" or simply "deceived." Delusion as a catchall category, then, served anti-Mormons well. Daniel Kidder, for instance, followed his *Mormonism and the Mormons* (1842) with a more generalized volume warning against an array of delusions. In the latter work, he associated delusion with credulity, witchcraft, astrology, "morbid acquisitiveness," "supernatural visitations," popular ignorance, and Mormonism. For Kidder, Mormonism surpassed them all. "The delusions possessing the body called 'Mormons, or Latter-day Saints,'" he concluded, "are some of the most extraordinary of any we have related."[12] Mormonism was thus portrayed as both symptomatic of and partly to blame for widespread popular gullibility, infidelity, and superstition. By gravitating toward behaviors long deemed controversial, anti-Mormons made sense of Mormonism, much as they had of Joseph Smith, by reassuring themselves that it was a familiar delusion. As one critic put it, "There's nothing new under the sun." The godly could weather outbursts of religious enthusiasm now as in the past.[13]

Mormon Spirituality and the Threat of Enthusiasm

The hypercompetitive voluntarism that followed disestablishment fostered anxiety about the ability of religious upstarts to upset established congregations. Most early anti-Mormons assumed that Joseph Smith drew his following from society's dregs.[14] These unflattering assessments by no means disappeared from later appraisals, especially as poor European converts flooded into Mormon centers, but critics found by the mid-1830s that Mormons often did not match the stereotype. As evangelist Nancy Towle expressed it, "I really viewed it strange, that so many men of skill, should be ... duped of them."[15] Anti-Mormons put the fact that some Mormons held middle-class credentials to good use (if Mormonism could dupe the respectable, all the more reason to be wary), but over time the assumptions about Mormonism's appeal only to the dissolute or destitute begged reassessment.[16]

Antebellum writers found in the concept of religious delusion a sturdy explanation of Mormonism's appeal and a reason to actively oppose the movement.[17] Separated from Joseph Smith by hundreds of miles, residents of Independence, Missouri, had only ordinary Mormons to contend with. By 1833, the old-timers had seen enough. Meeting in July, non-Mormons drafted a list of grievances before making their point with tar, feathers, and some rough handling of the Mormon printing press. The county's gentlemen wrote that the Mormon "fanatics" were "characterized by the profoundest ignorance, the grossest superstition, and the most abject poverty." The sect of "pretended Christians" had a corrupting influence on slaves, offered free blacks a share in their Zion, and boasted of their imminent possession of the county. Of the Mormons' "pretended revelations from heaven—their personal intercourse with God and His angels—the maladies they pretend to heal by the laying on of hands—and the contemptible gibberish with which they habitually profane the Sabbath, and which they dignify with the appellation of unknown tongues," the Missourians had "nothing to say," though they warned that Mormon "swarms" would soon wrest civil government from civil hands.[18]

The list of grievances encapsulates the century's anti-Mormon mantra but betrays considerable ambivalence about Mormon religiosity. Taken at face value, it designates religiosity as a minor irritant only, yet several "secular" grievances seem disingenuous. The alleged overture to free blacks, for instance, appeared in the local Mormon paper and seemed innocuous enough to prompt Mormon hypotheses that it was a deliberately exaggerated pretense. After all, on hearing that some had taken offense, the Mormon editor had promptly run an apologetic explanation.[19] As for tampering with slavery, many Mormons moved to Missouri from the Northeast and some brought antislavery sentiments with them. By contrast, overtly abolitionist Germans in Missouri were never harassed. The Mormons, moreover, like many Northerners, had repudiated abolitionism as too drastic a solution to the slavery problem.[20] So, while some historians have called attention to the cultural divide separating the Mormons and their Upper South–transplanted Missouri neighbors, others have emphasized the contradictions in anti-Mormon rhetoric. This latter narrative casts the conflict as a Protestant orthodoxy loathing a threatening heresy but existing within a political climate that made anti-Mormon claims leveled in wholly religious terms problematic.[21]

Ultimately, the Missouri grievances underscored the limited utility of traditional interpretive categories. This is especially true of the historiographical debate over the secular or religious nature of the Mormon conflict. Voicing one side, Kenneth Winn found that "the Missourians displayed a relative indifference to the actual content of Mormon theology," but that argument holds only if religion is reduced to doctrine at the expense of religious practice and experience.[22] Delimiting religion in this way was in fact a central thrust of the nineteenth-century polemics. Where pre-Reformation usage of "religion" had routinely related to ritual obligation, in the Euro-American West after the sixteenth century, religion was increasingly identified with belief and theology.[23] It should come as no surprise, then, that critics coded the early LDS practice-heavy conceptualizations of faith and community as nonreligious. If anti-Mormons sometimes exhibited little or no interest in the nuances of Mormon thought, its exegetical formulations, and the like, they typically expressed deep misgivings about Mormon religiosity. As anti-Mormons opposed the more ecstatic elements of Mormon religiosity or countered Mormon claims of divine power, they rehashed arguments about the cessation of biblical miracles and the reasonableness of Christianity. At the same time, they also ruminated on the fragility of the human psyche and the causes of mental illness. In other words, by drawing too stark a line between the secular and the religious in the nineteenth century, one risks clarifying with contemporary lenses what was muddled for historical subjects. Whatever political, economic, or cultural divide existed between the Latter-day Saints and their skeptics, perceptions of real religion clearly remained in the mix.

Anti-Mormons fixed the Saints on the radical end of a spectrum that had been taking discursive shape for some time. At one end was what Protestants termed "formalism," which named a skeleton of religious life that had devolved into lifeless form, cultural habit, or intellectual abstraction. At the other end of the spectrum was "enthusiasm," a term used to designate religious craziness—at worst those religiously insane or, at least, those falsely inspired. In her examination of the battles over religious experience, Ann Taves suggests that false experience proved as troubling to Anglo-American Protestants as false belief: "In contrast to sectarian and schismatic, which were linked to false ecclesiology, and heresy, which was linked to false doctrine, enthusiasm defined illegitimacy in relation to false inspiration or, more broadly, false experience. Enthusiasm, unlike schism or heresy, located that which was threatening not in challenges to ecclesiology or doctrine but in challenges to that most fundamental of Christian categories—revelation."[24] By the early nineteenth century, Protestants had contested the religiosity of the French Prophets, Quakers, Shakers, and successive waves of revivalists. Not surprisingly, earlier enthusiasts often served as the denunciatory model for later culprits. Early American evangelicals, for example, found that they had to walk a fine line, arguing for an immediate, miraculous infusion of the Holy Spirit in the "new birth" but at the same time warding off association with the infamous French Prophets.[25] Enthusiasm's bitterest opponents tended to be intellectual elites who, though they rarely decried religious experience generally, were inclined to oppose particular practices or groups in naturalistic terms. Protestants employed these Enlightenment strategies in their sectarian contests; as a result, nineteenth-century polemics offer a confused mingling of rationalistic, historical, and doctrinal arguments.[26]

Enthusiasm remained fashionable in anti-Mormon formulations, but delusion was arguably the more common term by the 1830s and 1840s. Like enthusiasm, delusion encompassed the religious and the naturalistic; it could describe one's false inspiration or one's mental state. That Mormons appeared sincere in their faith was hardly a moderating note in anti-Mormon literature—truly believing in Mormonism was precisely the problem. Apart from their relationship to their allegedly fraudulent prophet, the elements of Mormon religiosity that exposed them to charges of delusion were the same that had figured in Anglo-American thinking about religious experience for at least the previous two centuries: tongues speaking, angelic visitations, bodily agitations, and faith healing. Unitarian Jason Whitman astutely summed up both the Mormon message and the challenge it presented to Protestants. The Mormons argue, he wrote, "what all admit to be facts, that, in the primitive ages of the church, there was among the disciples the power of speaking with tongues and of working miracles; that, at the present day, no denomination of Christians possesses this power." Whitman was as uncomfortable with Mormonism as anyone but conceded that with biblical precedents in hand, a degree of plausibility attended its message.[27] Anti-Mormons thus inherited a sensitive problem. They felt to discredit radical expressions on the religious fringe but had to do so without disgracing religious experience generally. They, like their antienthusiast predecessors, found tools in Enlightenment narratives but learned to wield them gently so as not to touch the validity of biblical miracles or more conventional religious experiences.

Perhaps no other aspect of LDS religiosity disturbed nonbelievers as much as tongues speaking. Mormons considered the gift of an unknown, heavenly tongue (glossolalia) and the miraculous ability to speak in ordinary languages the speaker had not studied (xenoglossia) to be profound manifestations of divine power. Scholars disagree about the origins of the practice in Mormonism, yet it is clear early Mormons expected it as evidence that God was again pouring out his spirit. The Book of Mormon railed against modern deniers of the miraculous by relating spiritual tongues, the Bible, and a "restoration" of God's ancient power.[28] Joseph Smith remembered that Brigham Young had first experienced the gift in 1832 in Ohio, though the practice prevailed in Ohio before that time and perhaps in the infant church's first months in New York.[29] Sidney Rigdon, who would become one of Smith's chief lieutenants, had split with Alexander Campbell because of a disagreement over the restoration of spiritual gifts including tongues.[30] Rigdon's congregation was thus ripe for Mormon elders armed with the message, according to a skeptical news report, that there "would be as great miracles wrought" through their preaching "as there was at the day of Pentecost."[31] The newly minted Ohio Mormons eventually experienced their spiritual outpouring, and glossolalia figured prominently among the gifts.

Future LDS Church president Wilford Woodruff recalled that in the spring of 1832 he first read of a new sect "that professed the ancient gifts of the gospel[;] they healed the sick[,] cast out devils[,] and spoke in tongues."[32] His statement reflects the fact that, scarcely two years into the movement's history, glossolalia had become a symbol of Mormon singularity.[33] The Saints' tongues probably caused them the greatest trouble in Missouri. Non-Mormon Missourians had "nothing to say" about tongues in their polished list of grievances quoted above, but their "*secret* constitution" provided a more candid appraisal of the Saints' spirituality. Mormons "openly blaspheme the Most High God," that statement read, "and cast contempt on His holy religion, by pretending . . . to speak unknown tongues, by direct inspiration, and by divers pretenses derogatory to God and religion, and to the utter subversion of human reason."[34] Though the ensuing violence had myriad causes, at least one participant reduced the trouble to the Mormons' ecstatic gifts. Mormon David Pettigrew, recalling the turbulent period, wrote that the "gift of tongues, I think was the cause, or means of the excitement." Pettigrew reported that "when they heard little children Speaking tongues," the non-Mormons became convinced the Mormons must go—especially once an observer converted after witnessing a display of youthful glossolalia. Pettigrew acknowledged non-Mormon fears of being "over run" by the Saints' gathering; nevertheless his statement is indicative of the deep suspicion occasioned by Mormon religiosity. Tellingly, tongues proved so controversial that the Missouri Mormon high council forbad the practice for an extended period following the 1833 violence.[35]

With the French Prophets, Shakers, and followers of Edward Irving in England in mind, critics had timeworn strategies to draw upon in countering Mormon tongues.[36] Daniel Kidder noted that tongues followed each Mormon advance and assumed that the practice functioned as a "species of jugglery" to amaze potential converts. He poked fun at Mormon apostle Orson Hyde, who had been slowed on a mission to Palestine because of the language barriers he encountered along the way. With tongues rampant in the Mormon camp, Kidder teased, why delay the trip "to learn the German language *scientifically*"?[37] After witnessing Mormon glossolalia, an anonymous tract writer remained unconvinced. The author had observed a young Mormon woman in a Brooklyn meeting uttering "certain sounds, altogether unintelligible to the audience" and was entertained by her interpretation thereafter. She had prophesied, she reported, that within a year Brooklyn would boast five hundred Mormons. The writer noted that fellow Mormons received this as "inspiration, a new tongue, a divine prediction," but since a year had passed without the prophecy's fulfillment, the author concluded that the Saints "did not know the difference between gibberish and an inspired tongue."[38]

Anticipating the American encounter with Pentecostal tongues by nearly three-quarters of a century, Mormons found themselves embroiled in a controversy over glossolalia that had been ongoing in Christianity since antiquity.[39] For various reasons, Mormon interest in tongues cooled across the nineteenth century; eventually a preference for xenoglossia replaced the zeal for glossolalia. The trend mirrored Joseph Smith's own preference. But if Smith eventually displayed reservations about glossolalia, his resistance to the bodily exercises that coincided with the Ohio tongues was immediate. The fits, shakes, and swoons that had animated American revivals found their way into early Mormon meetings and caused a stir within and outside the church.[40] Leading Mormons denounced the exercises as false (Smith generally affirmed those manifestations that enjoyed clear biblical precedent) as they became acutely aware that the displays could discredit the gifts they deemed legitimate. Skeptics quickly caught wind of the Mormons' spiritual exertions. In early 1831, E. D. Howe published reports of the "wildest enthusiasm" among the Latter-day Saints. They would "fall, as without strength, roll upon the floor, and, so mad were they that even the females were seen in a cold winter day, lying under the bare canopy of heaven, with no couch or pillow but the fleecy snow." Predictably, the non-Mormon accounts made no distinction, as Mormons would, between these behaviors and speaking in tongues: "At other times they are taken with a fit of jabbering that which they neither understand themselves nor any body else, and this they call speaking foreign languages by divine inspiration."[41] Smith and his allies effectively controlled the spiritual fits. By the 1840s, the Mormon paper reiterated the warnings by invoking the French Prophets as an example of spiritual delusion. The Holy Spirit, it maintained, would never rob God's people of control over their bodies. LDS ambivalence about ecstatic spirituality, in other words, led Mormons to the very framework that had cast their experiences as delusion. Ironically, in the rush for distance from unpopular enthusiasts, the Mormon editorialist, possibly Joseph Smith himself, directed readers to a standard evangelical handbook for an account of the French Prophets.[42]

As in the case of tongues speaking and fits, Mormon claims of healing by faith were contested because these miracles were similarly amenable to outside observation. William Swartzell witnessed the failed healing of a man who had ingested mercury and summed up the event caustically: "So much for Mormonism *versus* Mercury!"[43] Another commentator gleefully related that after several failures to heal the sick, Joseph Smith "saw it necessary that some way should be devised to continue the deception of his credulous followers," so he issued a revelation about some of the sick being "*appointed unto death.*"[44] Mormons, though steadfast in their conviction that God would heal the sick when faith was sufficient, nevertheless came to recognize that their proselytizing efforts could be hampered if the church elders answered every skeptic with a healing. The matter was eventually settled. Yes, the Saints experienced miracles, but those experiences were for their own benefit and were not intended to convince unbelievers.[45] The directive against public healing predictably drew anti-Mormon comment. William Harris charged that Smith's moratorium was intended to shield his chicanery from detection. With the restrictions in place, he fumed, observers were limited to the Saints' own accounts, which were composed by "bigoted and interested persons."[46]

More troublesome for anti-Mormons were apparently successful healings. When an inquisitive group from neighboring Portage County, Ohio, visited Joseph Smith at Kirtland, the conversation turned to the apostolic age. Smith then surprised the group by approaching Elsa Johnson, whose arm was withered by chronic rheumatism, and commanded her to "be whole" in the name of Jesus. Johnson immediately lifted her arm and thereafter resumed household tasks without difficulty.[47] The scene was enough for Ezra Booth, a Methodist minister, who, after his later disaffection, described how observable evidence could as easily ensnare the unwary as expose Mormonism. In justifying his beguilement, he explained that his faith in Mormonism had been "built upon the testimony of my senses."[48] In an ironic turnaround, anti-Mormon Booth was left trumpeting a spiritualized epistemology against what Mormons would have understood as empirical vindication. In a similar example, Mary Ettie V. Smith recalled that her family's conversion to Mormonism resulted from the healing of her mother's deafness. Promised by a missionary that "if she would consent to be baptized, the deafness with which she was afflicted . . . would in a very short time be removed," Smith's mother became a Mormon. The entire family was convinced when immediately after baptism Smith's mother's hearing improved and was eventually restored. A short time later, Joseph Smith himself healed the leg of Mary Smith's brother. "With all these astonishing evidences before us," she concluded, "how could we doubt Mormonism?" Like Booth, though, many of the Smiths, including Mary herself, came to doubt Mormonism and reinterpreted the healings' causes.[49] Obviously, Mormons and their detractors both enjoyed complicated relationships with faith healing. Though Mormons could benefit from public feats of faith, they came to understand that empiricism could cut both ways for an evangelistic church. Anti-Mormons could ridicule failed healings, but the Mormons' sporadic successes begged explanation.

Some made short work of apparent healings by assuming that Mormons had taken credit for what doctors had really accomplished. However, La Roy Sunderland took a more novel approach.[50] In *Mormonism Exposed and Refuted* (1838), Sunderland, at the time a Methodist minister, linked Mormon claims not only with other religious impostors but with nonreligious curers as well. In offering something of a cross-cultural explanation of curing practices, Sunderland was ambivalent yet serious about the successful healings. Though persuaded that spiritual healers were frauds, he nonetheless believed they might actually heal some people: countless examples demonstrated "the power of the imagination over the nervous system, and how susceptible the human mind is to that influence." Sunderland not only articulated the beginnings of a theory of religious experience, which he would later elaborate, he also provided a paradigm that affirmed the healing accounts but discredited Mormon healers.[51] While his naturalistic perspective verged on a modern strategy for narrating religious experience, what linked Sunderland and other critics was the conviction that Mormon healers had perpetrated an unforgivable sham. The ritual act of healing bound Mormons together in a new social reality, but for the skeptics the rituals took a core element of Christianity, faked it, and constructed a deluded community on that sandy foundation. Ironically, though healing remains one of Christian history's signal continuities, it polarized Mormons and their observers in unmistakable ways.[52] Indeed, Mormons proved most controversial in their timing, as late-century Protestants abandoned miracle cessationism for faith healing in droves. Like the early Mormons, these late-century evangelicals argued from a primitivist perspective: faith healing returned one to an earlier, purer form of Christianity.[53]

Adding to the discomfort caused by tongues, fits, and healings was the fact that Mormons maintained regular interaction with supernatural beings. Joseph Smith's first religious experiences were heavenly visitations, but less prominent Mormons also found themselves in company with angels and devils. While other American Christians made similar claims, Mormon narratives of the unseen world bolstered charges that their religious experiences were mere delusions. Supernatural manifestations, like the other spiritual phenomena, had precedent in the Bible but were increasingly controversial in the period of Mormon beginnings. Whereas evangelicals had routinely seen Satan and angels in turn-of-the-century revivals, by the time Mormons entered the fray evangelical visitation accounts were as likely to occasion a smirk as reverent awe, as Christine Leigh Heyrman has noted.[54] Though they appear now as a bridge between the ecstasy of the early-century revivals and the spiritualist heyday at midcentury, the Mormon claims in the 1830s and 1840s struck most critics as ready for the trash heap of antiquated superstition.

Mormons' literalist hermeneutic with regard to spiritual beings prompted skeptics to firm up Reformed stances on miracle cessation. Many writers went beyond arguments that simply located miracles in antiquity. In particular, their critiques were tinged with naturalizing assumptions that formatted Mormon claims not as misreadings of the Bible but as pathology. In other words, Mormon visions or visitations were less likely to enter anti-Mormon writings as exegetical problems than they were lumped together with folksy fascination with witches, goblins, or fairies. In 1829, the *Paines-*

ville Telegraph reported that Joseph Smith claimed to have been visited by a "spirit," and editor E. D. Howe no doubt chose his words carefully.[55] Unlike Mormons, who would have preferred the word "angel," anti-Mormons chose language that distanced such experiences from the Bible. The *Vermont Telegraph* stated that Smith claimed he could communicate with "spirits" at will;[56] according to E. G. Lee, Mormon Martin Harris "had always been a firm believer in dreams, and visions, and supernatural appearances, such as apparitions and ghosts";[57] Howe wrote in 1834 that the Smiths' neighbors knew them to be "ignorant and superstitious—having a firm belief in ghosts and witches."[58] Howe wove such beliefs into an account of how one might descend into religious delusion. In doing so, his idealized sense of true religion came through clearly enough. One's mind and soul, Howe wrote, were refined in the embrace of "simple philosophical truths." Given his preference for philosophical truth over religious experience, Mormon emphasis on the latter seemed to Howe to take Saints in a downward spiral. Starting from mere false ideas, Mormons were set on a course to madness: "He who embraces falsehood and error, will sink deeper and deeper in the vortex of folly and madness; wild vagaries, apparitions, intercourse with the spirits of other worlds . . . will dance through his imagination in shapeless confusion . . . and thus we find him enveloped in the fatal cords of fanaticism."[59] For Howe and other anti-Mormons, contact with supernatural beings was evidence not of blessedness but of an unsound mind. Seen against a backdrop of similar narratives of evangelical experience before and after Mormonism's founding, the anti-Mormon material fits within what could be described as an almost Protestant/Enlightened explanatory tradition. Though Protestant moderates and enlightened skeptics differed in their understanding of true religion, their narratives of false religion were quite similar. Targets like Mormonism drew disparate commentators toward one another in the debates over authentic experience.[60]

Religion, Madness, and the Search for Rational Faith

Mormons' ecstatic gifts earned them a prominent place in often-contentious antebellum conversations about religion and mental health. Decorous Christians had long associated religious enthusiasm with madness, but the antebellum discussions were enlivened by an advancing professionalism in medicine, the proliferation of asylums, and the spiritual efflorescence described in the foregoing pages. Recent scholarship has demonstrated that by the 1830s and 1840s, the concept of religious madness had moved beyond the realm of sectarian polemics to a prominent if controversial place in standard medical explanations of mental illness. Moreover, sectarian polemics had themselves become thoroughly tinged by the naturalizing approaches of the more scientific narratives.[61] Far from comprising competing narratives, however, the sectarian and scientific accounts functioned as reinforcing explanations. Nonprofessionals who faced aberrant behavior with a threatening or confusing religious component often fused the two strains into a single explanation.[62]

There was no antebellum consensus on religion and madness, yet the various strands of thought worked against early Mormon religiosity. While antebellum officials became increasingly less likely to ascribe patients' mental problems to "moral causes" such as religious excess, many of the period's physicians harbored deep misgivings about American religion. Perhaps more significant for anti-Mormonism was the fact that nonprofessionals continued to blame religion for their loved ones' illnesses long after the medical establishment had grown more cautious.[63] Custodians of the nation's emerging asylum system found themselves in an awkward position, recognizing as they did religious connections in their patients' histories. At the same time, they sought support from religious bodies or benevolent societies, whom they did not wish to offend by suggesting that religion was directly to blame. Tellingly, one study of New England's McLean Asylum found that superintendents tended to underreport religious factors.[64]

On the other hand, some physicians cared little about offending the Protestant establishment. Amariah Brigham's *Observations on the Influence of Religion upon the Health and Physical Welfare of Mankind* (1835) flatly asserted what hosts of Americans steadfastly believed: religion could and did cause insanity.[65] Though evangelicals excoriated him for having maligned Christianity, Brigham consistently affirmed his commitment to an admittedly rationalistic version of Protestantism. Despite his recognition that religion itself had been refined over time, he worried that modern Christians were prone to "unenlightened" ideas about Christianity's true nature. He argued that Jesus sought a "uniform morality" only and that, far from being the stuff of the "supernatural," the "fruits of the spirit" were the "natural *results* of the exercise of the moral and intellectual powers of man."[66] Brigham, in short, was no evangelical Christian.

His rationalistic perspective regarding the Holy Spirit went to the heart of his concern about religion and the mind. After documenting the dangers of theaters and balls, he expressed shock that Americans failed to see the peril of the nation's religious revivals.[67] The effects of such meetings were disastrous, leading to "diseases of the nervous system . . . epilepsy, convulsions, hydrocephalus and insanity." Brigham pointed to revival preachers' sensationalist emphasis on "feelings" as the culprit and demanded that Christian clergy study "anatomy and physiology" along with the scriptures to guard against irrationality. If the revivals really exhibited God's power, he reasoned, then why not accept the claims of the French Prophets or followers of Edward Irving?[68] Brigham's rambling, nearly 400-page critique of revivalism not only reveals the tension within Protestantism regarding religious experience, it also demonstrates how perceived excess on the fringe could be wielded against expressions in the evangelical mainstream. For evangelicals carving out a middle ground, the forging of discursive distance with Mormonism became critical in their contests with rationalists.

Unsurprisingly, religion figured prominently in the annual or biennial reports of the nation's antebellum asylums. Most institutions were keeping systematic records and making regular reports by the 1840s; their patient lists, often maintained in tabular form, graphically demonstrate the belief that religion threatened mental health.[69] For example, when the Pennsylvania Hospital for the Insane listed twenty-eight of its patients with "religious excitement" as the "supposed cause" of their insanity, only cases resulting from ill health, loss of property, and "grief" outnumbered those determined to be brought on by religion. (Causes ranged from "celibacy" to "lactation too long continued,"[70] "intense study,"[71] and "tight lacing."[72] Potential causes at other institutions included "dread of a future state,"[73] "predisposition excited by novel reading" or "insolation in a tropical climate,"[74] "opium eating,"[75] and "musical excitement.")[76] The lists, in other words, would fall short of modern scientific standards. The physicians compiling these reports understood the limitations of such explanations; they often stipulated that they simply listed causes as surmised by admitting friends or family members. Even so, these doctors offered what explanations they could of the untrained initial diagnoses before relating their subsequent experiences with patients.

Physicians and admitting friends or family worked with what understanding of mental illness they possessed, but their explanations were laced with nineteenth-century perceptions of race, gender, class, sexuality, and religion.[77] Thomas Kirkbride, the physician-superintendent of the Pennsylvania Hospital, appended an explanatory note below the table of causes. Of those cases of "religious excitement," he wrote, "four were unquestionably produced by the delusion of '*Millerism.*'" While religious causes proliferated in the reports, in other words, only a handful of religious movements were themselves listed as causes. Some institutions went so far as to tabulate the religious affiliation of their patients, though one hardly finds Presbyterianism cited as a cause of insanity or its dangers detailed by superintendents. Millerism, spiritualism, and Mormonism, on the other hand, were featured as "causes," and each drew focused attention in the reports.[78] Whatever their personal perspectives, most superintendents found it difficult to avoid the issue of religion. Tellingly, a Connecticut facility listed the following as the fourth question on a survey given to those admitting new patients: "Is the patient a professor of religion? if so, of what denomination?"[79]

Asylum administrators were often skeptical of the stated causes of their patients' troubles. One officer wrote that his report's table of causes could not enjoy "even the merit of an approximation to truth."[80] Some physicians made sense of the apparent religious components of their patients' histories and the notoriously unhelpful "cause" lists by distinguishing between what they considered actual causes of insanity and events or behaviors that simply triggered or exacerbated the disease.[81] A superintendent in Maine thought it worth several pages to address the problem of causation since it provoked "popular interest" more than any other. He attributed insanity to "two different orders of causes"; one was "constitutional" and the other was "exciting" influences. While such a perspective might have removed blame from religion since it could be viewed as an exciting cause only, the superintendent instead seized on religion to explain spikes in asylum admittance. "Of the 87 cases admitted during the past year," he wrote, "13 were attributed, with as much certainty as can ever be obtained on this subject, to *religious excitement*." The unusually large proportion of cases with a religious connection, he surmised, was due "no doubt, to the extraordinary variety and vehemence of the religious movements that have characterized the past year." Not only had the year 1841 seen a "remarkabl[e] awakening of enthusiasm" among traditional churches, "Mormonism, Millerism, and other eccentric manifestations" had "agitated the public mind" to an alarming degree. With such "moral epidemics" sweeping the nation, he concluded, it was no wonder that so many predisposed to insanity had been "overthrown by their resistless force."[82]

Authorities offered variations of this perspective, typically refusing to regard religion as a primary cause of insanity but allowing for some connection between the two. Sometimes, their postulations took the form of unscientific contemplations on the differences between true and false religion. One official wrote that religion "rarely, if ever, induces insanity" but stipulated that it must be "unalloyed" with other things and "rightly and wisely" brought before the mind.[83] An Illinois official concluded that when religion became irrational, when "natural science loses itself in the mythical," it became a danger to those predisposed to insanity. "That the truths of the Christian religion," he wrote, "brought before the attention by any ordinary induction, ever produced insanity . . . by itself, we should infer that those great, comprehensive and impassioned minds which, in Edwards and Whitfield [sic], glowed with such religious fire, would supply cases in proof. On the contrary, those brought to us as of that character, are quite as frequently like him, 'Who never had a dozen thoughts in all his life.'"[84] While Jonathan Edwards and George Whitefield could appear as models of reasoned religious devotion in retrospect, accounts such as this muted the New Light controversy they sparked and the earlier polemic surrounding their innovations.[85] A new crop of enthusiasts thus called forth a Protestant history more unified than historical subjects had known. In these depictions, representations of a single Protestantism, or even a unified evangelicalism, depended on a deluded, irrational "other." False doctrine or religious experience, then, emerged not primarily as a theological problem. Rather, deviance from the Protestant mainstream could be viewed as pathological or, at least, as a complicating problem for those with mental trouble.[86] A Massachusetts report could contrast the "pure, gentle, and benign principles of the Prince of Peace," which had a "soothing and consoling influence," with "conflicting systems" of belief that tended to distract the mind. It was a "mistaken view" of Christianity, not true religion, that led one "into the mazes of delusion."[87] As a result of the reports' effort to scold delusion without maligning real faith, professionals' explanations could veer sharply toward the devotional.[88] Such reports thus portrayed Christianity in a bifurcated way. With deluded faith threatening minds and true piety rescuing the afflicted, medical professionals became unintended authorities in the authentication of religious claims and experience.

Warnings about the dangers of religious fanaticism targeted Mormonism. In one example, Mormonism functioned as the animating cause in one woman's turn to madness. In the Ohio Lunatic Asylum's 1841 report, its superintendent wrote that an "affectionate mother and devoted wife" was visited during her husband's absence by a stranger who "announced himself in the double capacity of a Mormon preacher and physician." The woman's "natural timidity" and "impaired health" left her prey to the Mormon's "startling message," a doctrinal "harrangue of a denunciatory and alarming character." The preacher's message had the effect of "tornado force," and the woman, unhinged by the experience, was admitted for treatment. The report concluded with a happy pronouncement of full recovery, but the passing mention of the woman's already impaired health compared with the lengthy condemnation of the Mormon preacher left little doubt as to the cause of her illness.[89]

"Monomania," the diagnosis in the Pascal Smith case detailed above, also cropped up in the asylum reports. Its ill-defined character in those texts helps explain its usefulness to anti-Mormons. This partial insanity, as in the Smith episode, described those who were by all accounts mentally well except for a particular obsession or preoccupation. One report explained that monomaniacs are "deranged but on one or a very few subjects"; while they might experience temporary delusions or seem intermittently melancholy, their "intellectual faculties seem but little disturbed."[90] In many reports, monomania went hand in hand with accounts of religious insanity. It could explain religious choices that struck loved ones or professionals as inexplicable. One account reduced "religious anxiety," a commonly listed cause of insanity, to monomania and stated that the anxiety was perhaps traceable to the physical strain associated with a "protracted religious meeting."[91] Monomania functioned similarly in anti-Mormon writings. Neighbors of early Mormon convert Martin Harris, for instance, often described him as upstanding and respectable—with the exception, that is, of his association with Mormonism. After putting his name to an affidavitlike attestation of the famed Book of Mormon plates, locals puzzled over the seeming contradiction between his respectability and his Mormonism. As a result, Harris garnered considerable notoriety as a monomaniac. He could also be made to typify any convert. E. D. Howe, who considered Mormonism the epitome of American irrationality, defined any Mormon as necessarily, at the very least, a monomaniac.[92]

Enlightened Christianity and the Problem of Mormon Evidence

While most Protestants saw no conflict in the commitment to Christianity and reason, Mormonism's spread forced issues to the fore—among them, the problem of biblical interpretation. For antebellum Protestants, reading the Bible was to be a straightforward, commonsense affair, but Mormons offered proof texts and prided themselves on the self-evident biblical premises of their faith. This left Protestant skeptics wondering if Mormons were too biblical or not biblical enough. To inoculate against the Mormon threat, the *Ohio Evangelist* called readers back to scripture: "A people ignorant of the Bible are always an easy prey to the ministers of delusion and error."[93] But, as anti-Mormon Tyler Parsons found in a debate with Mormon Freeman Nickerson, it was not always that simple. Parsons claimed victory in their 1841 exchange before Boston's Free Discussion Society but candidly related that, after hearing the opposing positions, two men in the audience came forward to defend the Mormon arguments. A "Mr. S.," Parsons wrote, remarked that "it was the duty of the christians to come out in support of the mormon faith" because the "Mormons supported all their books and dogmas." Mr. S. concluded: "All the difference . . . between them was, the Mormons believed the Bible to the very letter, while the christians believed it figurative and spiritual." Parsons' self-proclaimed vindication followed, though he admitted that at least one of the sympathizers "intended to become a christian of the Mormon stamp."[94] The literalist hermeneutic that Mark Noll has described as characterizing antebellum approaches to the Bible not only colored much anti-Mormon writing, it left some Protestants susceptible to the logic of Mormon religiosity.[95] Mormons and their antagonists alike could wonder why the other would not simply follow the Bible. Jonathan Turner, for instance, bristled at Mormon usage of the Bible, writing that though "the Mormons . . . hang around the Bible," they amounted to "vermin" who "suck their vigor from the most noble forms; but that does not make them an organic part of such bodies."[96] Though he found that the Saints twisted its meanings, Turner admitted that they too grounded their arguments in holy writ.

Among the interpretive issues begged by Mormon religiosity the Holy Spirit was paramount. Paradoxically, though Mormons rooted their arguments for experiential religion in the Bible, Protestants became aware that experience could trump scripture for Mormons. Hence, the editor of the *Christian Palladium* lumped Latter-day Saints with Quakers and Shakers, charging that each group emphasized the Spirit in such a way as to "undervalue and discard the *Book of God*."[97] E. D. Howe found that religious impostors always waged war on true religion under the false banner of the Spirit: "Here is the sure refuge, the fast hold, of every impostor. This something, which is the *Spirit*, or the *Holy* Spirit, has been the standing, unequivocal, incontrovertible and true witness for at least 24 false Messiahs, for Mahomet, who is considered the prince of impostors, and for nearly fifty others who have come with pretended commissions from Heaven."[98] Radical expressions thus seemed to force a choice between word and Spirit. Protestants routinely chose the former and resisted what they took to be a purely sensationalist epistemology. The Bible uncorked the spiritual flows for Mormons but checked the same currents for detractors. As a result, Mormon spirituality was recast as dangerous mysticism. At the same time, in the stereotype Mormons' own ambivalences about common sense and experience evaporated. The popular evangelical preacher Nancy Towle provided a vivid account of how this recoding worked. After reading the Book of Mormon, she was willing to grant that Mormon miracle talk seemed "according to the attainment of the primitive disciples." Yet she concluded that Mormons misconstrued the Spirit and therefore failed to re-create ancient Christianity.[99] Towle attended a meeting where Joseph Smith "turned to some women and children in the room; and lay his hands upon their heads; (that they might receive the Holy Ghost.)." Eliza Marsh, one of those blessed, turned to Towle and remarked: "What blessings, you do lose!—No sooner, his hands fell upon my head; than I felt the Holy Ghost,—as *warm-water*, go over me!" Towle was disgusted. "I was not such a stranger, to the spirit of God, as she imagined;—that I did not know its effects, from that of *warm-water!*" Joseph Smith bore the brunt of her revulsion. "I turned to Smith, and said 'Are you not ashamed, of such pretensions? You, who are no more than any ignorant plough-boy of our land! Oh! blush at such abominations! and let shame, forever cover your face!'" The prophet's response was characteristic. "'The gift,'" he countered, "has returned back again, as in former times, to illiterate fishermen."[100] Towle's evangelicalism had critiqued liturgical formalism for generations, but in her encounter with Mormonism the Holy Spirit became the potentially explosive variable.

Her account had more in common with a Unitarian point of view than she might have intended. Jason Whitman, writing from the latter perspective, concurred with Towle but went further, impugning evangelical Christianity in general out of a conviction that Mormonism's success stood as evidence that a "large portion of the community" misunderstood the Spirit. In describing what he regarded as "pernicious errors in regard to the influences of the Spirit," Whitman blasted revival culture as falsely leading people to "believe that they can certainly tell, from their own feelings at the time, when the Spirit is specially operating upon their hearts; that they can distinguish the operations of the Spirit from the workings of their own minds." Whitman reasoned that the spiritual subjectivity touted in the revivals fostered an inordinate emphasis on bodily display or emotionality. Most problematic, he argued, was the tendency of evangelicals to judge the veracity of theological points on the basis of their spiritual sensations. This, of course, is precisely what evangelicals accused Mormons of doing. Whitman's "mind over feeling" message echoed in evangelical anti-Mormonism despite the fact that the antiformalist tracts could run in the opposite direction.[101]

Alexander Campbell, as leader of the rationalist wing of the restorationist movement he helped launch, could assume he had Mormons in a evidentiary trap when he asked rhetorically, "Can they shew any spiritual gift?"[102] The Mormons' collective yes was ineffectual since Campbell had already fought that fight. He had been willing to see his movement's ecstatic wing go rather than capitulate on cessationism. The spiritual giftedness question nevertheless reflected the twin commitments of his brand of Christian primitivism. His strict Biblicism amounted to a prescription for America's denominational angst, but his demand for a demonstration of gifts was timely in an indirect sense. Though he did not seriously expect a display of spiritual gifts, Campbell worked in an extended tradition of argumentation that placed New Testament miracles at the fore. Anti-Mormons like Campbell found the Saints wanting for critical evidence, but Mormons proved adept enough at contemporary evidential strategies to keep critics busy.

Christian thinkers had long touted the reasonableness of Christianity and by Joseph Smith's time had been honing their arguments for more than two centuries. E. Brooks Holifield, who regards the "evidential" strain in antebellum American theology as its most prominent feature, has demonstrated how Enlightenment skepticism put Protestants on the defensive. Critiques from the likes of David Hume and, especially, the rise of Anglo-American deism forced Christians to stake the limits of human reason while demonstrating that "rational evidence confirmed the uniqueness and truth of the biblical revelation."[103] Indeed, Holifield finds few groups more obsessed with Christianity's rationality than the antebellum theologians and sees their publishing "flood" as "an unprecedented shift in theological interests."[104] High regard for the evidences of Christianity had been apparent since antiquity, but by the 1830s and 1840s Christian argumentation had become elaborate. A Baconian style of theological reasoning, characterized by empiricism and inductive modes of thought, commanded wide appeal in the early nineteenth century, and theologians argued in terms of "internal" and "external" evidences. The former consisted of claims like the internal consistency of scripture and the latter typically related to the historicity of biblical miracles or prophecies fulfilled.[105] Heirs to these argumentative styles, most antebellum Protestants—theologians and populist preachers alike—minimized any contradiction between reason and revelation and could appeal to both. In early Mormonism's cultural context, evidential logic was almost second nature.

It was the emphasis on biblical miracles in the antideist polemics that put anti-Mormons in a sensitive situation. Miracles, after all, had served Protestants in paradoxical ways. Along with providing evidence against what they perceived as hyperrationality, Protestants countered Roman Catholic arguments that its miracles supported its uniquely true doctrine and ecclesiastical superiority. Sometimes, Protestant divines invoked a multitiered distinction between miracles and mere "wonders" in an attempt to have it both ways.[106] In this way, Mormon claims for the miraculous existed in a vexed Protestant matrix. Mormons seemed quite cognizant of the place of miracles in Christian apologetics and, in particular, of the fact that American theologians had long argued for biblical miracles on the grounds that they had been verified by numerous witnesses.[107] Predictably, Mormon miracles and their witnesses became the focus of anti-Mormon attention.

Early associates of Joseph Smith, even those with spiritual confirmation of his mission, craved empirical verification no less than their anti-Mormon counterparts. Martin Harris, Smith's scribe, felt relief at having Book of Mormon manuscript pages to show his considerably less convinced wife. More compelling, he thought, was what he took to be outside verification from an academic authority.[108] Still unable to assuage his doubts fully, Harris yearned to see the metal plates Smith claimed to be translating. Similarly, Oliver Cowdery offered his assistance to the young seer and was presented with a revelation that he understood to be a sign of Smith's prophetic powers.[109] After experiencing the dictation process firsthand, a period he described as "days never to be forgotten," Cowdery rejoiced with Harris when the text promised that others besides Smith would be privileged to see the mysterious plates.[110] A revelation followed informing Harris, Cowdery, and David Whitmer that "it is by your faith that you shall obtain a view of [the plates]," and that after "you . . . have seen them with your eyes, you shall testify of them, by the power of God." Shortly afterward, the three men claimed to have been shown the plates and other ancient artifacts by an angel. They signed an affidavit describing the experience. They wrote that they had "seen the plates," that they knew of the book's veracity because the Lord's voice had declared it, and that "an Angel of God came down from heaven" to show them the relics. A few days later, eight other men—all Smith or Whitmer kin—asserted that Smith had shown them the plates. Their joint statement was matter-of-fact. They had "handle[d] [the plates] with our hands" and described the engravings as having "the appearance of ancient work." Having "seen and hefted" the plates, they concluded their account with a word for potential skeptics: "We lie not, God bearing witness of it."[111]

Anti-Mormons were thus met on the closing pages of the Book of Mormon with the problem of witnesses. Their responses varied. Some, like Baptist David Marks, chose to dismiss them because of their obscurity. Marks, who had been an evangelist since the tender age of fifteen, met the Whitmers in New York; they told him that "an angel had showed them certain plates of metal, having the appearance of gold, that were dug out of the ground by one Joseph Smith." Marks was neither convinced nor impressed with their conviction that additional miracles would follow.[112] Later, after reading as much of the Book of Mormon as he could stomach, Marks contrasted the introduction of Christianity with that of Mormonism. "None of the works of Christ and the apostles were in secret," Marks wrote, but "the origin of this book is hid in the dark." As for the witnesses, all the Mormons could offer was "the testimony of twelve men whom we do not know." Marks's speculation about the motivation of these farmer-witnesses was echoed by a generation of anti-Mormons. He wrote that the "gospel of Christ presented to its apostles no temporal gain, but the loss of all things; the 'Book of Mormon' has a copy right secured, that its witnesses may '*have the temporal profit*.'"[113] In a different kind of critique, William Harris wondered if Smith might have somehow fooled the Book of Mormon witnesses. Even if the witnesses were honest men, Harris reasoned (he later charged that they were not), "what would be easier than for Smith to deceive them? Could he not easily procure plates to be made, and inscribe thereon a set of characters, no matter what, and then exhibit them to his intended witnesses as genuine? . . . And if it were necessary to give them the appearance of antiquity, a chemical process could easily effect the matter." Whether or not Smith had plates was beside the point, Harris continued, since many of the witnesses had since left the church.[114] As it had with David Marks, the relatively small number of witnesses to Smith's plates struck Harris as a distinction between Mormonism and Christianity. Christ had presented "evidence of his Divinity" to more than his apostles, he contended; "nearly every miracle" on record "was performed in the presence of great multitudes." Since Jesus had apparently offered public proof wherever he went, Harris wondered why eleven witnesses of reportedly questionable character would convince anyone.[115]

La Roy Sunderland offered an even more elaborate rationale for dismissing Mormon witnesses, which he linked to a more general dismissal of Mormon miracles. He charged that the Mormons, like other "radical errorists," were strangers to scripture and could not "perceive the vast, the momentous difference between the miracles recorded in the Bible, and the juggling tricks of Smith."[116] Sunderland cataloged the impostors who had claimed similar powers, noting, for instance, that native tribes of New Zealand also claimed intercourse with departed spirits. His cross-cultural analysis associated Mormon practice with the primitive and barbaric, yet Sunderland could not avoid the question of Mormonism's relationship to Christianity's miracles. He did so awkwardly, making a distinction between dramatic and conventional miracles without describing a critical difference. If true, he wrote, the Mormons' claims would place them "on an equal footing with the apostles." Protestants could confidently know such claims were false and still maintain their belief in the "operations of the Holy Spirit by which all christians believe sinners are convinced of sin, and the heart is enlightened and sanctified to God." With that murky differentiation in place, Sunderland could sound his deepest concern. If it were true that God inspired modern individuals beyond what he revealed "by the light of nature," then those messages must be accepted as "religious knowledge without error or mistake." As satisfying as such revelatory certainty was for the Latter-day Saints, Christians like Sunderland found the antipluralist implications of the Mormon message not only a blow to the all-sufficiency of the Bible but also an awkward fit in a republic where varieties of Protestantism were hard pressed for unity to begin with.[117]

Sunderland was unsure whether Mormons were practicing sleight of hand or erroneously ascribing divine causation to natural processes. On the one hand, he routinely explained Mormon success in terms of cunning and deceit; on the other, he maintained that some "mysterious events" were actually natural processes. His inclination toward the disenchantment model prompted an extended discussion of authentic miracles and their distinguishing marks. Since Sunderland's "marks" seem to have resulted from his reasoning backward from a rejection of Mormon claims, he predictably found Mormon miracles wanting.[118] Though he dodged the question of tongues or healing, preferring to compare Book of Mormon miracles with the Bible, Sunderland nonetheless buttressed the validity of biblical accounts while locating them firmly in antiquity. His elaborate, scientific-sounding framework for testing miracles and their witnesses was idiosyncratic. Nonetheless, other Protestants would have approved because his framework provided little room for modern miracles, Mormon ones least of all, and because its empiricist rhetoric comported with the era's theological mainstream.[119]

That Mormon religiosity was perceived to run beyond the pale of true religion was perhaps most powerfully conveyed in the curious claim that Mormonism amounted to atheism. Modern readers might not expect Mormon accounts of visions, revelations, and additional scripture to relate to *un*belief. But in a context fraught with danger on all sides, more than one anti-Mormon conflated what moderns see as opposite ends of a spectrum. The association of hyper-religiosity with a-religiosity, in fact, had enjoyed currency in religious polemics since at least the early eighteenth century, when Anglican ministers charged that religious nonconformity was "virtually indistinguishable" from skepticism and that their respective proponents were in league against true religion.[120] Such a framework was put forward in the first extended anti-Mormon publication. Alexander Campbell, having set out what he regarded as the Book of Mormon's internal inconsistencies and grammatical atrocities, dismissed its author/translator as "this Atheist Smith."[121] Campbell's impostor thesis logically provided for such a conclusion.

Since at least the mid-seventeenth century, Anglo-American deism drove Protestant concerns about infidelity and atheism. Though enjoying unprecedented hegemony and church growth, Protestant commentators between the American Revolution and the Civil War engaged in a considerable amount of hand wringing over the spread of unbelief.[122] Writing in the late eighteenth century, Hannah Adams charged that American deists, unlike the Europeans who had confined their speculations to privileged circles, had stridently peddled their infidelity to the masses. Deist demagoguery from the likes of Thomas Paine, she insisted, had not just "diffused infidelity among the lower orders of society," it had "even led to atheism."[123] John Hayward's *Book of Religions* (1843) articulated a prevalent assumption about atheism's two-pronged menace. He divided atheism into two equally troubling branches: a "*speculative*" atheism that denied the existence of God and an ostensibly more common, "*practical*" atheism that professed religious belief but acted "contrary to this belief."[124] This latter understanding, rhetorically indistinct from hypocrisy, framed the voluminous references to Mormon atheism. David Marks assumed that the Book of Mormon "had been written originally by an *infidel*."[125] E. D. Howe agreed that it "must have been written by an atheist."[126] Ex-Mormon Warren Parrish charged that Joseph Smith and Sidney Rigdon were "notorious infidels."[127]

And James Hunt argued that Mormon leaders, far from revealing God's will, had only revealed themselves to be "stupid Atheists."[128] Since religious reference writers could equate atheism with mental illness, these insults in anti-Mormon writings could relate to imposture or delusion, depending on the author's needs.[129]

Additionally, anti-Mormons worried about the ways atheism and Mormonism might combine as reinforcing threats. John Ellis, in an exasperated note to the editor of the *Christian Palladium*, lamented a skeptic's association of Mormonism with Christianity. According to Ellis, the infidels had mockingly documented Mormon miracles and, by so doing, "they aim (as they think) a deadly blow at the very root of Christianity." In response, Ellis turned the tables by listing the similarities between "Sectarism and Infidelity." Skeptics had taken aim at the mere "extravagances" of the Christian faith, he fumed, and had thereby camouflaged their own affinities with Mormonism. Those "two monsters" had united to "make war with the saints." They used different means—one "storms and thunders," the other "smilingly" talks folks out of their faith—but Ellis wondered why a more formal alliance between Mormons and skeptics had not yet been struck.[130] In such accounts, Mormonism or skepticism took on a menace far outstripping either's numbers. Imagined in unholy tandem, the pious could nevertheless call for doubled effort in an ironic siege. Mormons mastered the siege narrative quickly themselves, making the alarmed cries of their opponents all the more striking.

Jonathan Turner, an Illinois college professor, extended this analysis into a sweeping account of American religious history. Writing in the shadow of Mormon Nauvoo, Turner left no doubt about his feelings toward the Latter-day Saints by headlining his work with a quotation from Deuteronomy 13:5: "And that prophet, or that dreamer of dreams, shall be put to death." Turner cataloged the perils of Mormonism but ultimately was concerned about the extent to which it sullied true religion's good name. He considered Mormons "the most dangerous and virulent enemies to our political and religious purity," though he saw their menace as an "*indirect* influence."[131] By stretching Christianity's boundaries to obnoxious lengths, Mormons were embarrassing the Great Tradition. The Book of Mormon might convince the "thoughtless multitude" of its divine authority, but Turner worried more that, because of it, thinking people would decide to have nothing to do with the Bible. His notion of fake religion dismissed Mormonism, but it also admitted to an alarming proximity between Mormonism and traditional Christianity. Sensing that Mormonism tarnished what it claimed to supersede, Turner rehashed the spurious but well-worn charge that atheists championed Mormonism.[132] Drawing on still another polemic, he imagined a threefold menace to the Union: "Mormonism, if suffered to spread extensively, and unite with Atheism and Romanism, its natural allies, will soon have power to disturb, not single states only, but the entire Union."[133] While Mormons, Roman Catholics, and atheists hardly claimed any natural affinity, in an early American scene with hazards lurking at every turn, it seemed satisfying to envision the complexities more monolithically.

AS ALMOST NO ONE was willing to admit, Protestantism's trust in the holy book and its individual reader had left it systemically prone to ecstatic readings and experiential strife. Writing against the prophet Matthias, newsman William Stone encapsulated what anti-Mormons unwaveringly believed: antebellum American religion had boiled over with dangerous levels of false spirituality.[134] A few years earlier Stone's New York Brick Presbyterian Church had been rent by a controversy involving his wife and ecstatic Christian women. The renegade women formed what mockingly had been dubbed the "Holy Club." They sought the restoration of apostolic power and immediate communion with God. They simplified their dress, met for intense prayer meetings, endeavored to work miracles, had visions and dreams, and healed the sick by faith.[135] When several Holy Club members were caught up in the Matthias scandal, Stone connected the dots and offered an angry critique of the course of America's religious history. Matthias, he warned, was no unique example but rather the culmination of "a series of delusions" that had been ongoing for years. He cautioned that, if left unchecked, the age's continued religious "ultraism" would devastate the nations' churches.

Though unsure of the underlying problem—be it "individual fanaticism, or enthusiasm, or madness; or combined, or individual imposture"—Stone found striking parallels between the various religious corruptions. Quoting another Christian writer, he reminded his readers that "when people become better than the Bible, they are very apt to be wrong."[136] Religious troublemakers had long claimed visions, dreams, miracles, speaking in tongues, and faith healing.[137] For Stone, underlying all those similarities was the common theme of madness. Even among religious impostors, he argued, there were those who "have themselves been partially deranged." How each impostor had come to his or her madness was less important than the fact that all of them had managed to "involve others in the same hallucinations."[138] He feared that young readers might recoil at the messy tale and blame Christianity. Monomania, he maintained, had absolutely no natural connection to true religion.[139] Though this statement evidenced more than a little discomfort with religion's ubiquitous danger, Stone concluded with a brief sketch of the "Kentucky enthusiasm" to bring readers back to the point of his book: that the Bible would vouchsafe religion against extremism.[140] That the Bible could as easily provide the jumping-off point for the Holy Club or Mormonism as tether its readers to a decorous version of the faith seemed lost on Stone.

Christians had long sought a balance between formalistic and enthusiastic religiosity along a fictive spectrum that ranged from disbelief to hyperbelief, and Mormons functioned for antebellum Americans at the far end of both sides of the gamut. More to the point, Mormonism provided the image against which Protestants could patrol their imagined community. Given their raucous theological and ecclesiastical diversity, early republic Protestants had an easier time identifying what they were *not*. Positioned just beyond the revivals' enthusiasm or the skeptics' "practical" atheism, Mormonism ironically numbered most of its committed opponents among the evangelicals. Joseph Smith himself was initially drawn to Methodist camp meeting piety but could never acclimate to the evangelical temperament. As recorded by a German convert, Smith recalled a "Revival meeting" where his mother and a brother and sister "got Religion." Smith "wanted to feel & shout like the Rest but could feel nothing." A turn to the Bible prompted a secluded prayer and resulting vision that eventually took Smith in radical directions. Smith saw "a fire towards heaven" and two divine persons who answered his first question—"Must I join the Methodist Church?"—by declaring that "none . . . doeth good no not one." Smith's disaffection seemed complete when, shortly after the vision, he "told the Methodist priest" of his experience and was answered that the modern age was not one "for God to Reveal himself in Vision." "Revelation," he was told, "ceased with the New Testament."[141] Though earlier Methodists had seen Jesus in droves, Smith's account rang anachronistically just decades later.[142]

Having encountered a religious world that mostly dismissed his experiential proclivities, Joseph Smith hammered out a distinctive creation that was viewed as merely the latest in a tradition of radical religion.[143] Because the Saints' spiritual powers had become associated with radical religion, mental illness, and social upheaval, non-Mormons interpreted their religious practice as a menace rather than a unique version of the Christian gospel. Moreover, with leaders regarded as duplicitous frauds and followers as deluded fanatics, anti-Mormons were disinclined to regard Mormonism as just another church. In response, the Mormons alternately trumpeted and suppressed their gifts. Increasingly, Mormons and their detractors agreed that the Latter-day Saints were a people apart—so much so that critics would almost universally adopt more alien analogs for the faith than the radical enthusiasts of the Protestant margins. Those alienating discursive tendencies are the subject of the fourth chapter of this book.

CHAPTER 3

"Fanaticism"
The Church as (Un)Holy City

In 1839, when Mormons abandoned their third community in scarcely five years, some questioned the wisdom of what they had called "gathering." In January Albert Perry Rockwood wrote a concerned letter to his father. "Last night we heard that the Prophets advise for the Brethren to scatter," he reported. "It is thought by some we shall not gather again in large bodies . . . still we do not know."[1] Mormons had come to recognize that living in communities apart constituted both a blessing and a burden. The fact that the Latter-day Saints envisioned their church as a holy city rendered their movement both inescapably conspicuous and utterly problematic. Mormons thought it reasonable to create communities on their own terms. Far from wishing harm, they maintained, they sought simply to live God's law and spread his word. Anti-Mormons agreed with the rights of conscience but found the living of the Mormon ideal far more troubling than a mere difference in denominational preference. What Mormons considered legal, practical, desirable, and democratic (electing church leaders as civic leaders, bloc voting, etc.), came to be viewed by many non-Mormons as clannish at best and tyrannical or un-American at worst.

Mormons and anti-Mormons could be found talking past each other about church and state throughout the nineteenth century. Looking back on the Saints' controversial stay in Illinois after Joseph Smith's 1844 murder, attorney and newsman George T. M. Davis could only lament that the Illinois legislature had granted "to a religious sect, powers and privileges, which no other denomination of christians would dare to ask."[2] Davis's statement at once highlighted and dodged the underlying problem facing both sides. The legislature had hardly bestowed rights on a church in granting the city of Nauvoo its charter—Mormons in Boston were not directly

LIEUT. GEN. JOSEPH SMITH,
Mormon Prophet.

influenced by it, for instance—but because the church found its ultimate
expression in the ideal of a Zionic city, boundaries between the ecclesiastical and the civic often lay in the eye of the beholder.[3]

The significance of the Mormons' passion for place is amplified by comparison with a religious tradition whose community rhetoric they closely
paralleled. Quakers caused a scandal in the age of Revolution largely due
to their transnational identity as a "nation of God." The Friends' "church
as nation" was so threatening to emerging states that even Quaker pacifism
was routinely cast as treasonous subversion. Nevertheless, into the nineteenth century Quaker identity resonated with the biblical language of "a
royal priesthood" and "holy nation." Believers spoke of the faith as "an holy

"The Only Sure Way," *Daily Graphic*, 6 December 1883 (L. Tom Perry Special Collections, Harold B. Lee Library, Brigham Young University, Provo)

Insign lifted amongst the Nations"; Friends would "hold forth a standard of truth and righteousness to the nations"; they prayed that "Zion may become the beauty of nations." Throughout, Quaker religious discourse fused Hebraic senses of nationhood with Christian tropes of being lights in the world.[4] Close echoes can be found everywhere in early Mormonism. The reliance on Hebraic themes, in particular, was critical for emerging Mormon identity. In fact, in sorting through the constituent elements of Mormon peoplehood, Charles Cohen found that the Mormons' "kingdom" rhetoric was not merely a function of LDS history or a sociological response to conflict, but instead a theological construct in place before Smith's church was even organized. The Book of Mormon, he contends, drew on the very themes in Hebrew scripture that had animated Quaker preaching. Mormons were to constitute a religious nation from the start. The character of the Mormon Zions flowed naturally from the logic of Smith's founding text.[5] A holy nation defined in terms of brick-and-mortar cities rather than a transnational community of believers rendered the Mormon Zion more controversial than any Quaker vision had been. And with evangelism replacing pacifism in the Mormon formula, the LDS kingdom refused to content itself with quietistic obscurity.

By the late 1830s the questions begged by Mormon communitarianism forced critics into new polemical strategies. While considerable overlap in themes persisted, anti-Mormons came to recognize that earlier critiques, which had concerned themselves with prophethood or the Saints' religiosity, simply could not account for Mormonism's solidity. As a result, commentators pushed beyond characterological judgments to evaluate Mormonism as a more or less cogent theology. Though this backhanded acknowledgment of Mormon religion reflected a Protestant bias for "religion as theology," it was framed from the start by questions of political power. In other words, granting the Mormons religion hardly redeemed Mormonism. Efforts to impugn a coherent Mormon*ism* built on traditional mistrust of Mormon leaders—after all, Protestants had long associated prophetism with political tyranny—but added that a Mormon thought system was itself malicious.[6] This development in anti-Mormon thinking in turn enabled critics to fashion a political anti-Mormonism that construed Mormonism as having both sociopolitical coherence and malevolent intent. James Hunt thus blended older and newer arguments when he wrote that "Mormonism . . . is a dangerous *ism*—dangerous to the ignorant and unwary, being calculated to mislead them in matters where the eternal welfare of the soul is at stake—dangerous to our political institutions and government, having a direct tendency to overturn the former and subvert the latter; dangerous to the Christian religion, having made more than a hundred infidels to one *true* believer."[7]

Such a perspective had its origins in the first frictions over Mormon communitarianism, but anti-Mormon ambivalence about mob rule mitigated justifications for a violent solution. After the brutal 1838 Missouri "Mormon War," though, political anti-Mormonism crystallized in the conviction that Mormonism constituted an ideology inherently at odds with republicanism and was thus unassimilable within American society. As LDS Nauvoo provided anti-Mormons with the most glaring examples of Mormon political mischief to date, they violently ended Joseph Smith's life and the Mormons' stay in Illinois. After 1848, similar conflicts were enacted on a still larger stage. As early as 1835, Mormons had been forced to defend their loyalty to American republicanism, even as they demanded that opponents honor its promise of religious freedom. A statement on civil power, unanimously accepted at an Ohio church general assembly, affirmed the necessity of man-made governments, each "instituted of God," and acknowledged the rights of "religious opinion." Those rights, the Mormons clarified in a telling line, could never justify "sedition nor conspiracy" whether they were constitutionally protected or not. The document concluded that it was fundamentally unjust to "mingle religious influence with civil Government," but Mormons and their enemies would time and again disagree about what such a statement might mean.[8]

The Political Burden of the Mormon Gathering

The first call for the Latter-day Saints to "gather" encapsulated the push and pull of Mormon community building. In New York, Joseph Smith's tiny Church of Christ received the "commandment" to "assemble together" with Ohio converts "because of the enemy & for your sakes."[9] What was true of the first gathering was true of each that followed: anti-Mormons provided the push behind the communitarian impulse. Gathering constituted a flight from immediate danger and the wrath awaiting the wicked at Christ's second coming.[10] An 1838 revelation summarized this defensive logic for communitarianism. In it, Mormons were reminded that "gathering together . . . may be for a defense, and for a refuge from the storm, and from wrath when it shall be poured out without mixture upon the whole earth."[11]

Yet gathering was not merely an act of retreat. Simultaneously going "out from Babylon" and "unto the Land of Zion," the Latter-day Saints were ever moving *toward* something as well.[12] Thousands found Smith's version of a "city on a hill" compelling, a vision first offered in the Book of Mormon. A "New Jerusalem" would be established on the American continent, the text predicted, where a "remnant" of Israel would be gathered in a "holy city of the Lord."[13] Shortly after the church's organization, Smith provided another vision of what the Saints might accomplish as Latter-day Israel. In an amplification of scattered biblical references to Enoch, he detailed the creation of an ancient "City of Holiness, even Zion" that would serve as a template for the Mormons' modern kingdom. The "Lord called his people Zion," the revelation read, "because they were of one heart and one mind, and dwelt in righteousness; and there was no poor among them."[14] Zion, then, named both the Mormons' city and the Saints themselves, with people and place woven together in a utopian quest for unity, purity, and socioeconomic equality.[15]

Blurring church and city as they did, Mormons found it difficult to demarcate the spiritual from the temporal. The Mormons were not alone in this. Nor was their paradoxical effort to reshape society by withdrawing from it unique. Communitarian experiments abounded in the nineteenth century's first half, as the nascent market revolution, widespread migration, and a host of related dislocations offered more questions than answers about the nation's social and economic institutions.[16] Shakers had been establishing separate enclaves since the late 1780s; by the 1830s, nineteen Shaker villages stretched from Kentucky to Maine.[17] The Harmonists, followers of the German pietist George Rapp, formed communities in Pennsylvania and Indiana beginning in 1804. Scottish philanthropist Robert Owen founded New Harmony, Indiana, in 1825. The Oneida Community, John Humphrey Noyes's perfectionist commune in western New York, survived for three decades after its formation in 1848. New England Transcendentalists established Brook Farm in 1841.[18] Followers of French utopian writer Charles Fourier set up more than twenty communes before the Civil War. Controversy followed each communitarian experiment, but none garnered the hostility that the Mormons' did. The reasons for the disproportionate response are detailed in the following pages, not the least of which was the Mormons' direct engagement with partisan politics. Joseph Smith and Brigham Young stand in contrast to earlier Anglo-American prophets, who, writes Susan Juster, contributed to the "reformulation" of politics but nevertheless stood apart from partisan wars because they "disdained the very idea of politics as outmoded, ungodly, and irrelevant."[19] It should be noted at the outset, however, that American Protestants were heirs to a communitarian narrative that inclined them to view the Mormon version with considerable suspicion.

The sixteenth-century Anabaptist revolt in Münster, Germany, lingered for later generations as a cautionary symbol of religious radicals' penchant for political upheaval. Despite persecution, Anabaptists had spread across parts of Europe by the mid-sixteenth century. Though they gained notoriety for emotional religiosity and adult baptism, their most enduring popular image was the infamous takeover of Münster by charismatic prophets Jan Matthys and Jan van Leiden. The Münster revolutionaries held off the combined might of European princes for nearly a year, and, while awaiting their apocalyptic triumph, remade the city into a holy commune.[20] They abolished private property and instituted polygamy in emulation of the biblical patriarchs, thereby ensuring that subsequent accounts of religious extremism would fuse concerns over religious, sexual, and political deviance.[21] Bequeathed both the Anabaptist narrative and the republicanized character of American Protestantism, nineteenth-century Protestants instinctively viewed talk of a concretized godly kingdom as a political grab for power.[22] William Stone surmised that New York prophet Matthias had taken his cue from Münster. "The similarity between the principal of this sect," wrote Stone in 1835, "known as John of Leyden, and Matthews, not only in doctrine, but in worldly observance . . . is so remarkable as almost to lead to the conclusion . . . that the more recent impostor had formed himself and his creed, designedly, upon the model of his ancient proto-type."[23] The image of Münster was so fixed in American minds that one anti-Mormon, sensing the similarities, accurately predicted Mormon po-lygamy: "I am not aware that the Mormons claim the privilege of poligamy, as yet. I presume they will, when they revise their creed."[24]

The ubiquitous references to the Anabaptist radicals in anti-Mormon literature signaled a more profound tension in Protestantism than the fear of insurrection, as real as that fear became in the face of surging Mormon power. The modern notion of religious "fanaticism," an unmistakably im-portant category for anti-Mormons, had itself been forged in the political crisis of Protestant beginnings. Significantly, Philip Melanchthon, Martin Luther, and John Calvin had formulated fanaticism's modern meaning not in their contest with Roman Catholics, but against the radical wing of their own burgeoning movement. Fanaticism in these early formula-tions described those Protestant iconoclasts who rejected both represen-tations of the divine and the legitimacy of secular power.[25] Those insisting on the immediate destruction of papist altars were convinced of the im-minence of God's kingdom, and Luther and his allies feared they would destroy everything in their fervency for millennial victory. "Civil society" and "fanaticism" were reflexively "conjoined," as Dominique Colas notes, from Protestantism's inception. The very duality of church and state was at stake in the iconoclast tumult. Luther's and Calvin's moderation on secu-lar civil society's legitimacy can thus be viewed as a critical feature of later American conceptions of religious liberty. But a violent paradox haunted that middle ground. The Anabaptist rebels played on Protestantism's main themes, after all. Luther himself had stoked the anti-Catholic fires, and his association of Rome with Babylon, coupled with the violent images scat-tered in his religious texts, made for an unmistakably apocalyptic vision. Moreover, his removal of the church and its priesthood as mediators of Christian salvation helped instigate the iconoclast protest in the first place. By "profaning Rome," Luther had "propelled fanaticism."[26]

Yet, from the first iconoclast riots in 1521 through Thomas Müntzer's Peasants' War (1525) and the Münster revolt (1534–35), Luther and his allies called for the radicals' violent suppression. Turning violently against what they helped create, the moderate reformers conjured fanaticism as an organizing motif around which their own visions might take shape. Importantly, eighteenth-century commentators would more clearly distinguish what had been equated earlier—the epithets "fanatic" and "enthusiast"—to emphasize that the fanatic put his deluded visions into action. In the discursive tradition framing anti-Mormonism, then, fanatic expressed the greater danger, though imposture and delusion had long been intertwined with it in various ways.[27] The legacy of fanaticism's categorical genesis is manifest in the following pages. Protestants, long wary of their own tradition's propensity to upset the mediating role of political institutions in fits of millenarian angst, violently opposed Mormon visions for fear of Mormonism's tyrannical and violent potential. The comparisons with Münster, eventually trumped by more alien analogs, admitted an embarrassing truth. Mormonism, for all the eventual talk of its foreignness, revived nightmarish memories from the Protestant past and stoked old fears.

ANTI-MORMONS HAD EARLY noted the Mormon yearning for a holy place apart. With each attempt to realize Zion, critics grew more wary of concentrations of fanatical power. When Ohioans first caught wind of the Saints' communitarian aims, they reacted with amusement. Newsman E. D. Howe found the Mormon plans audacious. Not only did they claim exclusive commissions from God, he reported in late 1830, the Mormons warned that those not heeding their call "to go to some unknown region, where God will provide a place of refuge for his people, called the 'New Jerusalem,'" would forever live in misery.[28] Much to Howe's dismay, the first Mormon gathering was in his own backyard.[29] Responses ranged from sarcasm to concern, but the seeds of the later political anti-Mormonism can be discerned in the growing awareness of Mormonism's potential political clout.[30] With communities under construction in both Ohio and Missouri from 1831 to 1833, the Saints found themselves answering two sets of critics at once.

Missouri's old-timers worried over the influx and could stand coexistence with the Mormons scarcely two years.[31] Religious chauvinism, rumors of Mormon evangelism of free blacks, and Mormon millenarian bombast combined with fears of economic and political domination to convince many of vigilantism's virtues. After drawing up lists of grievances, Jackson County residents tarred and feathered Mormon leaders and wrecked Mormon buildings in July 1833.[32] Threats, beatings, burnings, and several bloody exchanges followed once Mormons resolved to stay; by the end of November, however, the Latter-day Saints had evacuated the county.

Though the Mormons had experienced violence in Ohio (Joseph Smith and Sidney Rigdon had been assaulted there in 1832), the ferocity of the Missouri attacks left both sides searching for meaning.[33]

The vigilantes offered justification in the months and years that followed. When Samuel Lucas, a self-admitted ringleader, was commissioned to pen the entry for "Jackson County" in Alphonso Wetmore's *Gazetteer of the State of Missouri* (1837), he defended the Mormons' banishment. He laid blame for the violence squarely at their feet; even so, Lucas admitted that it was the Mormons' potential for harm that had sparked the tumult.[34] Alarmed by the "audacity of the outrages [they] contemplated," Lucas opted for the image of a locust swarm to express the danger. Old-timers feared they would be overrun. But contemplated outrages, dubious overtures to free blacks, and "threatened association" with Native Americans offered little Mormon malevolence to document, so Lucas resorted to stock anti-Mormon insults regarding Joseph Smith and the Book of Mormon. In his conclusion, Lucas made short work of western Missouri's complex politics: "To this county, then, this mass of human corruption was moving to an alarming extent, when, in self-defence, the good citizens of Jackson put in execution the good old law."[35]

The argument of self-defense was well received in Jackson County but elsewhere commentators reacted with ambivalence. The *Missouri Republican*, for instance, sounded unsure of its position. Its editor granted that Mormons were a "sect of fanatics," but he found the mobbing "wholly at war with the genius of our institutions, and as subversive of good order as the conduct of the fanatics themselves." After issuing the rebuke, however, he backtracked, wondering if violence was "the only method which could have been effectually put in practice to get this odious description of population out of the way." His effort to portray the fracas as orderly verged on the comical. The citizens had democratically voted to raze the printing house, he reported, and had then done so with the utmost decorum. While press reactions varied, most accounts echoed the *Republican* in evincing equal measures of condemnation for the mob and suspicion that the Mormons deserved what they got.[36]

LDS attempts to recover lost Missouri properties did little to sway public opinion; if anything, they spurred perceptions of fanaticism. Mormon leaders in Ohio had initially instructed their refugee brethren to seek redress through established channels, but a revelation in late 1833 sounded a call to action. It offered an extended parable that rebuked the Saints' impieties and included an ominous directive: "Gather together the . . . strength of mine house . . . and go ye straitway unto the land of my vineyard, and redeem my vineyard."[37] The revelation's instructions answered the Saints' fundamental political problem as they recognized it. Missouri governor Daniel Dunklin, according to a letter from Missouri church leader John Corrill, was willing to aid in the recovery of Mormon lands but would not leave troops to guarantee long-term protection. The Mormons, Corrill understood from his exchange with Dunklin, should organize into "independent companies" and, "armed with power and liberty," defend their homes against further aggression.[38]

Pursuant to Smith's late December revelation, Mormon leaders spent months gathering men, money, and goods. "Zion's Camp," as their volunteer force came to be known, left Ohio in the spring of 1834; despite efforts to disguise their intent, the "armies of Israel" found it difficult to avoid attention.[39] In the face of rising tensions, Dunklin offered conflicting advice. In February he had confirmed the Mormons' right to reclaim their homes.[40] By June, with Mormons marching toward Missouri, Dunklin reconsidered his cautious encouragement of an organized defense. In a letter released to a national audience, he laid out the Mormon problem. Still convinced of the Mormons' "clear, and indisputable right" to reclaim their homes, Dunklin nevertheless blamed the conflict on the "eccentricity of the [Mormons'] religious opinions and practices." The underlying logic was ambivalent: the Mormons had a right to defend their property, but, since their religious oddities had prompted the violence, there was no end in sight if they persisted in their Mormonism. His new advice—simply to move somewhere else—followed from these premises.[41]

The Zion's Camp march provided fodder for the church's enemies. Howe's *Mormonism Unvailed*, which went to press shortly after the Zion's Camp adventure, called readers' attention to what the camp illuminated about Mormonism.[42] The means by which the Missourians had rid themselves of their "fanatical neighbors," Howe cautioned, "were wholly at war with every principle of right, and the genius of our institutions." But he urged readers to consider the reasons why Missourians had felt threatened.[43] What sparked the Missouri violence was precisely what Howe feared of Ohio Mormonism: its potential "secular power."[44] For Howe, the clashes of 1833 had revealed the real motivation behind the Mormon gathering: "This [political domination] they calculate to accomplish by concentrating their forces in particular neighborhoods."[45] What Mormons had seen in terms of religious goals appeared to Howe and other critics as a calculated plan to accumulate political power. Sadly, the Zion's Camp episode predicted the future. Repeatedly put on the defensive in the early 1830s, Mormons would militarize and craft overtly political strategies for protection. In combination, the two developments made a prophet out of Howe. The critics helped create what they most feared about the Mormon gathering.

Also predictive of coming trouble was the internal crisis that brought down Smith's Ohio community. The Mormon bank there failed during the national panic of 1837, and Mormons experienced economic and faith crises in turns.[46] Droves of disaffected Mormons rejected Smith's leadership or left the church. In the apostate accounts, scholars have identified a common thread that paralleled anti-Mormon worries—namely, that Smith's leadership amounted to political tyranny.[47] Warren Cowdery, Oliver's Cowdery's brother, then editor of the Ohio Mormon paper, stopped short of leveling charges against Smith by name but cautioned readers about authoritarianism: "If we give all our privileges to one man, we virtually give him our money and our liberties, and make him a monarch, absolute and despotic, and ourselves abject slaves or fawning sycophants."[48] Though the Kirtland economy hardly hinged on Smith alone, for many mired in the crisis the question of prophetic authority became a critical one. Prophetic leadership was innocuous in the abstract, but when church leaders seemingly directed the local economy into oblivion, even Mormons grew wary about their church's hazy boundaries between sacred and secular.[49]

A second round of Missouri violence brought internal and external concerns about Mormonism to a head. Hoping to avoid a reprise of the 1833 bedlam, Mormon leaders sought non-Mormon help in determining where to settle. Even with a promising agreement in place, trouble came quickly to the new Mormon gathering in 1838.[50] As with the Ohio debacle, internal discord spilled over into non-Mormon relations. Unwilling to risk the previous year's upheavals, Mormon hardliners threatened LDS dissidents to keep quiet or leave the area. Preaching in late June from Matthew 5, Sidney Rigdon issued a thinly veiled warning that dissenters, like salt without its savor, ought to be cast out. Reports of another Rigdon sermon promising "a war of extermination" with any mob arrayed against the Mormons circulated throughout the summer.[51] The spark igniting the new tumult came in an August scuffle involving rowdies spurred by an anti-Mormon candidate for the state legislature who tried to bar Mormons from voting. Exaggerated reports sent both sides into action, and armed conflicts followed in Daviess, Carroll, Ray, and Caldwell counties. By autumn's end, violence had taken lives on both sides, and the Mormons, pursuant to Governor Lilburn Boggs's infamous executive order that the "Mormons must be treated as enemies and *must be exterminated* or driven from the state," were forced to flee Missouri.[52]

For this study, the significance of this bloody Mormon/anti-Mormon conflict rests in the ways it configured a "political" anti-Mormonism. The first effects of the 1838 clash were discernible in the Mormons' own accounts; many had grown uneasy with the militancy within their ranks. At the height of the crisis, two LDS apostles signed affidavits charging fellow Mormons of excessive measures. Thomas Marsh, president of the church's council of apostles, charged that Joseph Smith had threatened those unwilling to take up arms and that Smith and Lyman Wight had ordered the confiscation of non-Mormon property. Even more alarming, Marsh asserted, a secret Mormon vigilante force known as the "Danites" had been organized to defend Latter-day Saints and to wreck enemy buildings. He alleged that Danite leader Sampson Avard had proposed deceit and assassination as responses to non-Mormon aggression. From Marsh also came Smith's notorious declarations that seemed to vindicate the long-standing comparisons of him with Muhammad.[53] Fellow apostle Orson Hyde confirmed most of Marsh's statements.[54] Armed with such accounts, Missouri officials were confident they could answer Mormon accusations of state-sponsored persecution.[55] Official investigation of the war began in November 1838, and the results were published in 1841.[56] The affidavits and supporting documents painted a picture of an aggressive, out-of-control Mormonism bent on Missouri's destruction. Historians have wrangled over the veracity of the accounts, but one truth that emerges is that the war's strains split the Mormon camp.[57] While non-Saints had only sketchy knowledge of the extent of LDS militancy, disillusioned Mormons offered details of the Danite organization and the fiery rhetoric of LDS leaders.[58] Mormon loyalists offered counternarratives and Smith blamed Avard, but the damage to the church's reputation, such as it was, had been done. Newspapers from as far away as Vermont picked up the details of the Danite accounts, and extended apostate reports supported the testimonies given to Missouri officials in 1838.[59]

By 1840 critics had the evidence they needed to characterize Mormonism as a political machine, a portrayal that could be easily deployed to top off the imposture thesis. But the impostor/dupe paradigm left too much unexplained. What kept Mormonism together in the face of such crises? What accounted for its continuing solidity? Critics refused to see the various details of the conflicts as examples of desperation in the face of violent opposition. Instead, they read Mormon history together with elements of Mormon writing to construct what earlier critics had shrugged off as an impossibility: a distinctive and coherent Mormon theology. In this way, the violence and political controversy became less a sociopolitical problem than a fatal flaw intrinsic to Mormonism.

The Discovery of a Mormon Theology

Prompted by violent conflict to seek clues to LDS intentions, anti-Mormons somewhat accidentally constructed a Mormon theology in a selective engagement with Mormon texts. The Book of Mormon offered some evidence of Mormonism's political ideology, but critics found a richer trove in Mormon apologetics and, especially, in published collections of Joseph Smith's revelations.

Tales of ruthless Danites under Smith's control perpetuated the practice of pinning Mormonism's ills on LDS leaders—ordinary Mormons themselves, as one eastern paper put it, were "more sinned against than sinners." But another way of framing the Mormon problem became increasingly popular after 1838, when critics assigned culpability to Mormonism as a system.[60] The Mormon system, moreover, came to be portrayed as both inherently antirepublican and prone to violence. This approach coalesced in a series of works published between 1838 and 1842 as Joseph Smith's most successful Zionic city was rising from the swampy banks of the Mississippi. More than a dozen anti-Mormon books appeared in 1841–42 to narrate the Missouri conflict and, importantly, to check resilient LDS growth. This discursive development was complicated by American commitments to religious liberty, but critics made novel distinctions to patch over seeming contradictions. Illinois anti-Mormons, for instance, sometimes posited *two* Mormonisms, one religious and one political, and made war with the latter while claiming to respect the former. Both Mormons and anti-Mormons, then, puzzled over the boundaries between religion and politics and made awkward distinctions to suit their own purposes.

The portrait of a cogent Mormon political ideology had been nascent in earlier anti-Mormon works. One writer took his cue from an influential Mormon book, Parley P. Pratt's *Voice of Warning* (1837). The anonymous author saw in Pratt's chapter on "The Kingdom of God" signs that Mormonism evinced dangerous aspirations.[61] Given Pratt's rhetoric about the literal establishment of God's kingdom—an "organized government on the earth"—the author worried that talk of a Mormon capital city was more political stratagem than eschatological prediction. Pratt's contention that "the nation and kingdom that will not serve that city shall perish, and be utterly wasted," the author concluded, revealed the Mormons' plan: "In the midst of all these high and cloudy pretensions of the Mormons there seems to be a political end in view."[62] Once accounts of the Missouri war became widely known, this strain of thinking predominated.

Another earlier anti-Mormon insight figured prominently in the postwar polemics. What became the most cited evidence of a Mormon system rotten at its core was a passage from one of Smith's revelations. Mentioned in Howe's *Mormonism Unvailed* (1834), its implications remained unexploited until after the war. Howe quoted a letter from Samuel C. Owens, chairman of a Missouri committee responding to the Zion's Camp march. In it, Owens excerpted the Mormon *Book of Commandments* (1833): "Again, they say that they never intended to get possession of Zion, (that is Jackson,) by the shedding of blood! But, in Revelation No. 54, given in Kirtland, Ohio, August, 1831 . . . we discover the following in the thirteenth verse, to wit: 'Wherefore, the land of Zion shall be obtained but by PURCHASE or by BLOOD, otherwise there is no inheritance for you.'"[63] This passage found its way into a host of anti-Mormon works written after 1838. The partially quoted verse, when combined with the accounts of Mormon aggression in northern Missouri, made for a compelling narrative of fanaticism. That later authors lifted the partial reference from Howe is likely, since the passage in its entirety is far less threatening than the quoted excerpt. The fact that the revelation actually *forbade* violence made little difference, since most critics were likely unaware of the full citation and all were aware of the Danite tales and growing Mormon power in Illinois.[64]

A work penned coincidentally with the Missouri war and revised shortly afterward is characteristic of the turn to Mormon theology. La Roy Sunderland's *Mormonism Exposed and Refuted* (1838) grasped for evidence that Mormon theology was the underlying problem behind its outrages.[65] Sunderland reviewed the standard list of religious impostors and derided Mormon spirituality, but his narrative turned on what he regarded as one of several "distinguishing characteristics" of Mormonism. Perhaps most alarmed by the Mormon belief that Mormon "preaching, and pretended prophecies and revelations, are 'SCRIPTURE' and of equal authority with the Bible," Sunderland worried that Mormonism's insistence on continuing revelation made Mormons unfit for American democracy.[66] When the Saints spoke of revelation, they did not mean the "operations of the Holy Spirit by which all christians" are convinced of sin but, rather, that God had made His will known to "such a degree" that the Saints could impart religious knowledge "without error or mistake."[67] With the specter of prophetic infallibility and antinomianism in view, Sunderland turned to Mormon texts for evidence of violent revelation. He copied passages from the *Doctrine and Covenants* about God smiting unbelievers and singled out an episode in the Book of Mormon in which one figure was inspired to kill a drunken antagonist.[68] Writing coincidentally with the Missouri war, Sunderland connected the "*spirit*" of those passages with events in the press. Fearing a Mormon/Indian alliance, he worried that the Saints' violent "creed" might inspire rounds of bloody conflict.[69]

Sunderland updated his book in 1841 after the Missouri investigation provided more evidence. He was confident that the later edition irrefutably demonstrated "the treasonable tendency of Mormonism" and gave "a clear exhibition of the . . . conduct of that arch impostor, J. Smith, Jr., and those concerned with him in spreading that wicked system."[70] Sunderland's prose was more urgent than it had been in 1838. He warned readers not to underestimate Mormon radicalism. While the nation had been "sleeping," the Mormons had constructed a system that threatened the nation.[71] In the second edition, Sunderland greatly expanded the material treating Mormon texts. He wrote that the *Doctrine and Covenants* had been "kept out of sight" and that a disclosure of its contents, when combined with the Missouri documents, would "show that Mormonism is, in itself, treason against the government of God and man."[72] All the while, Sunderland kept an eye on progress in Nauvoo, Illinois. After detailing a press report of the Mormons' temple cornerstone–laying ceremony and its attendant military display, he wondered why anyone had been surprised by the Missouri war or how anyone could doubt a repeat in Illinois.[73]

Sunderland's portrayal was echoed by a host of titles published in 1841 and 1842. Most quoted generously from Howe's *Mormonism Unvailed*; with several authors borrowing from each other, readers were left with a web of cross-pollinating polemics that cast false prophet, false scripture, and a violently treasonous theology as a fanatical triumvirate.[74] An 1841 *Anti-Mormon Almanac* offered an account of Mormonism's "treasonable tendency" along with astronomical calculations and interesting facts.[75] It, too, found Mormon notions of revelation politically troubling. Agreeing with Sunderland's oversimplification—that "*Mormon writings, it is assumed, are of equal authority with the Bible*"—the almanac highlighted the "Zion with blood" passage and another from the *Doctrine and Covenants*. The latter promised church elders that, when "moved upon by the Holy Ghost," their spoken words would be "Scripture." That the revelation pertained to the entire Mormon priesthood and not Smith alone evidently made little difference, since the quoted material served as the foundation for alleged slavish obedience to prophetic dictates.[76]

William Harris's *Mormonism Portrayed* offered perhaps the most explicit charge that LDS theology was inherently at odds with American political institutions.[77] Apparently ghost-written by Illinois anti-Mormon Thomas Sharp, the Harris/Sharp text plumbed the political ramifications of Mormon emphasis on revelation. Sharp noticed a dangerous theme in Smith's revelations, especially those instructing Mormons to "heed . . . all [of Smith's] words & commandments."[78] "Mark this revelation," he urged, "for it is important in a political point of view." If the Saints were obliged to obey Smith "both in things spiritual and temporal," then was not "Mormonism inimical to the institutions of our country?" With Smith's law ostensibly superior to civil law, Smith controlled Mormon votes, and, should Mormons come to command a majority in Illinois, then the state would have a fanatic for its de facto dictator. Therefore, Mormonism constituted "a total subversion of Republicanism, and the establishment, in effect, of a despotism."[79] Sharp vacillated on the question of religion, however. With Mormon communitarianism cast as a political scheme, he explained Missouri's violent response with the assertion that non-Mormons had no problem with "the mere religion of the Mormons." Because he refused to see LDS concepts of revelation or community as religious, Sharp's view of Mormonism as politics was essentially an extended version of the imposture thesis and a discourse on secularization: "There can be no religion in this, every one knows."[80]

Professor Jonathan B. Turner rivaled Sharp's rhetoric. The united Mormon community, he wrote in 1842, constituted the "most dangerous and virulent enemies to our political and religious purity, and our social and civil peace, that now exist in the Union."[81] Like the other critics, Turner turned to the *Doctrine and Covenants*, which he dubbed Mormonism's "BLACK Book." The "whole design of it," he declared, "is, to concentrate power and resources around Joe Smith."[82] As an ardent abolitionist, Turner was well versed in the denunciation of concentrated power.[83] Though noting that the revelations constructed an ecclesiology respectful of the "voice" of the church, Turner dismissed those passages by characterizing Smith as a "democratic monarch."[84] His quip about democracy revealed much about anti-Mormon anxieties. No law barred Mormons from gathering, and, should they choose to vote in a particular way, who could gainsay them? A disestablished polity was simply not suited to manage revelation. The critics stretched the imposture thesis as far as they could, but granting the Mormons a treasonous theology came dangerously close to granting them status as a religion. Though detractors multiplied assertions that Mormonism amounted to politics and not religion, their turn to the Mormon revelations subverted the point. The Mormon religion was the problem in significant ways, but critics could scarcely admit it and had no idea how to address it. Anti-Mormon violence can thus be read as a systemic failure of American disestablishment. Anti-Mormons feared Mormon fanaticism, but beneath those expressions lay an admission that the American state was ill equipped to arbitrate religious claims. Mormonism exposed the American fantasy that religion and politics could be easily defined and separated.

The Politics of Expulsion

Acknowledgment of a Mormon system almost amounted to an oblique admission that it was a religion, but the protections such recognition might have provided did not materialize in the 1840s and 1850s. The sad story of Mormon Nauvoo and the Saints' subsequent exodus resulted primarily from the assertion that its menace went beyond the actions of any one leader. For Mormons, the consequences were devastating. Remarkably, with each attempt to insulate themselves from trouble, Mormons looked more and more fanatical to critics. The rhetoric on both sides soared until chilling cries that Mormonism must be "blotted out" became commonplace. Throughout, religion's definitional instability loomed large, as did democracy's. The Mormons' exile elided glaring questions. Was democracy defined at the local, state, or national level? Did a theology's political ramifications make it nonreligious? Who was to blame if a religiopolitical ideology was considered subversive? Anti-Mormon ambivalence on these points calls attention to the ways Mormonism served as a surrogate for broad questions concerning religion in the republic.

Among the objections to Mormon Nauvoo were its place in state politics, its charter, its radical religiosity, and, especially, its suppression of internal dissent. At first, Illinois welcomed the Mormon refugees. Early peace and promise notwithstanding, the seeds of discord sprouted as the most successful pre–Utah Zion matured.[85] In party politics, the Saints first benefited from, then were damned by, a new political environment.[86] Unlike Missouri, which had a clear Democratic majority, western Illinois in the early 1840s was evenly divided between Whigs and Democrats.[87] Both parties mobilized in search of the LDS vote, with competing expressions of outrage at Missouri's treatment of the Saints.[88] Mormons initially tried to maintain political neutrality but found it increasingly difficult to refuse the overtures of officials and office seekers.[89] The Saints then began a politically dangerous game of promising support to the highest bidder.

This political dance was disastrous for the Mormons. Had they stayed loyal to one set of political suitors, they might have enjoyed that side's continued protection. As it turned out, both parties concluded that Mormon support was unreliable. By 1842 the Saints were politically isolated.[90] The only thing that could unite Whigs and Democrats in 1840s Illinois was distrust of the Mormons. An "Anti-Mormon Party," the brainchild of Warsaw's Thomas Sharp, drew support from both older parties. Many Hancock County residents agreed that they could put aside their political differences to counter the Mormon threat.

Governor Thomas Ford maintained that Mormon promises "flattered both sides with the hope of Mormon favor," and Illinois politicians hurried a city charter bill through the legislative process unopposed.[91] The resulting charter confirmed an already existing ecclesiastical council's informal leadership, a blurring of church and state many Mormons considered logical and practical.[92] With the charter in hand, the Saints believed they had secured an unassailable legal foundation for Zion.[93] Since the charter included two subsidiary powers as well, creating "a body of independent military men" (called the "Nauvoo Legion") and "an institution of learning," Nauvoo's political, military, educational, and judicial institutions seemed securely in the hands of the Mormons themselves.[94] The LDS Presidency, consisting of Joseph Smith and two appointed "counselors," rejoiced. The legislature, the presidency wrote, had "come forth to our assistance, owned us as citizens and friends, and took us by the hand, and extended to us all the blessings of civil, political, and religious liberty." The chartered militia, they concluded, would enable the Saints to "perform our military duty by ourselves" and thus "show our attachment to the state and nation as a people" as well as "proving ourselves obedient to the paramount laws of the land."[95]

Though the Mormons regarded their "Nauvoo Legion" as protection, non-Mormons looked upon it with fear. The charter stipulated that it could be called up by either the mayor or the governor to defend city laws. Non-Mormons worried that it might be used against them.[96] After the charter passed, Mormons staged a community celebration and invited non-Mormons to share in Nauvoo's budding success. Artillery fire announced the arrival of Legion officers, the LDS *Times and Seasons* reported, each of whom led a cohort of Mormon militiamen. Thereafter, Lieutenant General Joseph Smith, accompanied by "his guard, staff and field officers," accepted an American flag from the Nauvoo ladies and reviewed the lines. Later, the entire procession, complete with choir and band, proceeded to the temple site where Smith presided over a religious service and laid the Mormon temple's cornerstone. This spectacle horrified at least one important visitor. Thomas Sharp, eventual leader of the state's anti-Mormon movement, traced his activism to that day's display of military, civic, and church muscle.[97] Others would say the same.[98]

The charter also empowered the municipal court to issue writs of habeas corpus, a provision that became controversial as Mormons used it to shield Joseph Smith from various legal charges.[99] Smith waxed defiant after his latest escape. He argued that the city court's power derived directly from the Illinois and U.S. constitutions. "All the power there was in Illinois she gave to Nauvoo," he contended, "and any man that says to the contrary is a fool." He warned that he would not "deal so mildly" with pursuers again. Should others attempt unlawful arrests, he warned, his people were "at liberty to give loose to blood and thunder." He urged the Saints to "be not the aggressor" and to forbear until struck on both cheeks yet insisted that Mormons would forfeit rights "only at the point of the sword and bayonet."[100] Governor Ford disagreed with Smith's assessment of Nauvoo's legal powers, whereas the Saints successfully portrayed attempts to extradite Smith to Missouri as unjustified harassment. One Illinois paper framed the whole affair as an instance of "persecution" and "oppression."[101]

Tensions smoldered until fractures within the Mormon community detonated deadlier conflicts.[102] The first major internal crisis came in 1842, after John C. Bennett had joined the Mormons in Nauvoo and quickly became one of Joseph Smith's trusted advisers. Bennett shepherded the city charter to passage and was elected Nauvoo's first mayor. A dramatic exile followed his meteoric rise, however, following a power struggle with Smith involving several issues, especially polygamy.[103] Bennett broke the news of Smith's radical marriage doctrine in a local newspaper. Thereafter, Smith's conflict with Bennett exploded in charges and countercharges of sexual misconduct.[104]

Bennett's expanded exposé, *History of the Saints* (1842), mixed revelations about the church's inner workings with embellished accounts of Smith's "plural marriage." The book's greatest influence was felt in western Illinois, since many eastern papers considered it a blend of conventional charges and outlandish tales that could scarcely be believed.[105] According to Bennett, Mormon leaders "were preparing to execute, a daring and colossal scheme of rebellion and usurpation throughout the North-Western States of the Union." The prophet and his "minions" planned to overthrow the governments of Ohio, Indiana, Illinois, Iowa, and Missouri and erect a "military and religious empire" headed by Smith "as emperor and pope." Bennett was confident that he had Smith cornered on polygamy. He described a multitiered system of wives and concubines at the disposal of Mormon leaders, portraying the system in exotic and Oriental terms. Armed with documents and Nauvoo hearsay about Smith's polygamous relationships, Bennett framed Smith as the "Pontifical head" of a growing "Mormon Harem."[106]

After the lurid stories about polygamy, Bennett returned to LDS imperial plans. With the Nauvoo Legion, the Mormons already possessed the means to establish a military and political state in Nauvoo, he warned. "As a military position, Nauvoo, garrisoned by twenty or thirty thousand fanatics, armed to the teeth, and well supplied with provisions, would be one of the most formidable in the world."[107] Bennett had reason to know, for no one, Smith included, had been more instrumental in the Legion's creation. Similarly, while Bennett made broad charges against the Saints for planning territorial conquest, he gave few specifics. His biographer speculates that Bennett himself had been so involved in the planning that he opted for generalities to avoid exposing himself to the charge of treason.[108] Whereas Smith's former confidant relied heavily on the image of Muhammad when describing polygamy, he exchanged Islam for Anabaptism in his chapter on empire.[109] Bennett considered the Münster revolt "the most striking historical parallel to the course of the Mormons." Moving beyond mere historical comparison, he charged that "Smith and his comrades" had "derived the ideas of many of their proceedings" from the Münster prophets. A brief outline of Anabaptism, he wrote, made it "quite evident" that the Saints "have taken [the Anabaptists] for models, and have copied their doings with as much accuracy as the spirit of the age would permit." Bennett found parallels in the two movements' social marginality, their prophetism, their emphasis on immediate revelation, and their militarism. He appealed to readers to stop Mormonism before Smith overthrew both the government and the national "social fabric" through the forced conversion of non-Mormons.[110]

Bennett's accusations struck many readers as fanciful, but his diatribe mixed hyperbole with accurate depictions. Evidence of Smith's polygamy was compelling, and his carefully worded denials left him open to lingering suspicion. Smith's overt turn to theocracy would have alarmed non-Mormons but this he also kept secret, though Bennett seems to have picked up on the LDS leader's early political theorizing. Though the Saints had long looked to a millennium where Christ's reign would replace human governments, Smith—in the closing years of his life—developed increasingly specific plans.[111] In April 1842 he received a revelation outlining a political kingdom of God but did not flesh out institutional particulars until later.[112] Between the April 1842 revelation and the 1844 establishment of a politically oriented "Council of Fifty," Smith initiated several close associates into what he called the "Quorum of the Anointed." Its purpose was to discuss and pray over church affairs and political issues.[113] Evidently Bennett was unaware of much that transpired in the spring of 1842, but his exposé revealed enough to alarm quorum members, who were constructing the beginnings of what Smith would later term a "THEO-DEMOCRACY."[114] Still, his embellishments, long reaches, and rhetorical flourishes undercut much of the damage Bennett might have inflicted. Smith's strenuous denials of the more outlandish aspects, combined with the evident lapses in Bennett's own morality, led many non-Mormons outside western Illinois to conclude that neither Smith nor Bennett could be trusted.

Polygamy's psychic and social toll forced Smith's hand in the summer of 1843. Urged by his brother Hyrum to dictate a revelation on polygamy, Smith obliged but failed to pacify his first wife or skeptical high-ranking Mormons.[115] The widening of the circle of secrecy was disastrous, since it made opponents out of some church members who had already been disturbed by Smith's other innovations.[116] Some chose to remain silent; others expressed uncertainty that time would set Mormonism right. William Law became their ringleader of Smith's detractors. Law had settled in Nauvoo as a wealthy, respectable convert and was quickly recognized for his leadership abilities. Smith made him a counselor in the LDS Presidency in 1841, but the relationship between the two soured as Law came to resent Smith's economic program, political activities, and plural marriages.[117] Eventually, Law presided over a dissenting "Reformed Mormon Church" and published the prospectus of a dissident paper, the *Nauvoo Expositor*. Promising to expose the polygamy and theocratic activities of Mormon leaders, the *Expositor* sent Smith and the city council into action.[118] When they destroyed the dissenting press, anti-Mormons had the evidence of Mormon antirepublicanism they needed and the county exploded. Thomas Sharp sounded the call to arms: "War and extermination" were "inevitable" and the only comment left to be made would be "WITH POWDER AND BALL."[119] Mormon leaders eventually turned themselves in, and anti-Mormons, seizing the moment, stormed the jailhouse and gunned down Joseph and Hyrum Smith.

Whatever Mormon hopes had existed for a peaceable stay in Nauvoo fell apart quickly. The spiral of violence sent both sides looking west for a resolution, as Hancock County's non-Mormons called a convention in 1845. Well acquainted with such meetings, the Latter-day Saints anticipated the convention's resolution.[120] Predictably, the assembly condemned the Mormons' "predatory disposition" and lawlessness. Satisfied that "no people, however quietly disposed, can live in the immediate neighborhood of the Mormons without being drawn into collision with them, and with a resort to arms for self protection," residents insisted that the Mormon era in western Illinois had come to an end.[121] Josiah Conyers, a physician from Quincy, was convinced that mob violence was not "levelled at Mormonism alone" but at "the constitution of our beloved country." Should citizens of Illinois "resort to forcible banishment, without trial, not only of the guilty, but of the innocent also," they should admit that either the Constitution was insufficient or that Americans lacked the "virtue and *intelligence*" to "administer their own laws." In the end, however, hotter heads prevailed.[122] When the Saints' exodus from Illinois moved too slowly for anti-Mormons, a full-blown battle punctuated the LDS retreat. Nauvoo thereafter quickly receded into small-town inconspicuousness. By 1851, the Mormon temple lay in ruins, French socialists had purchased much of the town, and, where over ten thousand people had lived, scarcely two thousand remained.[123]

Brigham Young, who had succeeded in securing ecclesiastical control against rival claims, managed the tensions of 1845–46 while seeking the Mormons' next gathering place. In the spring of 1845 Young sent letters to governors (except those from Missouri and Illinois) and President James K. Polk seeking advice. Specifically, the Mormons asked about relocation to Oregon country, a solution offered by politicians Henry Clay and Stephen Douglas, newsman James Arlington Bennett, and others since the late 1830s.[124] Only Governor Thomas Drew of Arkansas responded.[125] His letter was polite but offered little hope that the Saints would find a suitable home in the United States. He therefore heartily agreed with the plan of emigration to "the Oregon territory—or to California—the north of Texas or to Nebraska," where the Saints could "test the practicability of [their] system beyond the reach of contention."[126] For others looking west with different aims in mind, on the other hand, an Oregon Mormon empire might do more harm than good. Illinois governor Ford, desperate to rid himself of his political nightmare, encouraged Mormons to leave but hinted that they best do so quietly, since he suspected federal officials might resist Mormon migration to lands both coveted by expansionists and held by wary rivals.[127] Sure enough, Young received multiple letters from Samuel Brannan, a Mormon contact in Washington, reporting that the secretary of war intended to "prevent our moving West . . . alleging that it is against the Law for an armed body of men to go from the United States to any other government."[128] Brannan eventually updated his report and clarified that the Saints could leave, but Mormon leaders must have felt utterly confused as to the course expected of them.[129]

The vast West provided the space for Mormons to envision a final kingdom. When LDS leaders struck out from Illinois in 1846, they had an admittedly hazy notion of where they were going; nevertheless, they were satisfied that it was better for Mormonism to wither in the Mexican wilderness than succumb to American mobocracy.[130] Newly "exiled from the United States," the Latter-day Saints secured isolation from white neighbors though the United States followed them west. With the signing of the Treaty of Guadalupe Hidalgo in 1848, the Saints were again an American problem. Anti-Mormonism transformed once Mormonism became less a local annoyance and more a national political issue.

THE SMITH MURDERS and the Mormons' forced exile were the result of the conclusions anti-Mormons had reached by the mid-1840s. The conviction that Mormonism represented a virulent political theology had gained such sway that the destruction of a dissenting press seemed to bear out warnings of the church's imperial aims. Fearing Smith's intentions and the presence of a sizable Mormon army, Illinois residents cared little for how the danger was removed. Thomas Sharp's leadership of the lynch mob that killed Joseph Smith rested on his conviction that desperate times had gone beyond legal remedy—an echo from the Missouri grievance lists a decade earlier. Since Smith had manipulated the apparatus of state, only extralegal means could answer the threat he preresented, so the argument went.[131] Sharp announced that the "law of God and Nature is above the law of man"—a perspective he had long despised when issued from Mormon lips.[132] Given the rise of political anti-Mormon sentiment, it is perhaps little wonder that Illinoisans failed to imagine a religiously pluralistic western Illinois. In 1841 the Illinois Anti-Mormon Party had anticipated the future crisis when it claimed to "have nothing to do" with the Mormons' "peculiar religious opinions," only "the influence which these people have obtained, and *are likely to obtain*, in a political capacity."[133] Before they knew of polygamy or had experienced much of the Saints as neighbors, Hancock County residents expected trouble. For members of the Anti-Mormon Party, conflict was inevitable even without any illegal activity on the Saints' part because Mormons, by virtue of their gathering doctrine, would wield local political power. For their part, the Mormons were hardly prone to visions of religious pluralism. While laudably and explicitly including "Catholics" and even "Mohammedans" in a city ordinance protecting broad religious liberties, which affixed a $300 fine and a six-month prison term for anyone ridiculing another's religious beliefs, they could not tolerate vocal religious dissent.[134]

While the resort to mob violence seems in step with the broader contours of antebellum history, anti-Mormon thinking had made considerably more room for violence by the 1840s than had existed earlier. One study of American rioting singles out the 1830s as perhaps the high-water mark for mob action in the United States.[135] American vigilantes attacked Catholics, gamblers, abolitionists, bankers, northern and southern blacks, and a host of others in addition to Mormons.[136] Although this convulsive pattern of social trauma had generated considerable alarm during the 1830s, Illinoisans of the mid-1840s were united in their approval of anti-Mormon violence. Tellingly, the attorneys for the accused assassins of Joseph Smith settled on widespread public approval as the crux of their case. Since the murderers had enacted community will, no one individual could be found guilty, they argued. To the horror, but not surprise, of the Mormons, the jury freed the mob's ringleaders.[137] Anti-Mormon formulations made such acquittals possible. Had Mormonism not come to be viewed as a cogent political and military threat, anti-Mormon violence would not have commanded such pervasive assent. Though earlier assessments of Mormonism had focused on individual leaders or a deluded crowd, the rise of political anti-Mormonism culminated in calls for collective retribution. One Illinois county citizens' meeting resolved that "the whole body should be held responsible for all lawless acts against the persons, or property, of our citizens" and be forced from the state, a viewpoint that followed logically from the anti-Mormon arguments against a Mormon system.[138] The Saints' flight from the United States hardly answered the questions begged by Mormon communitarianism. Although relocation to the Great Basin and eventual territorial status ensured that the Mormon problem would not be any one state's alone, it spawned conflict with the federal government that would last more than a half century.

CHAPTER 4

"Barbarism"

Rhetorics of Alienation

Writing for the majority in the landmark case *Reynolds v. United States*, Chief Justice Morrison Waite casually laid bare a central dilemma of American law when he observed that the "word 'religion' is not defined in the Constitution." Waite insisted that in lieu of any constitutional definition, the Court was left with "the history of the times in the midst of which the provision was adopted" as a guide to "ascertain its meaning."[1] He ended up at Thomas Jefferson's 1802 letter to Connecticut Baptists and, in the process—to paraphrase legal historian Sarah Barringer Gordon—made history by interpreting it.[2] Viewed from the perspective of many years' worth of often-bitter debate, the Court's reliance on Jefferson's "acts v. beliefs" dichotomy scarcely resolved religion's definitional conundrum.

If the high court was unsure in 1879 about what exactly religion was, most Washington politicians had long known what it was not. In an 1860 report to the House Judiciary Committee, Congressman Thomas Nelson of Tennessee wrote that when the founders had secured the free exercise of religion, "they did not mean to dignify with the name of religion a tribe of Latter Day Saints disgracing that hallowed name, and wickedly imposing upon the credulity of mankind."[3] Nelson's denial of Mormonism's religiousness rested on the central thrust of early anti-Mormonism. Freighted with sectarian polemics and theological taxonomies, "religion" in mid-century political discourse meant "Protestantism." Mormons swam against the cultural and political currents when they assumed that polygamy would be protected as a religious practice. Representations of Mormonism, moreover, cut to the heart of American thinking about history, religion, race, and nation. Indeed, the Latter-day Saints' geographic exodus from American centers of power anticipated the discursive trajectory of postbellum anti-Mormonism. Increasingly, Mormonism was construed as religiously

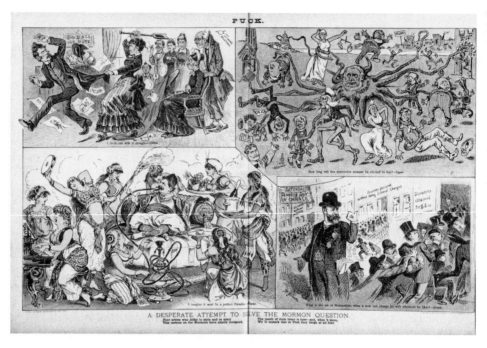

"A Desperate Attempt to Solve the Mormon Question," *Puck*, 13 February 1884 (L. Tom Perry Special Collections, Harold B. Lee Library, Brigham Young University, Provo)

and culturally alien, and the racialized and gendered forms of those constructs hint at the opposition's place in the cultural hierarchies undergirding westward and overseas expansion. In its complex transition from a fake religion to an alien one, Mormonism functioned like a screen upon which Americans could project their crises. Its influence in the nineteenth century was thus indirect: it was perceived as a threat, creating a critical forum for some of the century's pressing ideological issues.[4]

What resulted from the *Reynolds* decision is familiar enough, as successively harsher legislation marked the beginning of polygamy's end for mainstream Mormons. What preceded the case is less understood. After all, when viewed against five decades of anti-Mormon sentiment, the Court's ruling might have signaled a different trajectory altogether. The opinion effectively dodged the question of polygamy's religiousness by asserting that government could suppress acts, religious or not, that stood in the way of civilization's progress. Seen in the light of calls in the 1840s and 1850s for Mormonism to be excised from the body politic for its essential un-Americanness, the *Reynolds* case can be read as tacit acceptance of Mormonism's religiousness — a moment of no small significance in the long

WOMAN'S BONDAGE IN UTAH.
THE MORMON SOLUTION OF THE "CHEAP LABOR" QUESTION.

history of anti-Mormon polemics. In practical terms, however, the ruling buttressed claims like Nelson's that Mormonism merely imposed on the category "religion." In particular, the Court's recourse to religious and cultural analogy signaled the extent to which notions of history, race, and the world's religions had come to set the agenda for various approaches to Mormonism. *Reynolds*, then, was a multihinged pivot point in Mormon-Gentile relationships, one that spelled eventual doom for polygamy but could, in the long run, make space for Mormonism among America's religions.

Empire(s) in the West

It was Mormonism's flight from the United States and Utah's subsequent status as a federal territory that drew it into larger conversations about the fate of the West, the spread of civilization, and the national character. Untangling the related arguments about Mormonism's "Americanness" and "religiousness" preceding the *Reynolds* decision highlights not only the fears about commingling church and state along Mormon lines but also the permeability of Jefferson's famed wall of separation. In this case, the wall's permeability was rooted in the fact that official positions trafficked in understandings of religion that depended on conventionally Protestant sensibilities. Seen in this light, it is no coincidence that *Reynolds*, which at least implicitly comported with allegations of Mormonism's a-religious character, appeared in the same historical moment with the National Reform Association's fight to amend the Constitution to explicitly declare the United States a "Christian" nation.[5]

Mormonism became Washington's problem once the United States followed the Mormons west in 1848. According to Mormon watcher John Gunnison, by 1852 Mormons regarded "themselves as placed in the position of our colonial fathers." Chafing at the heavy-handed rule of "*foreigners*," the Latter-day Saints spent the next half century begging to be left alone — alone, that is, in an independent state stretching from San Diego to Denver.[6] With so much at stake in determining just what kind of West the nation would have, politicians in the 1850s, 1860s, and 1870s could hardly leave the Mormons alone. In the 1830s and 1840s, national commentators had imagined successively western spaces as possible Mormon ones — from Wisconsin to "Upper California" to Oregon — but a sea-to-shining-sea America closed the social safety valve and left Washington without another West for the Mormons.

Mormons troubled American minds already divided about the West. Heirs of Jefferson's vision imagined it as an agrarian paradise offering economic opportunity and the renewal of republican virtue. Others were less optimistic. In a famous 1847 sermon, Horace Bushnell, Congregationalist pastor and heterodox theologian, considered the West a "great problem."[7] Already threatened by "Romanism" and a "relapse towards barbarism," the West was further complicated by Mormonism.[8] That Mormonism "could gather in its thousands of disciples in this enlightened age, build a populous city, and erect a temple, rivalling in grandeur, even that of the false prophet at Mecca" left little doubt for Bushnell that the West constituted an American dilemma.[9] Because they had long been associated with the dark side of the western experience, it is curious that modern historians of the West, in the estimation of one prominent scholar, almost routinely overlook the Mormons. Indeed, nineteenth-century commentators tended toward the other extreme.[10] A nascent Mormon kingdom became an embarrassing impediment to the advance of a more powerful one, as Bushnell had hinted. In his call to civilize the West, he rallied Christians to "not cease, till a christian nation throws up its temples of worship on every hill and plain." Bushnell envisioned an entire continent circumscribed within the "bounds of a new Christian Empire." In the way of that dream stood tens of thousands of Latter-day Saints busily erecting their own Rocky Mountain "theo-democracy."[11]

The 1850s represent the last years of what one scholar has called the "local tradition" of anti-Mormonism and the first years of the clash between Mormon and federal empires. Postannouncement anti-Mormonism was largely subsumed within a federally directed antipolygamy crusade, which lent energy to those concerned with the Saints' domestic habits and those opposed to the LDS theocracy.[12] By the early 1860s, the general terms of the conflict had been more or less set, and a "national antipolygamy ethic" both incorporated and overshadowed the varieties of anti-Mormonism that had predominated earlier.[13] In response, Mormons defended polygamy as a religious right and tried to secure local self-rule. That Republicans linked slavery and polygamy in the 1850s came as no surprise. Mormonism's new geography ensured entanglement in the issue of national destiny as surely as the South's peculiar institution did.

Bitter disputes between Mormon leaders and federal appointees set the stage for congressional consideration of Utah territorial matters during the tumultuous Kansas-Nebraska controversy of 1854. Mormon patriarchs, it turned out, were "far less controversial" targets in 1850s political discourse than were slaveholding ones.[14] The Kansas-Nebraska Act embodied Stephen A. Douglas's ideals of congressional nonintervention and localized sovereignty, but the Utah question demonstrated just how far national leaders were prepared to let local democracy go. During the act's debates, John Clayton of Delaware took the opportunity to regret the passage of the Utah bill of 1850, partly to embarrass Douglas, wondering if it had been "judicious [to] erect a territorial government for Utah" given its "peculiar institution" and "a Mormon theocracy, virtually established by law."[15]

Connecticut's Truman Smith, who had praised Utah's territorial government in 1850, similarly regretted his support of Utah's "Organic Act"; in a complete reversal, he singled out Utah as evidence of the danger of the popular sovereignty position.[16] With the slavery question in view and thinking he had Douglas exposed, Smith asked: "Did you intend to confer on the people of Utah the power to introduce *polygamy*, for that appertains to one of the domestic relations?" With Utah a state, Smith surmised, Congress had best prepare for Brigham Young as a member. "Has the honorable chairman [Douglas] considered whether [Young] is to bring his forty wives to the Seat of Government; and if so, I would ask in what part of the city is he to establish his harem?"[17]

Attacks like Truman Smith's put popular sovereignty's supporters on the defensive. Some assumed that Mormons would eventually rid themselves of the "monstrous absurdity" of polygamy and thereby validate the popular sovereignty principle, but Iowa's Augustus Caesar Dodge took another approach.[18] He found arguments against popular sovereignty to be based on "a presumed or asserted incapacity of American citizens to comprehend either their duties or rights, and their inability to govern themselves," a position he believed was un-American but one that nonetheless required him to defang Mormonism. Dodge did so by associating it with Shakerism, which, he implied, constituted a harmless set of religious eccentrics. Sects were "apt to go to extremes," he granted, but no one had presented a proposition to drive Shakers out. Both Mormons and Shakers were "doubtless in gross error," but they were "gradually diminishing before the intelligent and enlightened Christianity of the day."[19]

So, if Mormonism figured in political speech as a surrogate for discussions of slavery, much of that speech was loaded with concerns about religion and the state. In perhaps the period's most wide-ranging harangue against Mormonism, Caleb Lyon of New York raged against a proposal to strike from a House territorial bill a provision that would make polygamists ineligible for land grants. To make his point, Lyon declared that an antipolygamy position was "worthy of Christian statesmen and Christian lawgivers." Couching the quarrel in this way put forward a series of durable polarities that left Mormonism on the wrong side of the boundary marking "Christian," "American," and "civilized." For Lyon, an "American Harem" reverted toward barbarism. As in the "Orient," he argued, Mormon homes featured jealousies among wives, a lack of "respect of parental authority," and probably "infanticide" since husbands no doubt struggled to support their sizable broods. Thereafter Lyon's call lost its moderate tone: "Let us, as Christians, follow and legislate in the doctrines of Christ, not of Joe Smith; let us take the holy Gospel, not the Book of Mormon. . . . Point me to a nation where polygamy is practiced, and I will point you to heathens and barbarians. It seriously [affects] the prosperity of States, it retards civilization, it uproots Christianity. . . . Let us nip this evil in the bud, for the sake of morality, religion, and Christianity."[20] Few stated the terms as starkly, but his conflation of Christianity, monogamy, and civilization nicely encapsulates the main thrusts of postbellum anti-Mormonism. Such perspectives were hardly invented in Washington. Anti-Mormon writers had been assembling these arguments since the 1840s, and the influence of prominent 1850s anti-Mormon voices on congressional talk is unmistakable.[21]

Calls for forceful action against Mormon theocracy and polygamy made such assumptions the stuff of party platforms. For the Republicans, of course, antipolygamy was a mainstay of their national identity. Speaking to the House of Representatives in early 1857, Vermont Republican Justin Morrill demanded military action, asserting that the "Mormons are quite as hostile to the republican form of government as they are to the usual forms of Christianity." Morrill found Brigham Young's sermons, in which he castigated non-Mormons for their prostitutes and infidelity, reminiscent of a Turkish ambassador's apology for Islam: "It is natural that the Mormons should sympathize more with Turks than with Christians. Accordingly, they do rank them higher in the scale of civilization, repeat their slanders, and assimilate their domestic institutions."[22] Turning exegete, Morrill derided the notion that "Divine revelation has made no progress" since the time of "Abraham or Solomon." If the Bible actually sanctioned polygamy, he continued, did it similarly sanction Lot's incest, Moses' murder of the Egyptian, or David's seduction of Uriah's wife? Taking turns as theologian and historian, Morrill joined the chorus of those limiting what could and could not be properly denominated religious.[23] Charging that the Latter-day Saints sought to "maintain and perpetuate, a Mohammedan barbarism" merely under the "guise of religion," he wondered if religion "might . . . be invoked to protect cannibalism and infanticide." Furthermore, since polygamy was abetted by an "ecclesiastical hierarchy" more powerful than "the Pope of Rome," Mormonism itself was "clearly repugnant to the Constitution of the United States."[24] Republicans had sharp rhetorical tools for dealing with purportedly un-American religious hierarchies, versed as many were in Know-Nothing anti-Catholicism.[25]

That anti-Catholic and anti-Mormon sentiment developed in tandem in the 1850s is clear, but Democrats, seeking their own place on the moral high ground, could rail against Mormonism just as vehemently. Though he had been friendly to the Mormons in Illinois, Stephen Douglas turned on the Saints when his popular sovereignty doctrine (not to mention his presidential aspirations) seemed imperiled. Speaking in Illinois in 1857, he presented himself as having been duped by the Mormons. Who could have known that Mormons would be guilty of anything other than religious "peculiarities?" Given the field reports, he continued, it seemed that "the inhabitants of Utah, as a community, are outlaws and alien enemies, unfit to exercise the right of self-government." Congress should "apply the knife and cut out this loathsome, disgusting ulcer."[26] President James Buchanan applied the knife, awkwardly, but stopped short of cutting out the Mormon ulcer. And, though Lincoln signed the first antipolygamy bill in 1862, he had far greater crises at hand than Mormons marrying in a distant desert. With the Civil War won, it fell to other Republicans to accomplish the dirty work of ridding the nation of its remaining barbarism.

The Problem of Mormon Whiteness

As the preceding survey of federal rhetoric demonstrates, in the hands of anti-Mormons religious analogy worked in tandem with Protestant versions of religious history to map a past, present, and future for American civilization. This is not surprising given the polemics of the preceding decades—it was a matter of months after the publication of the Book of Mormon before skeptics fit Joseph Smith with Muhammad's mantle, situating Mormons with other fanatics on the religious fringe. The analogies became richer as years passed, spurred by the explanatory problem of polygamy. Peoples of Asia and Africa were added to a generic Islam in the postbellum years as analogs for Mormonism, rhetorical strategies that both reflected and created new senses of racialized identity and history. Theology and exegesis were (mostly) absent from official talk, but the religious sensibilities undergirding antipolygamy existed as powerful "givens" in various explanations and sometimes as featured conversation pieces themselves. Jan Shipps's provocative suggestion that polygamy pushed Mormons from sectarian "difference" to foreign "otherness" begs important questions—what accounts for the prepolygamy period's greater violence, for instance—but her framework at least charts a midcentury tonal transition.[27] Increasingly, anti-Mormon rhetoric drew on fashionable understandings of human difference, especially emerging theories of racial difference and religious development. As a result, Mormonism, despite its own racialized sense of religious purity, came to inhabit the vexed space between white and nonwhite in American minds.[28]

Whatever liberalizing tendencies might have inhered in the Supreme Court's 1879 refusal to decide polygamy's religiousness were undone when Chief Justice Waite left Jefferson and went on to situate polygamists among the "uncivilized." "Polygamy has always been odious among the northern and western nations of Europe," Waite opined, "and, until the establishment of the Mormon Church, was almost exclusively a feature of the life of Asiatic and of African people."[29] Waite's tripartite grouping of the world's peoples reflected an understanding of race, lineage, and history that rested on Protestant readings of the Bible. Though obviously not the only theory of racial history promulgated in the nineteenth century, Waite's was prominent precisely because it was thought to comport with the biblical account of the Noachian flood. In the popular formulation, Noah's three sons, Ham, Shem, and Japeth (or Japhet, Japheth), begat three broad groupings of peoples emerging from Africa, Asia, and western Europe, respectively. Mingling biblical exegesis, race prejudice, and selected "scientific" insights, postbellum thinkers worked in the liminal space between an earlier period's creative engagement with race as a primarily theological problem and a turn-of-the-century context in which scripture was "dethroned" as the principal text to be reckoned with when theorizing about race.[30]

Mormons fit awkwardly into this schema. Their shared commitment to conventional racial taxonomies—albeit with some uniquely LDS modification—prompted their own aggressive claims to whiteness. In the blend of authoritarianism and egalitarianism that defined early Mormonism, race seems not to have garnered special attention initially.[31] The Book of Mormon's language—that "black and white, bond and free, male and female . . . all are alike unto God"—might have tilted the movement toward a more radical inclusiveness were it not for the twists and turns of early Mormon history.[32] In the 1830s, Mormons took a moderate enough course on slavery to alienate slaveholding neighbors. Their reactions dampened Mormon enthusiasm for evangelizing slaves. An 1835 church statement conveyed Mormon intentions to avoid interference with "bond-servants, neither preach the gospel to, nor baptize them, contrary to the will and wish of their masters."[33] At first, tactical retreats from black evangelism lacked doctrinal explanations. A few African Americans were ordained in a universal male priesthood, but Mormon practice and policy in early Utah turned against full black participation. Brigham Young made more of the legendary "curses" of Cain and Ham than Smith had—though a cryptic reference to cursed lineage in one of Smith's revelations became a main justification for later Mormon exclusionism—and, gradually and somewhat haphazardly, Mormons erected doctrinal frameworks around their denial of priesthood to any man found to be of African descent.[34]

Mormons' own race prejudice notwithstanding, in the church's first decades anti-Mormon antagonists routinely invoked racial epithets as knee-jerk insults. For instance, in 1833 when the souring of Mormon/non-Mormon relations prompted old-time Missouri citizens to organize, their list of demands charged that Mormons were "elevated . . . but little above the condition of our blacks."[35] Set on their heels by such talk, Mormons spent considerable ink despairing over their disappointed assumption that shared whiteness might mitigate religious bias. Mormon leader Parley Pratt angrily recounted the rhetorical tactics of the church's opponents. "This murderous gang" of anti-Mormons, he wrote, "were denominated citizens, white people . . . while our society . . . were denominated Mormons, in contradistinction to the appelation of citizens, whites, &c, as if we had been some savage tribe, or some colored race of foreigners."[36] In a similar vein, some Mormons understood their exodus as a renunciation of white society. "We are not accounted as white people," Heber Kimball acknowledged bitterly, "and we don't want to live among them. I had rather live with the buffalo in the wilderness."[37] Mormons should not have been surprised to find that anti-Mormons would weave increasingly elaborate descriptions of just how far they stood apart. In the decades after 1845 anti-Mormon estimations of Mormon whiteness deteriorated, an ironic development when viewed against the contemporaneous embellishment of Mormon racialism.

By midcentury, commentators found that polygamy not only constituted a ready analog to the non-Christian and nonwhite, it also begged questions about Mormon bodies. Were Mormons simply *like* nonwhites in their familial or religious practices, or were Americans witnessing a new, threatening racial category in the making? Even apart from polygamy and despite the overwhelmingly white makeup of early converts, observers strained to find a difference in the physical appearance of Latter-day Saints. Writing in 1851, an anonymous author fantasized that Mormon religious mischief was apparent on Mormon faces. In this highly stylized account, two Mormon elders happened onto a peaceful village and made trouble. Inviting readers to "take a glance at their physiognomy and appearance," the author described the older preacher as possessing "a visage at once striking and unprepossessing." The Mormon's "intellect, marred by low cunning—fanaticism mingled with, if not overpowered by, hypocrisy," shaped his facial features: his lips "vainly endeavored to curb an habitual contemptuous smile" and "eyes now flashing with scornful pride, now raised to heaven with an air of sanctified humility."[38] Religious fanaticism was not always as obvious. An alternate line of reasoning held that because Mormons looked and spoke like other Americans, extra vigilance was called for, since one could not be sure where the Mormon threat might emerge. With some acknowledgment that the nature of the Mormon menace was similarity, arguments about difference became even more trenchant.[39]

Late twentieth-century scholars thus found in nineteenth-century Mormonism a rich case study in the evolution of American thinking about ethnicity.[40] Historical subjects lacked such a flexible category, however, and were left to address Mormonism with clumsier rhetorical tools. In an awkward but telling report on the state of military installations in the West, U.S. Army surgeon Roberts Bartholow explained Mormon peculiarity in racial terms. For Bartholow, Mormon children became the victims "of all the vices of civilization" that older societies "have been ages in reaching." As evidence, he referred to a "preponderance of female births," high infant mortality rates, and the prevalence of "gelatinous types of constitution" among Mormons. Though the veneer of empiricism gave Bartholow's report scientific credibility lacking in more literary arguments on the same theme, the results were similar. "It is a curious fact," he observed, "that Mormonism makes its impress upon the countenance." Unsure whether to credit a temporal environment, "a purely sensual and material religion," or "the premature development of the passions," Bartholow could nonetheless detail a "Mormon expression and style": "The yellow, sunken, cadaverous visage; the greenish-colored eyes; the thick, protuberant lips; the low forehead; the light, yellowish hair; and the lank, angular person, constitute an appearance so characteristic of the new race, the production of polygamy, as to distinguish them at a glance." The "new race," as he termed it, amounted to a fearsome melting pot. The allegedly recognizable "physical peculiarities of the nationalities" of older Mormons were utterly "lost" in the unnatural practice of Mormon polygamy.[41] Bartholow's backhanded compliment to Old World racial stock stands in stark contrast to more straightforwardly xenophobic depictions of Mormon demography, typically expressed to underscore Mormon alienation from American institutions. Time and again, it was said that Utah Mormonism was made up primarily of (poor, uneducated) European converts with only "the principal leaders and a few others . . . natives of the United States."[42] How could those unacquainted with American institutions and burdened by Mormonism's erroneous ideology and practices possibly be trusted with democratic political institutions? This unstable characterization of Mormon bloodlines reflects the ambivalence inherent in the broader American engagement with race.

In 1865 scientist John Draper pulled various strands of contemporary theorizing together in an explanation that both extends and contextualizes Bartholow's account. Draper's rested on the assertion that societies, like bodies, develop according to natural law. Grounded in a mythology of order and predictability, Draper fused history, religion, race, and empire into something of a recipe for American success. With an eye on past empires, he wrote that nations undergo unceasing change but, generally, in a "helpless and predetermined way" through various stages of development.[43] The rate of development in turn hinged on environmental factors. Climate, in fact, did most of the heaving lifting in Draper's explanation of racial difference. Caught between robust environmentalism and a sense of racial superiority, he could both deny race's "absolute unchangeability" and reify whiteness. After noticing Jews as examples of race's variability (common origins yet varying complexions, so his argument went), he identified the "Indo-European" race as a "homogeneous family, derived from a common stock." Awkward though it was, Draper's philologically defined white race remained historically coherent, while other peoples, defined variously, were heirs to malleability and historio-environmental contingency.[44]

Relapsing into environmentalism, Draper described American whiteness in terms of regional variation. Temperature differences ensured that southern labor patterns were seasonal, its work less pressing. The northerner, by contrast, "must be industrious." Cold not only inculcated northern urgency, it provided periods conducive to "forethought and reflection." Southern whites resembled "Asians" in Draper's tale. In the contrast between the progressive West and the inert, tradition-bound East, Draper could sound dire warnings.[45] He decried the immigration of "stagnant Asiatic tribes" (Chinese and Japanese) to the American West, predicting a "flood . . . to come" if the current wave were not curtailed. He especially worried about the "political power of polygamic institutions." Fearing racial hybridity, Draper noted that "the sentiments of Asiatics" had "already obtained a firm root in Utah." The migration of Mormons westward had only intensified their political threat: "As men approach the confines of Asia, they seem to be affected by its moral atmosphere."[46]

Draper's theorizing, idiosyncratic though it may have been, was nevertheless in step with what Tomoko Masuzawa has described as a fundamental transformation of Euro-American identity. Whereas eighteenth-century Euro-Americans tended to group the world's peoples into four categories—Christian, Jewish, Mohammedan, and "others"—comparative philology in the late nineteenth century helped remap religious groups based on shared locations of origin and what were thought to be three distinct language families: Semitic, Aryan (or Indo-European), and Turanian (or Oriental). This perceived correspondence between religious and linguistic places of origin was amplified by the tripartite schema of world communities based on Noah's sons. These sometimes competing, sometimes complementary frameworks jumbled science with exegesis, associating Christianity with this or that religious tradition or language family. As Masuzawa notes, this reordering eventuated in drives both to Hellenize Christianity and to Semitize Islam. In any case, it left unquestioned in most Western minds the inferiority of Asia and its religions.[47] Writing that Buddhism, Islam, and Judaism "are all of Asiatic origin," Draper found that, despite the awkward fact of Christianity's own origins in "Asia," the "irrepressible tendency of Europe is to philosophy" where Asia's was "religion." Grateful (or hopeful?) that European Christianity had thrown off its Asiatic origins, Draper could fret over cultural/religious relapse in the form of Mormonism or Chinese immigration.[48]

Asia thus rivaled Islam as the analog of choice for antipolygamists.[49] Given the prominence of Asia in the racialist imaginations of the mid-century intellectual elite, this should come as no surprise. Still, some irony accompanied this development. Take, for instance, Draper's assertion that "fifty years ago it would have been thought incredible that a polygamic state should exist in the midst of Christian communities of European descent."[50] Congressman Thomas Fitch apologetically echoed a similar sentiment on the House floor in 1870 while arguing *against* antipolygamy legislation: "I am not unmindful of the deep disgrace to the nation that the barbarous social practices of the Asiatic should be unblushingly pursued among a Saxon people in this noon of the nineteenth century."[51] What these Asia-heavy conceptualizations obscured, of course, was the original historical connection that anti-Mormons drew for polygamy: the radical Protestants of sixteenth-century Münster. In an 1842 exposé, Mormon defector John C. Bennett pointed to the Anabaptists as Mormonism's "most striking historical parallel," but, even earlier, anti-Mormon Tyler Parsons had accurately anticipated Mormon polygamy because of the resemblances he discerned between the two movements.[52] In late nineteenth-century America, these Christian/European comparisons largely lost their charm.

The references to Asia called forth a timely, though complicated, nexus of race, religion, and empire, a point not lost on legal historians. Legal scholars have located the *Reynolds* decision in both antebellum and Gilded Age legal temperaments and in the latter have found connections with a burgeoning American imperialism. In her description of the federalization of U.S. marriage law, Sarah Gordon has detailed the debt *Reynolds* owed to antislavery and the responses it offered to constitutional questions prompted by abolitionism.[53] For Nathan Oman, *Reynolds* hearkens back to the 1850s less than it portends an imperialist turn at century's end. By responding to Mormon arguments that polygamy was protected under the Constitution with analogies to the British regulation of Indian religious practice, Oman notes, antipolygamists not only constructed Mormons as racial outsiders, they buttressed ideologies grounding American domination of racial minorities at home and abroad. As Oman demonstrates, the legal implications of antipolygamy before and after *Reynolds*—the liberation of racial minorities before and the suppression of them after—help set *Reynolds* in a heretofore-unappreciated place in American legal history.[54] The Court's decision, seen in this context, fits precisely within those narratives that chart the radicalism of leading Republicans in the 1860s, the compromise of that vision during the years 1872–77, and the eventual turn of prominent Gilded Age Republicans to the politics of empire and its concomitant strains of racism.[55]

Rhetorical recourse to British imperialism in India came with certain problems, however. For one, Indian peoples fit within philologically oriented narratives of "Aryan" culture, as Sanskrit formed the foundation of the Indo-European language family. And, while Indian examples (primarily "suttee," an Anglicized Sanskrit word for Hindu widows' ritual suicide, and "Thugee," the infamously murderous tradition of East India) became the discursive volleys against Mormon claims of free exercise, it remained true that the British Raj had been soft on Indian polygamy. Antipolygamists did not notice the India/Asia/Aryan interpretative dilemma, but Mormons and some liberal Republicans ensured that British toleration of polygamy would not go unnoticed. One strategy was to turn the game of historical analogy around by locating polygamy in less alien historical contexts. Utah's territorial representative, William H. Hooper, cited Martin Luther's permissive stance on polygamy and assembled biblical passages where polygamy was allegedly "not only tolerated, but explicitly commanded by the Almighty." His point, though primarily intended to cast polygamy as a Christian practice, underscored a more fundamental claim made in an 1870 House speech: "The Mormon people are a Christian denomination." Hooper could even grant the counterreasoning, for argument's sake, because, as he noted, even non-Christian polygamy was tolerated under British rule.[56]

Liberal Republican James Blair agreed. Though expressing no love for Mormonism, Blair pointed to the British precedent as a guide for U.S. policy. He too acknowledged polygamy's biblical precedent: "Upon almost every page of the old Bible we find polygamy." He wondered, given polygamy's standing in the Bible, how Mormon polygamy had come to be so despised. Had not the Baptists, Congregationalists, Episcopalians, Methodists, and Presbyterians all declared Indian polygamy "not contrary to divine law" in the 1850s? Blair added that, since the treaty that secured the Mormons' Great Basin kingdom had expressly recognized "their" religious freedom, how could American Protestants disallow Mormon polygamy on the grounds it offended Christianity?[57] His perspective, which was "already anachronistic" in its sensitivity to minority religious practices in 1872, garnered no support (or even comment) in Congress. In the context of surging postwar confidence in the nation's civilizing potential, Blair's kind of toleration smacked of pro-Mormon apologetics.[58]

Mormon Women, the Ungrateful Objects of American Pity

Rhetorically entangled as they were in contests over American civilization, Mormon women were prominent subjects of late-century portraits of Mormonism. It might seem curious to find Mormon women in tiny rural outposts writing as if they lived in the glare of the national spotlight, but, given the voluminous chatter about them and their families, it is perhaps not surprising. These obscure figures seemed to sense that the "case for or against Mormonism rested on its women," as Claudia Bushman has written.[59] Given the formidable links Americans made between gender and civilization, it is no wonder that Mormon women dominated anti-Mormon literature during the 1870s, 1880s, and 1890s. In Gail Bederman's classic study of masculinity, middle-class whites remade late-century American manhood through ubiquitous references to race.[60] The racialization of Mormons went hand in hand with representations of Mormon women, with the women functioning as representatives of civilization's march or decline. Mormon women denied their prescribed roles as tyrannized victims, however. In the initial response to LDS defiance of the Morrill Act (1862) and thereafter, antipolygamists flirted with "defense of the defenseless" as the central justification for their crusade. In opposition to antipolygamy legislation, Eliza Snow, in 1870, protested: "Our enemies pretend that in Utah, woman is held in a state of vassalage—that she does not act from choice, but by coercion—that we would even prefer life elsewhere, were it possible for us to make our escape. What nonsense!"[61] National commentators were puzzled when the expected flood of grateful women failed to materialize during President Buchanan's 1857 Utah invasion. For the remainder of the century, few in Washington or in the press seemed to know what to make of Mormon women. In 1873 the New York Woman Suffrage Association memorialized Congress, certain that female votes would rid Utah of its polygamy. Less than twenty years later, federal legislation *stripped* Utah women of that same right in hopes of finally stamping out plural marriage. Resting as it did on what Christine Talbot has called the "impossibility" of Mormon women's consent, antipolygamy never fully reconciled its stated aims with the realities of these women's lives.[62]

LDS leaders knew that polygamy would generate legal and political issues. Though western travelers went to Utah to see the Mormon curiosity, Latter-day Saints insisted that it was un-American to question another's religious convictions.[63] The Mormons' first public announcement of polygamy, after all, was a carefully scripted event that had anticipated the spectacle. Orson Pratt's 1852 sermon set the terms of their defense. Indeed, his doctrinal framework was itself the defense. Anticipating arguments that polygamy was merely "a kind of domestic concern . . . in no way connected with religion," Pratt contended that since Mormon polygamy sprang from a coherent theology, it amounted to a constitutionally protected religious practice.[64] While insisting that polygamy was a religious as well as a "domestic" concern, Pratt nevertheless assumed that outsiders would disagree.

Most outsiders did. Indeed, polygamy so dominated postannouncement anti-Mormon thinking that it obscured earlier critiques of Mormonism. In novels, exposés, and plays, writers enumerated polygamy's horrors and called readers to mobilize against the Mormon threat. Polygamy's power to captivate the imagination is evident in American fiction; by century's end, more than fifty novels took up Mormonism as their central focus.[65] Terryl Givens has shown that anti-Mormon fiction offered readers a caricature of exaggerated "otherness" and a venue insulated from the stigma of religious persecution. For Givens, anti-Mormon fiction helped transform the nature of the threat: "Physical and psychological coercion define the action, and Oriental, exotic characteristics define the villains. These representations contributed effectively to the refashioning of Mormonism from a religious sect into a secular entity, whose unpalatable religious features could the more easily be made the objects of public ridicule and censure."[66] Laurence Moore has added that sexuality was fit for nineteenth-century print only when connected with religious deviance. Protestant ministers attacked sexual misconduct in anti-Catholic polemics "before they had Joseph Smith to kick around," and readers were met with equal measure of righteous indignation and titillation in both genres.[67] Disclosures of sexual depravity sold well, and more than one author stretched their scant knowledge of Mormonism to meet market demand. According to one scholarly assessment, novelist Orvilla S. Belisle's work was so outlandish that it must have been written to capture the royalties offered by eastern publishers.[68] Similarly, the exposés by Maria and Austin Ward, respectively titled *Female Life Among the Mormons* (1855) and *Male Life Among the Mormons* (1859), mixed scattered details relating to actual persons and events with highly creative embellishments.[69] Less misleading depictions were typically no less lurid.

Antipolygamy portrayals drew heavily on the captivity narrative tradition, on anti-Catholic tropes, and on traditional anti-Mormon themes. In their fascination with coercion and secrecy, the fictive depictions took up what David Chidester has described as the traditional tests for religious authenticity that could be agreed upon by both Enlightenment rationalists and Protestant devotionalists.[70] On both counts, polygamy's religiousness was found wanting. Mormon polygamy could thus relate to the imposture thesis in two ways: by providing the motive for Mormon hierarchs' duplicity and by offering evidence of the means through which they pursed theocratic ends. The links drawn by anti-Mormons between polygamy and theocracy were so complicated that untangling them is difficult. Efforts to weigh which was the greater threat in American minds—theocracy or polygamy—risk missing how interrelated and mutually dependent the two were thought to be.[71]

Nonfiction accounts trafficked in the same devices but were reinforced by evidence gleaned from outsider observation and insider exposé. Even so, many reports were ambivalent. For every breathless tale of female slavery was another acknowledging the orderliness and general respectability of Mormon life. Solomon N. Carvalho, company artist for John C. Frémont's 1853–54 exploration of the West, arrived in tiny Parowan, Utah, ill and unable to continue with the expedition. Nursed back to health by Mormons, Carvalho spent time in various communities and interacted with Latterday Saints across the social spectrum. In ten weeks at the Mormon capital, Carvalho "never heard any obscene or improper language; never saw a man drunk; never had my attention called to the exhibition of vice of any sort"; and observed "no gambling houses, grog shops, or buildings of ill fame, in all their settlements." Such moral circumspection gave him pause. Deeply troubled by polygamy, Carvalho was sure that it produced effeminate men, discontented women, and a turbulent society. Still, the two polygamous families he described in great detail were by his own admission happy. Inimical as Carvalho found polygamy to be with "human progress," he struggled to reconcile the practice with what he had experienced in Mormon country: "Certainly, a more joyous, happy, free-from-care, and good-hearted people, I never sojourned among."[72] Two decades later, Elizabeth Kane encountered a similar puzzle. On an extended trip through Utah with her husband, Kane vacillated between revulsion at the foreignness of Mormonism and admiration for what its women had accomplished in the desert. Mormon wives understood eastern standards of respectability and domesticity. Even before the railroad's arrival in 1869, they had mustered an approximation of eastern refinement. After dining with a polygamous family in Scipio, Kane could not bring herself to censure the sister wife. "Ought I to despise that woman?" she wrote. "She certainly came up to Solomon's ideal of a virtuous wife."[73]

Less flattering appraisals abounded, as most lacked the positive experiences that tempered the Carvalho and Kane narratives. In particular, disillusioned Mormon women proved highly influential. Standing in awkward contrast to a profusion of women's defenses of polygamy, the voices of Mormon women offered bitterly divided accounts of female freedom in Utah. Fanny Stenhouse, one of the most compelling, represented both sides of the divide in turns. An English convert to Mormonism, she had accompanied her husband during his European missionary labors; after gaining a reputation for their articulateness and refinement, the Stenhouses settled into Salt Lake City's elite circles. As a member of the Mormon intelligentsia, she defended Mormon positions. Richard Burton, in his famous *City of the Saints* (1862), stated that it was from Stenhouse that he had first heard polygamy "learnedly advocated" by a woman.[74] Her subsequent disillusionment and opposition brought her far greater acclaim, eventually connecting Stenhouse with such luminaries as Susan B. Anthony, Elizabeth Cady Stanton, and Harriet Beecher Stowe. Her two accounts of polygamy, *Exposé of Polygamy* (1872) and *"Tell It All"* (1874), were popular with national readers, wildly so in the case of the latter; for years afterward she lectured in venues from Boston to Australia.[75]

Exposé of Polygamy was the more restrained of the two accounts. Here, Stenhouse described her conversion to Mormonism, her shock at learning of polygamy, and her growing disaffection with the faith. Though convinced that polygamy made women miserable, she offered a subtly complex picture of the practice. In England, she had seen how polygamy had troubled traditional family patterns, though, she added somewhat awkwardly, it offered some advantages. Not only did polygamy increase opportunities for marriage, thus gaining acceptance among young, "silly" British converts, but also "ill-mated" women could seize on emigration and polygamy to improve their lot.[76] Published shortly after Stenhouse left the LDS Church, the book somewhat protected former friends and credited Mormons with good intentions, though it left no doubt of the author's profound relief. "I am a free woman," Stenhouse exulted, "free from the bondage of superstition. . . . I feel the pleasure of the captive who shakes himself free from his chains."[77] In her second work, Stenhouse named more names and took aim at Mormon sensitivities, including its temple rites. *"Tell It All"* also added historical material from her husband's writings. This book's more strident, sensational tone pushed Mormonism further toward the margins. Whereas she had merely come to see things "in another light" in the first volume, in *"Tell It All"* Mormonism emerged "strange, wild, and terrible."[78]

Stenhouse's writing directly influenced another renegade polygamous wife. Ann Eliza Webb Young, who had joined Brigham Young's massive household as a plural wife in 1868, reminisced that *Exposé* had first awakened her to the dangers of polygamy. After breaking with Young in 1873, she wrote her own exposé and became a sensation on the lecture circuit. Her book, *Wife No. 19*, likewise traced a "life in bondage," and, in dedicating it to the "Mormon Wives of Utah," she inverted the Mormon master narrative. Non-Mormons were agents of "liberation," not persecution; life in polygamy resulted from ignorance, not faith. "This Christian realm is not 'Babylon,' but The Promised Land."[79] Buttressing American self-perceptions as they did, antipolygamists celebrated these works as evidence of absolute Mormon male power and non-Mormon female freedom. In casting monogamous women as the only real agents, antipolygamists denied or ignored other Mormon women's voices and choices—the very dismissals they laid at the feet of the Mormon hierarchy.

Mormon women loyalists defended their way of life. In account after account, they maintained that they had not been coerced in their choices and that holy faith guided their communal lives; their personal pain notwithstanding, they lived out a biblical sacrifice that merited the state's protection. In an 1880 interview, Jane Snyder Richards candidly acknowledged the emotional burdens of polygamy but explained that she had longed checked her desire to complain because she had "entered that state voluntarily."[80] Helen Mar Kimball Whitney, though similarly admitting her difficulties—her voluminous writings were littered with biblical tropes of sacrifice—refused to concede that polygamy made women slaves. What polygamy molded, she wrote, were better Christians. LDS women bravely stood with Sarah, Rachel, Leah, and other godly women as "lawful and honored wives."[81] Polygamists with "pure motives" had "their souls . . . expanded, and in the place of selfishness, patience and charity will find [a] place in their hearts."[82] Martha Hughes Cannon pushed still further, insisting that polygamy actually enhanced women's opportunities. As the nation's first elected state senator and a practicing physician, Cannon hardly conformed to the stereotype. "A plural wife is not half as much a slave as a single wife," she said in an 1896 interview. With more time and independence than monogamous wives, she wrote, Mormon women were free to pursue public lives.[83] The paradoxical blend of Mormon feminism and patriarchy notwithstanding, such public defenses often obscured the deeper pain of Mormon women. Jane Richards, for instance, admitted to counseling other plural wives to keep their sorrows private. In her published tracts Helen Whitney wrote obliquely of the psychic trauma she experienced because of polygamy, but her private narratives vividly portray the emotional toll her sacrifices exacted.[84] On both sides of the polygamy divide, then, public representations failed to portray accurately the complexities of Mormon life. Instead, published attacks and defenses left polygamy reduced to a thin symbolic marker of Mormon otherness or cultural resistance and identity.

Representations of Mormon men were also polemical. On the eve of the Civil War, eastern depictions contrasted an effeminate Mormon culture with the more manly agents of American political or military power. Race discourse routinely fused with gendered language, as in the case of a popular women's health guide warning that polygamy degraded female health and threatened "the whole stock." "The Mormons of Utah," it concluded, "would soon sink into a state of Asiatic effeminacy were they left to themselves."[85] With wives in ample supply, easterners sometimes imagined Mormon society as stunted in its masculinity—an admittedly odd turn given rampant fears of Mormonism's penchant for theocracy and violence. In cartoons from the Utah War, Mormon men cowered behind female hordes or plural wives waging battle in place of their men folk. Others fantasized about pretty Mormon ladies flocking to manly liberators.[86] Valorization of self-control as the marker of middle-class manliness placed Mormon men on the wrong side of civilization. Given widespread assumptions about polygamous sexuality, men were easily cast as savages in formulations of Mormon barbarism. In one prominent medical manual, the author noted polygamy's presence in biblical and Christian history, but its dangers became clear in his caution for sexual moderation. Health and happiness in marriage, he emphasized, are "seriously curtailed by sexual excess." Overindulgence exhausted the nervous system, increased one's susceptibility to disease, and limited one's "sexual satiety."[87]

Well-informed historical observers and modern historians agree that nineteenth-century Utah was no hedonistic hotbed, but, in the popular imagination, representations of Mormon men fit nicely with broader characterizations of Mormonism as a system fully out of control. Ambivalence on the question of Mormon control—did it evince an overabundance or lack of it?—mirrored a tension in the broader American discourse of civilization. Indeed, manly restraint itself began to lose its charm during the very years polygamy swelled in significance. As a "primitive masculinity" came to compete with the more civilized versions, Mormon men stood in a more complex cultural matrix. Near century's end, when Americans became increasingly obsessed with muscularity, sexual virility, and "primitive" fitness, barbaric harems could potentially produce as much longing as dread.[88] Rather than being marked by an apparent lack of sexual differentiation, which had often been the charge when Americans appraised the gender arrangements of "native" cultures, Mormon savagery was grounded in perceptions of gendered extremes that emerged as inflated caricatures of American norms. Mormon patriarchs offended female delicacy with a superabundance of domestic coercion. Mormon men themselves were eventually not so much sissies as they were hyperexamples of masculine power and sexuality.[89] In esteeming Mormonism as an alien religion, Americans could pull back from what they feared they had become.

With polygamy's growing political significance, some found it necessary to collapse Chief Justice Waite's tripartite scheme for world peoples. In the debates over the 1882 Edmunds Bill, Representative Ferris Jacobs Jr., of New York, reduced the human family to "two grand divisions." His dualism—"Asiatic" polygamy on the one hand and Euro-American monogamy on the other—stretched history and geography to the near-breaking point.[90] The diversity and complexities of peoples, places, and history melted away in the clash of cultures that antipolygamists like Jacobs discerned in the Mormon problem. This kind of binary made for powerful partisan oratory and potent colonialist rationale. As Christine Talbot has demonstrated, the 1870s saw a metaphorical turn to physiology and "contagion" in anti-Mormon rhetoric. Seen in light of the relationship between individual bodies and the body politic, efforts to cast Mormons' light-skinned bodies as racially "other" or to characterize Mormonism as uncivilized in gendered terms appeared intellectually fashionable.[91]

ANTI-MORMONS LET POLYGAMY do the lion's share of the work in the various formulations of Mormon foreignness. A highly publicized exchange between U.S. vice president Schuyler Colfax and Mormon apostle John Taylor exemplifies the subtle but significant change in Mormon/non-Mormon relations. Colfax had defended the antipolygamy prerogatives of the Grant administration in Utah during the autumn of 1869. One line in his speech particularly kindled the apostle's indignation. Colfax had opened his address with a curious setting of the debate's terms: "I do not concede that the institution you have established here, and which is condemned by the law, is a question of religion." Taylor thundered back that such a statement could scarcely be taken seriously given polygamy's doctrinal and practical importance in Mormon life. "With us it is 'Celestial Marriage,'" he wrote. "Take this from us and you rob us of our hopes and associations in the resurrection of the just. This not our religion? You do not see things as we do."[92] In denying polygamy's religious basis, Colfax participated in a device that had framed anti-Mormonism's first four decades. But Colfax's move also anticipated developments that would significantly alter anti-Mormonism. Where Mormonism itself had borne that burden for decades, polygamy increasingly became the rhetorical battleground for what could be rightly considered religious in American culture.

This development was perhaps as historically accidental as it was a conscious tactical maneuver. Though committed anti-Mormons were quick to remind that polygamy "is not the only un-American thing among them," no antagonist could deny that polygamy by far constituted the best entrée for discussion of any Mormon error.[93] With others, polygamy functioned not so much as a lead-in to other themes as the shorthand, symbolic stand-in for all of Mormonism's faults. Still others came to see little threat in Mormonism beyond its polygamy. With polygamy such a glaring marker of seemingly radical difference, in other words, Mormon distinctiveness beyond the practice seemed less distinctive. As one military report put it, the "marked peculiarity of their religion is the claim of a religious right to have a plurality of wives. In other respects their religion does not offend public opinion."[94] Such an account dramatically understated the ways Mormonism had offended public opinion, but it is nonetheless telling in its reduction of Mormonism to that single practice alone. Hostility to the

LDS Church unquestionably localized on polygamy, but, more specifically, much of the argumentation surrounding Mormon otherness depended on polygamy because of the growing intellectual significance of "scientific" racial theories advanced in the United States and Europe. With so much riding on polygamy ideologically, Mormonism stood to be substantially defanged by its renunciation.

And so it was. Before the 1890 polygamy manifesto, which officially (though not in reality) ended the practice, James Blair hinted at additional ideological developments that would work toward at least grudging inclusion of a polygamyless Mormonism under the umbrella of American religion. After arguing for the biblical and legal standing of Mormon polygamy, Blair outlined in broader strokes the politically problematic intersection of Protestant hegemony and questions of religious authenticity. In contemplating *Webster's* entry for "religion" ("any system of faith and worship . . . true or false religion"), Blair wondered how Mormonism or polygamy could be construed as nonreligious. Who could disprove Mormon claims? he asked. "Shall we take a Jew to prove the Christian religion, a Catholic to prove the Protestant religion, or *vice versa*; a Methodist to prove the Presbyterian, or a Presbyterian to prove the Baptist religion, or *vice versa*?" For Blair, religious claims simply could not be adjudicated by Congress or American courts. "Whether Jew, Christian, Mohammedan, Pagan, Turk, Hindoo, or Swedenborgian," he concluded, "true or false, we are bound to protect them in the free exercise thereof."[95] His capacious sense of religion and religious freedom could hardly compete with the louder voices condemning polygamy. But, with polygamy officially discountenanced and Mormon theocracy in shambles, subsequent iterations of Blair's vision could foresee space, however conflicted, for Mormonism in the republic.

CHAPTER 5

"Heresy"

Americanizing the American Religion

Anti-Mormon hostility unquestionably gained momentum as commentators discovered or inflated the "Oriental" or "Asiatic" character of Mormon life. Mormonism, hardly an imported or foreign tradition, demonstrates how central the perception of cultural deviation has been in the maintenance of homegrown religious variety.[1] The persistent (and still lingering) problem of categorizing Mormonism reveals as much about American negotiations of religion's conceptual boundaries as it does about Mormon belief or practice.

The increasingly "scientific" study of religion cut in another direction. Caught between older understandings of religion (that were essentially theological) and newer ones (that countenanced the possibility of non-Christian "religion"), late-century Mormonism found itself in "a period of general uncertainty and taxonomic indeterminacy," but one that has worked toward the gradual inclusion of previously marginalized religious groups.[2] A place at the table of American religions depended as much on the nation's acquiescence to less theological conceptualizations of religion as on Mormon renunciation of polygamy.[3] Mormons stood to benefit as theology's hold appeared to weaken before more universalizing or pluralizing comparative taxonomies. But since theology preserved much of its sovereignty, if in admittedly less explicit ways (one scholar describes it surviving as "half-disguised theological presuppositions"), approaches to Mormonism could remain little changed despite religion's substantial reframing after 1870.[4] Ironically, mainstream Mormonism's graduation to "religion" and "theology" left it susceptible to withering late twentieth-century doctrinal attacks from conservative Protestants—the group least likely to grant a Mormon theology early on.[5]

This chapter charts the beginnings of Mormonism's acceptance as an

THE GREAT CONGRESSES AT THE WORLD'S FAIR.

"The Great Congresses at the World's Fair," *Cosmopolitan*, March 1893
(Harold B. Lee Library, Brigham Young University, Provo)

American religion without muting its ongoing challenge to those very categories, but with an eye to the paradoxes of late-century American approaches to religion and history. Mormonism's move up from an alien to a merely false or heretical religion offered Latter-day Saints new opportunities in the processes of assimilation and accommodation, though not without pain and communal loss. The LDS Church was transformed when Mormons mixed concessions with new forms of resistance but emerged only half respected as an American faith. The weight of Mormonism's own history demanded recognition but left it on ever-contested categorical territory. When an anonymous author chided an infant Mormonism for its lack of history, the writer unwittingly hinted at logic that would lead later Americans to partially include it under the umbrella of American religion. Wondering what "proof" Joseph Smith and the earliest Mormons could offer of their honesty, the writer reasoned that "they can give none but their own assertion; they have no sacrifice to make—no loss of fortune or reputation to sustain—they are in a land of liberty. . . . [The early Christians] had to forsake their relatives, leave their possessions, and forfeit their [reputation]. Scourging and torture, imprisonment and death, were often staring them in the face. . . . Thirteen apostles, all, save one, sealed their testimony with their blood. So, whether their religion was true or false, they proved their honesty."[6] True or false, then, Mormonism made a case for

"The School Question," *Leslie's Weekly*, February 1876 (L. Tom Perry Special
Collections, Harold B. Lee Library, Brigham Young University, Provo)

honesty with its stubborn presence and eventually found a less turbulent,
if still contentious, place in American culture.

Mormonism in the Crowd of World Religions

Symbolically, the most tumultuous period of Mormon controversy came
to a head in October 1893. In the charged public atmosphere of that year's
"Parliament of Religions," held in concert with the World's Columbian Exposition in Chicago, Mormonism's vexed status as an American religion
became clear. Repeatedly turning to the parliament/exposition, historians
have found deep meaning in the spectacle. William Goetzmann finds that
Americans arrived at a "plateau of self-definition" with the fair's composite
display of capitalist and scientific advances. John Burris writes that the
nineteenth-century exposition tradition played a decisive role in the development of the human sciences and that the religion parliament, in particu-

lar, played a pivotal role in the development of the modern field of religion.[7] At the unprecedented event, representatives of various faiths received invitations to a gathering that its organizers assumed would both celebrate human brotherhood and underscore Christianity's superiority. Though presented as illustrative of religion's global diversity, the organizers ensured that the congress reinforced Western, Protestant-centric assumptions and priorities.[8] Native American traditions were categorically excluded on the assumption that Christian diversity could stand in for American religious diversity. African Americans were numerically underrepresented, appearing as converted Christians only. "Asian" religions, though much was made of their participation, were allotted considerably less speaking time than their Western counterparts. So, while the parliament stood as a critical moment in the rise of religious pluralism (one scholar called it "sweeping testimony to the progress of the inclusionary ideal") and an East/West encounter of lasting intellectual significance, its paradoxical aims ultimately contributed to the broader exposition tradition's colonialist mythmaking.[9] Due to the ideological tension between enlightened toleration and Christian triumphalism forged from Protestant millennialism and ascendant notions of progress, culture, and race, religious traditions found themselves on uneven ground at the parliament. The modern project of comparative religion thus emerged from both the Enlightenment's intellectual legacy and the violence of colonial conquest.

Given the significance scholars attribute to the exposition and parliament, the dramatic part Mormonism played—or, more precisely, did not play—at the congress becomes all the more intriguing. Historians have documented Mormonism's slight at the congress and the event's substantial influence on it. In short, Mormons experienced both the insult of underrepresentation and the sting of exclusion.[10] Once word of the congress found its way to Utah, church authority B. H. Roberts emphasized to his superiors that Mormon participation might help remove the lingering cloud over the church's national reputation. To his dismay, Roberts found that none of the three thousand invitations were intended for his church. Incensed at the slight, Roberts wrote parliament organizers but to no avail. The LDS First Presidency then appealed to the parliament president and sent Roberts to Chicago to lobby congress officials directly. In Chicago, Roberts was told that the Protestant-dominated body feared Mormonism would prove a "disturbing element" because of its polygamous past. Roberts shot back that since many conference attendees represented polygamous traditions, Mormonism's recently renounced practice could hardly be a disqualifying factor. Eventually, Roberts learned from a sympathetic personal secretary to the parliament's general committee chair of the depth of the committee's anti-Mormonism. The secretary, Roman Catholic Merwin-Marie Snell, shared the Mormon's suspicion that the congress's professed toleration masked an aggressive Protestant bias. The Catholic and the Mormon each made public accusations of bigotry. Roberts warned that the parliament's history had been "blurred with blunders" and that despite the committee's "pretensions to toleration," a "spirit of narrow bigot[r]y" would forever mar the event.[11]

Where Mormon religion had failed, Mormon arts and agriculture met with huge success at the exposition. Utah's agricultural displays were widely heralded, and the Mormons' choir finished second in the choral competition to considerable acclaim. Similarly, Mormon women were cast as critical allies of national women leaders, while Utah mining was extolled in superlatives. According to Konden Smith, Mormons appropriated the secular at the exposition. Though non-Mormons contributed to the Utah exhibit, the LDS Church was unmistakably invested in its success. Not only was the exhibit unexpectedly given a central location, organizers ensured that it was impressive. Smith writes that it "functioned as a secular back door by which the LDS Church entered upon the stage of national legitimacy."[12] These temporal achievements and the church's downplaying of its unpopular theology offered risks as well as rewards, but, with the echoes of national opprobrium still ringing in their ears, Latter-day Saints relished their moment in the sun. Mormon leaders were deeply impressed by the Chicago experience. Their subsequent adjustment to self-representation make it reasonable to trace the modern church's public relations savvy and image-consciousness—not to mention its distaste for public debate of LDS theology—to the eventful autumn of 1893.[13]

Whereas early nineteenth-century thinkers contrasted "true religion" with various fraudulent approximations of it, by the turn of the twentieth century leading minds had come to see religion as a universal category subject to intercultural comparison. This new universalism had roots in the eighteenth-century Enlightenment but became widespread and influential by the 1880s and 1890s, just as Mormons emerged from their battle with the federal government. Though the later comparative projects favored "scientific" frameworks, science was itself deeply implicated in colonialist ideologies, and Protestant assumptions continued to hold sway. In the short run, therefore, the older and newer approaches generated remarkably similar judgments on Mormonism. Knowledge of the world's faiths undeniably increased from the mid-eighteenth century to the early twentieth—a popular schema for organizing "world religions" tellingly grew from four to ten or twelve over that span—but Mormonism did not benefit immediately from the expanding views of religion. For instance, though "sect" and "denomination" gradually morphed into terms describing only intrareligious divisions, Mormons did not simply transform into a Christian denomination. A Mormon "religion," in other words, could function as easily as a discourse of othering as it could credit Mormonism with substance or respectability.[14] With anti-Mormonism as a lens, the eighteenth- and late-nineteenth-century traditions of religious comparison seem less disparate.

Prominent in the new science of religion was evolutionary thought in all its nineteenth-century variety. Ideas about progressive religious development had cropped up earlier, but during the formative years of religion's scientific study, evolutionary thought commanded wide assent and largely formatted its narratives. Beginning in the eighteenth century, European commentators had posited a unitary history of civilization. Nations, societies, or peoples could be viewed, they explained, as being at one of several possible stages on a single scale of progress.[15] After the 1870s, this loose set of assumptions hardened into powerful explanations buttressed by scientific data and purportedly verifiable principles of social change. The Darwinian strains of evolutionary thought featured randomness in their account of biological change, however, which may help explain the relative weakness of Darwinian perspectives in American thinking about religion. Better suited to the comparative religionists were the so-called neo-Lamarckian theories, which oriented biological adaptation toward an alleged developmental goal.[16] In these progressive models, the religion of civilization—Christianity—was ubiquitously cast as "new" while non-Christian faiths routinely found themselves labeled "old." This device worked in tandem with scientific appraisals of savagery. Contemporary or not, one looked into humanity's distant past when viewing the racial or religious other. Through its wide appeal, evolutionary thought became the "secular counterpart" to the mantra of Christianity's civilizing mission for the world.[17]

These theories of unilinear development did not preclude the possibility that all peoples, given the requisite resources and time, could mount civilization's heights. Most forcefully, however, another of evolution's bequeathals stamped out latent possibilities of this sort. Grounded in genetic science, a racist hereditarianism surged alongside the hierarchies of progress. If progressive frameworks could potentially spark a kind of dynamism in cross-cultural comparisons, eugenics ensured that a "stasis of . . . hierarchy" reigned supreme between the 1870s and the turn of the century. By 1910, an "*innateness*" grounded in race had "begun to overshadow" all other concomitant principles of evolution. When combined, then, notions of progressive civilization and genetic racism doomed some groups to perpetual savagery. In describing "primitive" religion, theorist James Frazer observed that "civilisation varies . . . directly with complexion." The new hierarchies fused religion and civilization so neatly, in fact, that only those traditions associated with recognized centers of civilization might count as properly religious—hence the new ten or so "world religions" represented at the 1893 parliament and in turn-of-the-century literature.[18]

Mormons fit ambiguously into the new science. After the polygamy manifesto, the slow demise of Mormonism's quintessential marker of otherness sapped the power of earlier alienating strategies. The whitening of Mormonism that ensued opened interpretive space for Mormons. Some pulled generously from liberal Protestantism; others pulled from the budding Protestant fundamentalist movement.[19] For a critical few decades around the turn of the century, the progressive apologists had the upper hand; they proclaimed Mormonism the future's religion because of its aggressive open-endedness, its theology's resonance with modern science, and its hopeful accent on human progress. In these formulations, apologists like B. H. Roberts could turn Mormon theological materialism into a badge of honor and cast creedal Christianity's spiritualized deity as an irrational superstition, the "absolute nonentity" of "paganized Christianity."[20] Similarly, Mormon luminary John Widtsoe could systematize Mormon thought under the title "Rational Theology" or offer "Joseph Smith as Scientist."[21] Confident of Mormonism's philosophical coherence and its harmony with cutting-edge science, Latter-day Saints appropriated the language of scientific progress, newness, and religious development in a formula that critiqued rather than celebrated traditional Christianity.

As a consequence, Mormons unwittingly participated in the secularizing tendencies of the new scientism. The scientific study of religion rallied believers of various stripes to a kind of solidarity against secularists, but the new classificatory systems also enabled a Western secular ideal.[22] Given this discursive paradox, the bifurcation of Mormonism into secularized and religious representations takes on an even more complicated frame. The modern construction of religion/religions went hand in hand with objectivity, facticity, rationality, and individualized market relations. Religion thus functioned as a "correlate" to modern capitalism and can be considered part of the "mystifying project of western imperialism" in the ways it obscured international inequity and exploitation. Seen in this light, the crystallization of Mormonism's double image in the 1890s entailed implications as lasting as polygamy's apparent renunciation. Mormonism's success in meeting Gilded Age secular standards left it at least half praised. Thereafter, its bureaucratization, industriousness, and emphasis on growth replicated corporate gauges of American achievement.[23] The implicit accommodations to secular ideals by Mormons and anti-Mormons alike helped elevate Mormonism to the realm of "American religion."[24] In the process, ironically, Mormons now occupied a greatly diminished space from which to critique American civilization. For Mormons, millenarian protest faded and then gave way to a politicoeconomic ideology of "celebration, complacency, and conservatism."[25]

Textbook Mormons and the Weight of Mormon History

Diverging representations of Mormonism at the turn of the twentieth century were crafted at the intersection between religion's science and a professionalizing field of history. Moreover, with the partial discrediting of theology in the wider intellectual world, history became all the more important as an arbiter of religious authenticity. Early anti-Mormons had derided Mormon theology due, in part, to the imposture thesis's interpretive power. But with polygamy waning and awareness of Mormonism's theology waxing, the newly reconfigured Mormons were still irresistible targets. Narratives of Mormon misbehavior retreated from polygamy somewhat, but tamer attacks still wielded considerable influence. The dramatic supernaturalism of the Mormon master narrative could easily be caricatured in light of the new professional standards. On the other hand, the sheer span and heroism of the Mormon story proved powerfully constitutive. As a result, ambivalence continued to characterize narratives of Mormon history despite the new "discipline's" concern for mere facticity.

The long Mormon/anti-Mormon scuffle demonstrates history's centrality in American negotiations of religious authenticity. Almost immediately, it dawned on critics that Mormons understood history's authenticating power. As early as the 1850s, historical sketches of Mormonism betrayed anxiety about the Mormon story's charm.[26] The legacy of Joseph Smith's martyrdom, for instance, ultimately explained Mormonism's resilience. In one account, Smith had won for himself "a crown of martyrdom" that galvanized the Latter-day Saints into a more united, resolute body. When "time has worn away from memory and tradition the insignificance," the author predicted, Smith's martyr legend would continue to "immortalize his name."[27] Writing for *Harper's* in 1851, James Johnston agreed that persecution was key to the movement's success. "By their inconsiderate persecution," anti-Mormons had "made him a martyr for his opinions, and have given a stability to his sect which nothing may now be able to shake." The explanatory punch of this argument ensured its periodic reappearance.[28] Mormons clearly resented the use of persecution as yet another excuse for attack, and they fought back. By the 1850s, opponents complained that Mormons could be counted on to recast every objection as "persecution."[29]

Critics were eventually forced onto new ground. One commentator reasoned that "high-sounding titles" and "temporal advantages" were responsible for the faith's continuing appeal.[30] Another credited Mormonism with combining authoritarianism and egalitarianism in a borrowed yet enduring formula. On the one hand, the faithful were "commanded to listen reverently . . . and to obey," but on the other, since "Mormons live under a democratical form of Church government," every man could aspire to high church office. Having combined the best of both ecclesiastical worlds, future Mormons had the "foundations on which to build." Through serendipitous scrounging from Christian tradition, the author concluded, "it will not be difficult to construct, uninterruptedly and understandingly, the edifice of Mormon History."[31] One *Harper's* editor acknowledged that among the American religious inventions, only Mormonism constituted "a distinctly new religion." With its "new law" and "new spiritual polity," Mormonism was not "merely a new interpretation of an old theology." The editor's ambivalence about Mormon newness cut both ways, however. Newness did not necessarily equal progress, since Mormonism stood cut off "from the main current of our common traditional Christianity." But its own sacred history gave Mormonism a solidity that evinced "a power of tremendous reality."[32] At century's end, Mormonism's "tremendous reality" existed in narrative tension with its massacres and its polygamy.

The late-century chroniclers of American religious history drew upon established narrative conventions but wrote, as was the case with comparative religionists, in a fluid intellectual setting. The leading historians of the early and mid-nineteenth century crafted epic accounts that underscored their sense of national destiny. Their histories displayed a "missionary commitment" in their progressive, providential narrative trajectories.[33] In the late-century reconstitution of the field, however, such "morally or spiritually edifying tales" fell out of fashion. Viewed now as researchers rather than expositors, modern historians relied on objective facts that revealed the past "as it really happened."[34] In the United States, this "disciplinarization" drew heavily on German historiography. The transatlantic exchange of students (from the United States) and ideas (from Germany) left American historians of the 1880s and 1890s distinguishing themselves from predecessors (mainly George Bancroft, Francis Parkman, and William Prescott) who had indulged in judgment and overt moralism.

The American professionalizers, though, had drawn selectively from their historiographical "prince," Leopold von Ranke, to imagine their work in this way. They translated his notion of historical "intuition" into an obsession with facticity and the correlating assumption that historical facts essentially explained themselves. The Romanticism that spawned the German historical renaissance was completely lost in translation. In the United States, cold facts reigned supreme in the decades just before and after 1900. Through the work of German-educated historians and influential German immigrants like Hermann Eduard von Holst, U.S. educational institutions—Johns Hopkins, Chicago, Harvard, Columbia, Michigan, and Wisconsin—adopted the graduate seminar, the doctorate in history, and the new scientific standards as building blocks in the making of professional historians. In their triumph over amateur-gentlemen predecessors, some scientific historians assumed that with the archives' exploration almost complete, all of the true stories would be told and history as an intellectual discipline would simply finish its work and conclude.[35]

Budding science offered modern scholars newfound authority, but it often affirmed conventional understandings of Mormon religious experience. I. Woodbridge Riley wrote of Mormon origins in 1902 from the perspective of modern psychology, gleaned from the best authorities at Yale, but his conclusions looked old rather than new. Joseph Smith's revelations and charisma, he asserted, resulted from psychic trauma, hallucinations, mental instability, and hypnosis. Riley abandoned the imposture thesis, it is true, but deployed a delusion framework in its place. Ultimately, his account did little more than recast earlier polemics in scientific language. In the preface to his book, Riley positioned himself against his predecessors: "Sectarians and phrenologists, spiritualists and mesmerists have variously interpreted his more or less abnormal performances,—it now remains for the psychologist to have a try at them." Previous accounts of Smith, he believed, had been "partisan." A scientific assessment of "the state of his body," his "mental abnormalities," and "physical ills" would break the explanatory impasse.[36]

The new religious historians deployed the modern methods erratically; when it came to Mormonism, they could not break free of the earlier master accounts. Late-century chroniclers softened their rhetoric but were at a loss for another candidate for their hierarchy's bottom rung. Torn by the scientific historians' passion for objectivity and the comparativists' zeal for hierarchy, most writers left open the question of how far down the scale religious legitimacy might extend, though they resisted letting it reach "on down to the Mormons."[37]

Noted theologian and church historian Philip Schaff wrote of Mormonism in 1855 that he would "fain pass over this sect in silence." Mormonism was "out of the pale of Christianity"; it had not "exerted the slightest influence on the general character and religious life of the American people."[38] By the 1880s, time had forced a partial reconsideration. In a paper for the newly formed American Historical Association, Schaff argued that the genius of the American state consisted in its independent but "friendly" relationship with Christian churches. Written as Congress first disenfranchised polygamists and then nonpolygamists alike in Mormon country, Schaff maintained that religious persecution was "impossible" in the United States. In the balance between liberty and the priorities of "order and safety," Schaff found significance for the Mormon story. In a reversal of his earlier work, he acknowledged that Mormonism had indeed influenced national religious life. Now, Schaff dedicated an entire section of his text to Mormonism and the ways it marked the limits of religious liberty. When a religion debilitates public morality and encourages criminality, he contended, it must be treated as a public nuisance. Remarkably, Schaff turned from the Mormon example to criticize anti-Chinese sentiment, noting that irrational fear of China's "heathen customs" stoked xenophobic abuse.[39]

Daniel Dorchester's *Christianity in the United States* (1888) considered American religious history as a tripartite competition between Protestantism, "Romanism," and various "Divergent Elements." His treatment of Mormonism's first period was just stock anti-Mormon characterizations, but the later period took a decided theological turn. Mormon doctrines of divine embodiment and the preexistence of human souls figured prominently, appearing before an extended analysis of polygamy and theocracy. On the last page of his sprawling 780-page tome, Dorchester dismissed Mormonism along with Catholicism in a Protestant rallying cry. He reassured readers that though Mormonism was "lifting her beastly, defiant head," it was a "local ulcer" only. In "a broad, dense environment" Mormonism would "have no sure lease of the future." As surely as in early national accounts of American religion, Mormonism was Dorchester's foil against which Protestant progress could be articulated, defined, and defended.[40]

Henry K. Carroll and Leonard W. Bacon, writing after the Mormons officially renounced polygamy in 1890, seemed unsure how to characterize polygamyless Mormonism. Carroll's *Religious Forces of the United States* (1893), which launched the "American Church History Series," aimed to "describe and classify" American Christian denominations based on census data. Carroll explained that, since he intended to cover "every denomination, regardless of the character of its faith or the fewness of its members," some surprising inclusions could not be avoided: "Thus Chinese Buddhists, Mormons, Theosophists, Ethical Culturists, Communistic Societies, and Spiritualists appear." Struck by the religious variety in the census data, Carroll proposed three grand divisions for American religious bodies: Christianity, Judaism, and "miscellaneous." Interestingly, he numbered Mormons among the Christians and proposed a subdivision that might suit twenty-first century Mormons: "Catholics, Protestants, Latter-Day Saints." Carroll explained that Mormons at least "make much of the *name* of Christ." In another passage, however, he hesitated to include Mormons in his tally of total Christians, writing simply: "We should naturally exclude . . . Latter-Day Saints." His vacillation marked the problem that post-manifesto Mormonism posed for modern classificatory systems that were torn between Protestant intellectual traditions and the new scientism.[41]

Bacon's *History of American Christianity* (1897), also of the "American Church History Series," conjured Protestant unity, much as Dorchester had done, in the face of bewildering variety and schism. His account of New World Christianity was unabashedly religious, with "controlling providence" replacing human causation at various critical junctures. Without polygamy, Bacon seemed unsure what to do with the Mormons, however. Only Mormons' founding imposture and the "solidity with which they are compacted into a political, economical, religious, and, at need, military community" remained as evils. The faith thus emerged less threatening but still happily distant: "It is only incidentally that the strange story of the Mormons, a story singularly dramatic and sometimes tragic, is connected with the history of American Christianity."[42]

Mormonism had been so thoroughly exoticized between 1850 and 1890 that few knew how to treat a more mundane version of the faith, at least until the U.S. Senate hearings of 1904–7 on whether to seat LDS apostle Reed Smoot ignited strident protests. There was enough recognizably Christian in Mormon teaching and practice, though, that Mormons and detractors alike would sometimes have to overstate the distance between their faiths once the most glaring markers of difference faded. And with Mormons themselves sometimes unsure which theological themes should go front and center, outsiders could be left with little contemporary grist for their explanatory mills. One well-intentioned Unitarian tract listed Mormonism last among the "Sects Not Calling Themselves Christian" and accounted for LDS theology with exasperation: "Mormans [sic] are in a sense polytheists, believing in a system of gods, all of whom were at one time men. Their belief about them is in confusion, and no satisfactory statement can be made from conflicting accounts and sermons."[43] Henry Carroll's account of Mormon belief, on the other hand, was drawn from the church's official "Articles of Faith," which did not emphasize Mormon singularities, and left him with the mistaken impression that Mormons affirmed the traditional Christian Trinity. When summarizing LDS Church organization, he found nothing particularly striking as it "includes features of both the Jewish and Christian systems." With polygamy and theocracy presumably in the past, Mormons of the 1890s suffered more from near-omission than from wide-eyed alarm. Heresy thus aptly describes Mormonism's status in American religion at century's end. Its heterodoxies of form and content lingered in reality and imagination, maintaining its perpetual marginality, while its resonance with the broader Christian tradition kept it at least "incidentally . . . connected" to those broader stories and identities.[44]

At the turn of the twentieth century, even writers with anti-Mormon instincts were content to leave the Mormon story as a narrative puzzle. Thomas Gregg had opposed Mormon power in his home state of Illinois, yet his *Prophet of Palmyra* (1890) stressed the "remarkable results" of Smith's legacy as well as his duplicity. For Gregg, the incongruities of the Mormon story remained a perplexing "mystery."[45] Hubert Howe Bancroft's *History of Utah* (1889) mixed older and newer priorities in American historical writing. Steadfastly committed to narrative and literary punch, Bancroft professed to leave readers to form their own opinions. He sedulously mixed Mormon and non-Mormon perspectives. This, of course, probably confused readers. Bancroft confessed to having opinions about Mormon faith but avoided mentioning them, so readers were told. Yet he acknowledged that because "beliefs enter more influentially than elsewhere into the origin and evolution of this society," he could hardly avoid accounting for the history and evolution of its "doctrines." As much as he wanted to stay in the realm of "material facts," Mormons pushed Bancroft onto unstable ground.[46] The resulting volume offered incoherence, arguably a more sophisticated way to avoid religion's historical complexities.

As it turned out, historians of the early twentieth century had little more patience for religion's mysteries than Bancroft. David Brion Davis, looking back on Mormon historiography in 1953, found that "the vast literature on Mormonism tends to treat the subject as everything but a religion."[47] In the century's first decade, muckrakers had a field day exposing covert polygamy, and the Smoot hearings and their aftermath revived the specter of theocracy. The historical and economic scientists pedaled secularized portraits of Mormonism, largely based on their own preferences and interests. Richard T. Ely's 1903 treatment of LDS economic history, for instance, rendered Mormonism an efficient "social mechanism" only. Academically trained Mormons, too, often interpreted LDS contributions apart from theology or religious practice. Ephraim Ericksen, trained at Chicago, wrote that twentieth-century Mormons best concerned themselves with "social ideals" rather than their "theological system," as if the two were separable.[48] What had originated as a polemical mainstay had in the complicated development of the modern academic disciplines become an implicit aversion to religion. Both paradigms denied Mormonism's claim to religion, if in different ways. Though scholars of religion in the twenty-first century have tentatively included Mormonism as an object of respectable analysis, the fascination blooms even as those same scholars increasingly wonder what it means to call anything religious.

Conclusion: Mormonism (Almost) Defanged

The excision of polygamy went hand in hand with other transformations in Mormon country. The net effect was so transformative that Thomas Alexander dubbed it a "revolution."[49] Thereafter Mormonism found itself in a less precarious position. Utah statehood in 1896 marked a dramatic change indeed, demanding new terms for national engagement with the Latter-day Saints. Though others have wondered if such a framework overstates the 1890s as watershed, at least regarding the influence of the polygamy manifesto on ordinary Mormon lives, many agree that Mormonism was fundamentally altered after the crisis of the 1880s and early 1890s.[50] Modern scholars have invoked various models to describe the changes in Mormonism, from "transition" to "transformation" or "accommodation" or "Americanization" or "assimilation"; each has its explanatory strengths and weaknesses. As Ethan Yorgason writes, Americanization and assimilation paradigms tend to assume a dominant, unitary American "culture" un-critically or even convey an implicit expectation of cultural "uniformity."[51] Further complication comes with Harold Bloom's provocative suggestion that Mormonism was Americanized from the start, a perspective with roots in portrayals that cast Mormonism as an outgrowth of evangelical ascen-dancy or democratized Christian populism.[52] Yet any discussion of Mor-mon "acceptance" in the twentieth century must be understood in light of Jan Shipps's classic study of LDS representations in national periodical literature. In her massive quantitative analysis, positive depictions of Mor-mons outnumbered negative ones only after World War I. A more favorable public image did not emerge until after the slow death of polygamy and Mormon displays of military patriotism in the wars of 1898 and 1914–18.[53]

From the perspective of anti-Mormons, the 1890s and first years of the twentieth century were littered with irony. Mormons acclimated to capi-talistic individualism, political-cultural pluralism, and less radical under-standings of marriage, but only after time and with debatable complete-ness.[54] For one thing, hundreds of LDS leaders and laypeople viewed the manifesto as a tactical public retreat only and discreetly sanctioned or par-ticipated in plural marriage ceremonies.[55] Many non-Mormons in Utah warned that the manifesto had been a sham. Influential clergyman Josiah Strong called for vigilance, arguing that, "by creating the impression that the Mormon problem is solved," the manifesto could actually "materially strengthen Mormonism."[56] Growing recognition of LDS stubbornness cul-minated in the dramatic Reed Smoot Senate hearings.[57] In the early 1890s, though, many observers outside Utah assumed that the previous decade's harsh legislation had quashed Mormon resolve and began approaching Mormonism as a newly monogamous tradition.

The destruction of Mormon theocracy was equally indecisive. LDS leaders of the twentieth century rarely imagined Mormon nationhood as had their counterparts of the 1840s or 1850s, and they did not directly pre-side over a Mormon political party as was the case in the 1870s and 1880s. Still, the importation of national parties into Utah failed to cripple Mormon political power in the state and across a significant portion of the West. New alliances and priorities that reconfigured regional politics may have actu-ally enhanced LDS leaders' political clout. Since most Mormons had in-stinctively moved into the Democratic Party and most Utah non-Mormons sided with the Republicans once the old parties evaporated, some promi-nent Mormon leaders worked to shift LDS numbers to the GOP. Mormon leadership moved to the Republicans before rank-and-file Mormons did, and the activism of partisan hierarchs on both sides spawned tension in the ranks and forced new adjustments to LDS political action.[58]

The shift to the Republican Party was expedient given the GOP's clout in Washington, but it put Democratic Mormons on the defensive. Troubled by the activism of Republican LDS apostles John Henry Smith, Francis M. Lyman, and Joseph F. Smith, Democratic authorities B. H. Roberts and Moses Thatcher proposed that Mormon leaders stay out of partisan squabbles. Rebuffed, they worked all the harder for the Democrats. In response, Joseph F. Smith charged both men with insubordination and called upon Mormon leaders to consult with ecclesiastical superiors before running for office. When Thatcher ignored the counsel and push ahead with his own campaign, he ran afoul of his superiors. Mormon leaders were now in an almost impossible position. Had ecclesiastical influence not been deployed, there may have been little political diversification in Utah. By responding with a "political manifesto" formalizing Smith's insistence on ecclesiastical oversight of authorities' political activity, however, the hierarchy strengthened its grip on LDS political engagement. While Roberts accepted the new arrangements, Thatcher, certain that such oversight amounted to un-American church interference, lost his place among the apostles and barely kept his membership in the LDS Church.[59] If late-century anti-Mormons had hoped to reduce Mormon political influence, they failed miserably.[60]

The church's financial power had long been seen as crucial to its political power. The first federal antipolygamy law, the Morrill Anti-Bigamy Act of 1862, checked the church's financial power by limiting property not designated for explicit religious use. The legislation of the 1880s was even harsher. As U.S. president Rutherford B. Hayes put it in 1880, "To destroy the temporal power of the Mormon Church is the end in view."[61] The confiscatory Edmunds Tucker Act (1887) and the economic dislocations of the early 1890s devastated the church financially. Church property was seized, some of its business ventures collapsed, the Mormons took on significant debt to offset the effects of the depression, and many Latter-day Saints hesitated to pay tithes in so unstable a climate. Church leaders responded with a less communitarian and a more corporate mindset, and, eventually, renewed emphasis on the payment of tithes.[62] The debt crisis lingered into the twentieth century but, despite a midcentury scare stemming from a deficit spending plan, the church had fully recovered by the late twentieth century.[63] In the short run the hammer blows of federal legislation took their toll, yet Mormons adapted to the corporate models that had so worried Brigham Young in the 1860s and 1870s. In the words of one historian, though LDS leaders deployed the church's corporate influence more selectively, they did so "more influentially than ever before."[64]

Similar irony applies to women's lives in Utah. "Americanization" left them a complicated legacy. Reactions to the polygamy manifesto were mixed, though many Mormon women were grateful for the document. Given all she had experienced as a plural wife, Annie Clark Tanner wrote that she was "easily convinced that [the manifesto] was from the Lord." She felt "great relief" at seeing polygamy go. Nevertheless, the independence of Mormon women weakened in the manifesto's aftermath. As Ethan Yorgason argues, between 1880 and 1920 their cultural authority declined: "The range of permissible models of gender authority narrowed, and these models became increasingly hardened and irrefutable. By the end of the period, little cultural space existed regionally from which to question or even discern alternative conceptions of gender hierarchy." In some ways, the suffragist rhetoric of Mormon women had mirrored national arguments, especially in the universalist strain holding that women were men's equals in every significant way. But, in what must have been a painful turnaround, Mormon rhetoric could also subvert the priorities of the national woman's movement. For one thing, Mormon women had called for suffrage from a distinctly LDS perspective. Polygamy freed them from household drudgery and permitted public roles, they insisted; it enhanced rather than limited their opportunities. Other polygamy defenses, moreover, acquiesced to contemporary notions of gendered difference. Since lust characterized the male nature and moral purity the female, so these arguments went, then polygamy managed society's sexual differences better. Relying on some of the very notions that tended to circumscribe women's public selves, Mormon women found themselves in a position not unlike their antipolygamy foes. By letting so much ride on polygamy ideologically, they left themselves susceptible to unintended consequences should that keystone crumble. By fusing suffragism and propolygamy, Mormon women could challenge notions of monogamous female independence or Mormon patriarchy; at the same time, however, they weakened their own authority in Mormon culture.[65] By the late twentieth century, Mormon women were more easily cast as loyal defenders of the old ways than as allies of the movement dedicated to gender equality. For instance, when Mormon women overwhelmed Utah's 1977 "International Women's Year" meeting with twice the attendees of any other state, they were there to vote down—rather than support—national feminist priorities.[66]

Mormon Americanization thus proved incomplete and complicated. National leaders got their symbolic victory with the polygamy manifesto, but Mormons then negotiated a complicated relationship with the broader society. Over the short term, the "cancer" and "excision" talk almost disappeared in polite society. Though general dislike of Mormonism was entrenched for decades still, it was nonetheless possible to discern the beginnings of a bifurcation of the Mormon image: lingering distrust vied with admiration for Mormons as all-American patriots. The seeds of non-Mormon acceptance of Mormonism resulted from the new ways Americans saw Latter-day Saints as part of a national capitalist or imperial machine. This potential role for Mormons had struck some early observers. John Gunnison, working for the federal government in the antebellum West, was fascinated by Mormons. He was struck by the ordinariness of LDS preaching but wondered at the foreignness of polygamy. Ultimately, he urged toleration. In contrast to the warnings that Mormonism impeded civilization's march, Gunnison saw Deseret as "a sound connecting link in the great empire chain." Mormons, walled in by uninhabited vastness, would serve as a bulwark against Native American aggression and as a way station for Pacific travelers.[67] Two decades later, legendary explorer John Wesley Powell argued that Mormons had developed an ideal settlement model for the nation's arid lands. The LDS cooperative spirit and communalistic ethic had done what "individual farmers, being poor men," could not achieve alone. Rugged individualism was doomed to failure, Powell wrote, and Americans had best imitate the Mormons' "coöperative labor" systems if they hoped to redeem the land from its "present worthless state."[68] Powell's account anticipated later positive appraisals.

Secularism dominated the reappraisals of the value of Mormons and Mormonism. Powell and his successors redeemed Mormonism by imagining its people apart from their religion. For Powell, the Book of Mormon and other LDS beliefs resembled the primitive Native American cosmologies that would inevitably wither under the glow of modern science.[69] Conceiving Mormon communitarianism apart from religion provided a way to avoid religion's polarizing complexities and to praise the temporal achievements of Mormon pioneers. This secularizing paradigm was critical to the post-1890 détente. It portrayed a Mormon people who could be celebrated as industrious Americans.

The secular impetus only increased with growing awareness of Utah's potential for industrial profit. Moderate commentators believed that railroads and mines were engines of American empire that could also civilize the Mormons. An anonymous *Daily Graphic* editorialist assured readers that railroads and rich mines had destroyed Mormonism's "ecclesiastical supremacy" and would "leave the Mormons in an unpopular minority in their own stronghold." He predicted that the East's "new fashions" and civilizing "spirit" would eventually erode Mormon zeal for polygamous insularity.[70] Tellingly, railroad interests had helped block early antipolygamy legislation to preserve anticipated profits in Mormon country and, in the rapprochement between church and nation, similar corporate interests proved significant.[71] The railroads did figure in Mormonism's transformation, but nineteenth-century observers underestimated Mormon capacity to flourish within modern rubrics.

When aspiring non-Mormon miners swarmed into Utah in the 1860s, they found that the Latter-day Saints had built agricultural villages at the feet of mineral-rich peaks. Once the eastern and western lines of the transcontinental railroad were linked in Utah, eastern capitalists could exploit mineral deposits, effective freighting lines, and, unlike most western spaces, a built-in labor and supply infrastructure in the form of established Mormon communities.[72] Their promotional material and government reports downplayed Mormon distinctiveness and accentuated Mormon industriousness or hospitality. Above all, they avoided extended discussion of the Mormon religion, unless it could be marketed to eastern travelers as a western curiosity worth seeing for oneself.[73]

One railroad pamphlet informed tourists that the history of Utah Territory was one of "unfaltering work" and that Salt Lake City was the "pioneer" of civilization's story in the West. Mormonism's "cardinal maxim" was agriculture, not polygamy. The capital's sacred spaces, its temple and tabernacle, became impressive architectural sites—all part of the evidence that "these people made the desert blossom." Effectively shrinking cultural distance between the Saints and tourists, the tract described Mormon homes and gardens with an accent on familiarity: Mormons had brought *eastern* seeds and *eastern* architectural patterns with them. The choice of religious analogs shrank the psychic distance, too. Mormon worship spaces mimicked "the Hebrews of old," and the Mormon congregant liked Sunday morning harangues no less than a "Scotch covenanter."[74] Another railroad's 1890 tract declared that no city in the nation's history "possessed greater certainty of a grand future" than did the Mormon capital.[75] Preserving enough mystery to pique readers' curiosity, Mormonism nevertheless emerged from these texts benignly—dramatically so given the protests still raging in other quarters. Boosterism of this sort suggested a template for

Mormon/non-Mormon cooperation at the turn of the century. Selective forgetting, an appreciation of Mormons' temporal contributions, and an eye on future market possibilities made for a workable reconfiguration. A sober, efficient, and secularized Mormonism could emerge from its polygamous past at least partially respected for the ways it seemed to partake of the nation's modern corporate spirit.

These secularizing portraits mirrored the Mormons' own representative strategies employed at the 1893 exposition and those of other religious minorities during the period. American Jews, for instance, were at the same time crafting self-representations that downplayed theirs as a *religious* community and instead framed Jewish life as an *ethnic* experience that comported well with American history, society, and political institutions. Such a strategy, as Beth Wenger has demonstrated, could deflect those strains of anti-Semitism with a strong religious edge. It could also resist efforts to "Americanize" Jews; arguments for ethnic singularity guarded social distinctiveness.[76] Representation as a quasi-ethnic group offered these advantages to Mormons and those interested in political or economic links with Mormondom. Chief among the resulting ironies, though, was the fact that just as variations of secularized peoplehood grew in prominence, antipolygamy and other forces were destroying the elements of Mormon life that had formed the basis for quasi-ethnicity in the nineteenth century. Polygamy had knit Mormon communities tightly, while bloodlines and dynastic connections had defined LDS leadership for at least two generations. These, combined with geographic isolation, local custom, communal resistance, and religious "peculiarity," had helped fashion a near-ethnicity for the Rocky Mountain Mormons. Each of these elements eroded in the very moment the railroad pamphlets constructed an attractive, modern Mormon people. The characterization of Mormons as a (secularized, ethnic) people could not quite hold, however, as it evoked a vanishing past more than an emerging present. Across the twentieth century, Mormons would less and less view themselves as a peculiar people. Increasingly, they recaptured a strain from earliest Mormonism: the Latter-day Saints constituted a Christian church.[77] Twentieth-century anti-Mormons would not contend primarily with Mormon peoplehood, either. Rather, they said, they opposed a heretical church and misguided pseudo-Christians.

By 1900, then, Mormonism hovered between Christianity and a non-Christian religion, between history and comparative religion, and between material reality and sacred myth. This ambiguity makes debates over Mormonism an unmistakably rich source from which to view American conceptions of religion. The reembedding of Mormonism's sacred words, spaces, and stories in the "real" world of politics might reduce it to the sum of its material advantages. But for those inside and outside the tradition who sense its "tremendous reality," a vexed mystery remains. The unfolding history of the hostile gazes that Mormonism still inspires reveals much about Americans' tortured engagement with a "peculiar people."

NOTES

Prologue

1. Joseph Young, "Remarks on Behalf of the Indians," 230. See also Cohen, "Construction of the Mormon People"; Flanders, *Nauvoo*, 1; Leone, "Mormon 'Peculiarity,'" 81; and Van Wagoner, *Mormon Polygamy*, 102.

2. Woodruff, "Fulfillment of God's Word," 61.

3. Hinckley and Wallace, "Interview with Gordon Hinckley."

4. Stahle, "Pres. Hinckley Addresses Journalists."

5. William O. Nelson, "Anti-Mormon Publications," 45.

6. Land and Siegel, "Glenn Beck and Obama's Christianity." For characteristic debates of Mormonism's Christianness, see Millet and McDermott, *Claiming Christ*; Blomberg and Robinson, *How Wide the Divide?*; Shipps, *Sojourner*, 335–57; and Paulsen, "Are Christians Mormon?"

7. Evangelical uses of "cult" typically rest within the word's negative popular connotation rather than analytic senses employed by scholars. See, e.g., Shipps, *Mormonism*, 46–51.

8. See Eliason, Introduction to *Mormons*.

9. Stark, "Rise of a New World Faith."

10. Davies, "World Religion." See also Davies, *Introduction to Mormonism*.

11. See Mauss, *All Abraham's Children*, 17–40, 158–211; Shipps, *Sojourner*, 289–301; and Epperson, *Mormons and Jews*.

12. See Givens, *By the Hand of Mormon*, 185–208.

13. Jensen, Woodford, and Harper, *Manuscript Revelation Books*, 12–13.

14. Cartwright, *Autobiography*, 342.

15. Givens, *By the Hand of Mormon*, 62–88; Underwood, "Book of Mormon Usage."

16. See Shipps, "From Peoplehood to Church Membership."

17. Influential popular works include Robinson, *Are Mormons Christians?* and *Believing Christ*, and Millet, *After All We Can Do*. For Benson and the Book of Mormon, see Givens, *By the Hand of Mormon*, 86–87, 241.

18. Damon Linker ("The Big Test") considers theological instability endemic to Mormonism.

19. For the formation of the modern LDS memory, see Flake, *Politics*, 109–37.

20. Feldman, "What Is It about Mormonism?"; Hardy, *Solemn Covenant*, 363–88; Paulos, *Mormon Church on Trial*, 101–6; Flake, *Politics*, 75–81, 95.

21. See Farmer, *On Zion's Mount*, 96.

22. Goodstein, "Huckabee Is Not Alone in Ignorance on Mormonism."

Introduction

1. See Halttunen, *Confidence Men.* Original spelling, grammar, and italics have been retained in quoted material unless otherwise noted.

2. Bacheler, *Mormonism Exposed,* 48.

3. Sehat, *Myth of American Religious Freedom.*

4. See Alexander, Review of Will Bagley, *Blood of the Prophets*; Bagley, *Blood of the Prophets*; Coates, Review of Will Bagley, *Blood of the Prophets*; Reeve and Parshall, Review of Will Bagley, *Blood of the Prophets*; and Walker, Turley, and Leonard, *Massacre at Mountain Meadows.*

5. See Kerber, *Women of the Republic.*

6. See David B. Davis, "Themes of Counter-Subversion."

7. Jan Shipps ("Difference and Otherness") is correct in segmenting anti-Mormonism into pre- and post-polygamy phases, characterizing the earlier as a matter of "difference" and the latter as one of "otherness," but such a framework tends to minimize the virulence of the earlier polemics. Difference, in other words, matters less if expressed in terms of mere sectarian preference than if one argued that a group professing to be religious was something else entirely, as early anti-Mormons did.

8. Bailey, "Anti-American Influences in Utah," 19. See also Flake, *Politics,* 12–33.

9. Chidester, *Authentic Fakes,* 17, 191–92.

10. Jonathan Z. Smith, "Religion, Religions, Religious," 269–71.

11. Jonathan Z. Smith, *Relating Religion,* 365.

12. Jonathan Z. Smith, "Religion, Religions, Religious," 269–71. See also Masuzawa, *Invention of World Religions,* 1–33.

13. Masuzawa, *Invention of World Religions,* 60.

14. See Styers, *Making Magic,* 4–5. For the influence of Enlightenment thought on conceptions of religion, see Harrison, *"Religion" and the Religions*; Jonathan Z. Smith, "Religion, Religions, Religious"; and Asad, *Genealogies of Religion,* 27–54.

15. Jonathan Z. Smith, *Imagining Religion,* 55.

16. Taves, *Fits, Trances, & Visions,* 6–19. Taves demonstrates how the two narratives of religious experience that predominated in early America—one polemical and the other comparative—became jumbled in sectarian conflict. This is especially apparent in anti-Mormon literature. Curiously, Taves virtually ignores Mormonism in her fine study.

17. For examples of such comparisons, see Conkin, *American Originals*; Hatch, *Democratization*; Holifield, *Theology in America,* 319–40; and Marini, *Radical Sects,* 7.

18. Kidder, *Mormonism,* 9.

19. For the late nineteenth-century shift in American thinking about religion, see Masuzawa, *Invention of World Religions*; Hutchison, *Religious Pluralism*; Fitzgerald, *Ideology of Religious Studies*; McCutcheon, *Manufacturing Religion*; and Burris, *Exhibiting Religion.*

20. See, e.g., Timothy L. Smith, "Ohio Valley."

21. The tidal wave of animosity aimed at early Latter-day Saints is all the more remarkable given some twentieth- and twenty-first-century appraisals of early Mormon-

ism. Renowned scholars have described early Mormonism as quintessentially American, but none have reconciled that characterization with its alienation from nineteenth-century American culture. See Bloom, *The American Religion*; David B. Davis, "New England Origins"; Hatch, *Democratization*; Remini, *Joseph Smith*; and Wood, "Evangelical America." Richard Lyman Bushman (*Joseph Smith: Rough Stone Rolling*, 559) attributes this view of Mormonism to a "belated recognition of [its] populist side." See also Bushman, "A Joseph Smith for the Twenty-first Century." Though LDS polygamy existed long before the 1852 acknowledgment of the practice, anti-Mormon literature did not feature it as a prominent theme until the mid-1840s. Even then, effective Mormon denial of plural marriage kept widespread polemical obsession at bay until the early 1850s.

22. See Butler, "Historiographical Heresy," 291.

23. Quoted in Noll, "A Jesuit Interpretation," 52.

24. Hamburger, *Separation of Church and State*; Gordon, *Mormon Question*, 13.

25. Mazur, *Americanization of Religious Minorities*. Mazur also anachronistically reads polygamy back into the earliest anti-Mormon agitation (p. 64).

26. Sullivan, *Impossibility of Religious Freedom*.

27. For some time, Mormon historiography moved little beyond nineteenth-century frameworks, since considerations of Mormon exceptionalism were routinely grounded in assertions about persecution or deviance from an alleged American mainstream. LDS scholars, attuned to the contradictions within anti-Mormon polemics, have, in simplistic analyses, reduced anti-Mormonism to unexamined "persecution" or, in more sophisticated ones, shown how anti-Mormons, pressed against ideals of religious toleration, had ample reason to cast Mormons in nonreligious terms. See Arrington and Bitton, *Mormon Experience*, 44–64, and Givens, *Viper on the Hearth*. Non-LDS scholars have typically either strained for neutrality, acknowledged wrongs on both sides, or charged Mormons with cultural deviance. One study of Mormon/non-Mormon relations in antebellum Illinois, while justifiably critiquing reductionist explanations by Mormon scholars, merely substitutes an anti-Mormon version: Mormon institutions and thought were fundamentally un-American. See Hallwas and Launius, *Cultures in Conflict*, 1–8. I self-consciously follow in the tradition of R. Laurence Moore (*Religious Outsiders*), who has found that a religious mainstream and periphery are largely fictive creations, that all sides had vested interests in positioning themselves and others on such a spectrum, and that Mormons, in their eagerness to appropriate "outsider" status, seem to have been very American in so doing. Such a framework denies neither the presence of anti-Mormon persecution nor the reality of Mormon heterodoxy or episodic culpability. See Givens, *Viper on the Hearth*, 13–14.

28. Winn, *Exiles*.

29. Gordon, *Mormon Question*; Flake, *Politics*; Mason, "Opposition to Polygamy" and *Mormon Menace*; Jones, *Performing American Identity*.

30. Givens, *Viper on the Hearth*.

31. Especially helpful were Flake and Draper, *Mormon Bibliography*; Fales and Flake, *Mormons and Mormonism in U.S. Government Documents*; and Allen, Walker, and Whittaker, *Studies in Mormon History*.

32. See Craig L. Foster, *Penny Tracts and Polemics*.

33. See Lawrence Foster, "Career Apostates"; Introvigne, "Devil Makers" and "Old Wine in New Bottles"; and Patterson, "'A P.O. Box.'"

Chapter 1

1. Reese, *Humbugs of New-York*, vi, ix–xii, 14, 19, 265. For "Matthias," see Johnson and Wilentz, *Kingdom of Matthias*.

2. That anti-Mormons saw their task as one of counterfeit detection is not difficult to illustrate. Note, for example, the titles of several early anti-Mormon works: Bacheler, *Mormonism Exposed*; Harris, *Mormonism Portrayed*; Eber D. Howe, *Mormonism Unvailed*; Lee, *The Mormons*; Livesay, *Exposure of Mormonism*; Orr, *Mormonism Dissected*; Parsons, *Mormon Fanaticism Exposed*; Sunderland, *Mormonism Exposed and Refuted* and *Mormonism Exposed*; Swartzell, *Mormonism Exposed*; and Samuel Williams, *Mormonism Exposed*.

3. The terminology here follows William Swartzell (*Mormonism Exposed*, iii), who referred to Mormonism as "Joe Smithism."

4. Forster, *Mahometanism Unveiled*; Eber D. Howe, *Mormonism Unvailed*; Eastman, *Noyesism Unveiled*; Grant, *Spiritualism Unveiled*.

5. For treatments of the period, see Halttunen, *Confidence Men*, xv, 1–32; Daniel W. Howe, *What Hath God Wrought*; Noll, *America's God*, 293–385; and Sellers, *Market Revolution*.

6. For disestablishment, see Curry, *First Freedoms*; Steven K. Green, *Second Disestablishment*; Hamburger, *Separation of Church and State*; Lambert, *Founding Fathers*, 236–64; and Sehat, *Myth of American Religious Freedom*.

7. For example, the attempts of conservative Virginians to establish Christianity (as opposed to a particular denomination) reveal that when they said "Christianity," they meant Protestantism. Their proposed test oath would have effectively excluded Muslims, Jews, Catholics, and possibly Quakers. See "Bill concerning Religion," in Buckley, *Church and State*, 186–88. Mid-nineteenth century Protestants would try to amend the federal Constitution to explicitly define the United States as a Christian nation. See Gaines M. Foster, *Moral Reconstruction*, 27–46, and Hutchison, *Religious Pluralism*, 78–82.

8. See Noll, *America's God*, 161–86. For the appeal of the period's "popularizing" Christian preachers, and the complications such an approach met in the South, see, respectively, Hatch, *Democratization*, and Heyrman, *Southern Cross*.

9. Schmidt, *Hearing Things*, 11.

10. See Halttunen, *Confidence Men*, 33–55.

11. See, e.g., Adams, *Dictionary of All Religions*; Baird, *Religion in America*, *Christian Retrospect*, and *Progress and Prospects*; Benedict, *History of All Religions*; Branagan, *Concise View*; J. Newton Brown, *Encyclopedia of Religious Knowledge*; Buck, *Theological Dictionary*; Evans, *History of All Christian Sects*; Goodrich, *History of the Church*, *Pictorial and Descriptive View*, and *Religious Ceremonies*; Hayward, *Book of Religions* and *Reli-*

gious Creeds; Milner, *Religious Denominations*; Parkman, "Religious Denominations"; Rupp, *He Pasa Ekklesia* and *Religious Denominations*; and Watson, *Biblical and Theological Dictionary*. For an important antecedent of these works, see Hunt, Jacob, and Mijnhardt, *The Book That Changed Europe*.

12. Adams, *Dictionary of All Religions*, advertisement, 1, 3, 6, 12, 23, 84–85, 106, 132, 156–62, 267–69.

13. Buck, *Theological Dictionary*, 1:title page, iv. See also Bowman and Brown, "Reverend Buck's *Theological Dictionary*." For a similar example, see Branagan, *Concise View*, iii–vi, 23, 45, 52, 92–95, 105–6, 110, 113–14, 116–18, 125, 128–29, 176.

14. J. Newton Brown, *Encyclopedia of Religious Knowledge*, 239.

15. Ibid., 615, 894. Though most Mormons eventually moved away from what most Protestants would regard as a "free grace" position, it would be anachronistic to regard their divergence from orthodoxy as complete by 1836. Indeed, the document most approaching a creedal formulation (Joseph Smith was a devoted opponent of creeds) by that time offered language that would have seemed innocuous had it come from another source. See Jensen, Woodford, and Harper, *Manuscript Revelation Books*, 75–87 (esp. 79). For Smith and creeds, see Richard Lyman Bushman, *Joseph Smith: Rough Stone Rolling*, 284–85.

16. J. Newton Brown, *Encyclopedia of Religious Knowledge*, 844.

17. The question of theology in the Mormon tradition is a complicated one. Generally, historians have described early Mormonism as emphasizing experience, narrative, and community over theology. The classic description is Richard Bushman's (*Joseph Smith and the Beginnings*, 187–88): "The core of Mormon belief was a conviction about actual events. . . . Mormonism was history, not philosophy."

18. Even moderate attempts to catalog American religious variety struggled to describe Mormonism. See Hayward, *Book of Religions*, 3, and *Religious Creeds*, 139–42.

19. Peter Harrison, *"Religion" and the Religions*, 16. According to Harrison, "The imposture theory was the most popular of all seventeenth and eighteenth century accounts of religion" (p. 16). The phrase "imposture thesis" of religion is Frank Manuel's (*Eighteenth Century Confronts the Gods*, 47–53, 65–69). See also Schmidt, *Hearing Things*, 85–86.

20. Mormons were as obsessed as anti-Mormons with deception and spiritual counterfeits. For examples in early Mormon revelations, see Jensen, Woodford, and Harper, *Manuscript Revelation Books*, 51–53, 125–29, 137–43, 147–51.

21. See Hughes, "Two Restoration Traditions."

22. Farmer, *On Zion's Mount*, 56.

23. See Richard Lyman Bushman, "A Joseph Smith for the Twenty-first Century," 164–66.

24. For the complications of religious "outsider" status, see Moore, *Religious Outsiders*.

25. Kitchell, "A Mormon Interview."

26. Skinner, "Changes of Mormonism," 87. On early Mormon universalism, see Underwood, *Millenarian World*, 53–56.

27. Mazzuchelli, *Memoirs*, 267–73. See also Grow, "Whore of Babylon."

28. See David B. Davis, "Themes of Counter-Subversion." The "only true & living Church" language appears in Jensen, Woodford, and Harper, *Manuscript Revelation Books*, 225.

29. As Richard Carwardine ("Religion and National Construction," 32) has written, "It was the multiplying divisions *within* [Protestantism] which proved just as likely to engender abrasiveness and strife."

30. This is also to say that when early anti-Mormons invoked the Book of Mormon, they typically did so symbolically, much like Mormons did. As Terryl Givens (*By the Hand of Mormon*, 64) has demonstrated, early Mormons were more likely to call attention to the fact of the Book of Mormon than its content. Givens here amplifies Underwood, "Book of Mormon Usage."

31. Mattison, *Scriptural Defence*.

32. See Lucy Mack Smith, *Biographical Sketches*, 148–51; Richard Lyman Bushman, *Joseph Smith and the Beginnings*, 121–24; and Hedges, "Refractory Abner Cole."

33. See Cole editorials in the *Reflector*, 30 June 1830, 53; 6 January 1831, 76; 18 January 1831, 84; 14 February 1831, 100–101.

34. See Campbell, "Delusions." Campbell's material was subsequently published as a tract with an introduction penned by Joshua V. Himes. See Campbell, *Delusions*. Himes later republished the Campbell tract with an expanded introduction of his own. Himes's (*Mormon Delusions*, iii) history of imposture included "Mormonism, Shakerism, Swedenborgianism, or any other *ism* depending on special prophecies of these *last-times* prophets." This last phrase is ironic given Himes prominent role in Millerism and Adventism. See Arthur, "Joshua V. Himes."

35. Campbell, "Delusions," 86. See also Eber D. Howe, *Mormonism Unvailed*, vii–ix, 12.

36. For exposés of Matthias, see *Memoirs of Matthias*; Matthews, *Matthias*; Stone, *Matthias and His Impostures*; and Vale, *Fanaticism*.

37. Johnson and Wilentz, *Kingdom of Matthias*, 3–11. See also Jessee, Ashurst-McGee, and Jensen, *Journals*, 86–95.

38. *Memoirs of Matthias*, 2; Stone, *Matthias and His Impostures*, 14, 16–17, 39, 45, 288, 293, 313; Vale, *Fanaticism*, 4.

39. Matthews, *Matthias*, [3].

40. Bacheler, *Mormonism Exposed*, 48.

41. Andrew F. Smith, *Saintly Scoundrel*, 114–19.

42. Lucas, "Jackson County," 96; M'Chesney, *Antidote to Mormonism*, 52; Lee, *The Mormons*, 6; Jonathan B. Turner, *Mormonism in All Ages*, 97, 102–3;52; DeLeon, "Rise and Progress," 527. See also Reese, *Humbugs of New-York*, 19; Sunderland, *Mormonism Exposed and Refuted*, 11; and Henry Brown, *History of Illinois*, 394.

43. Badger, "Matthias the Prophet."

44. For Mormonism and Islam, see Givens, *Viper on the Hearth*, 130–37; Green and Goldrup, "Joseph Smith, an American Muhammad?"; Arnold H. Green, "Muhammad–Joseph Smith Comparison" and "Mormonism and Islam"; Thomas S. Kidd, *American*

Christians and Islam, 26; James K. Lyon, "Mormonism and Islam"; Marr, *Cultural Roots*, 185–218; and Perciaccante, "Mormon-Muslim Comparison."

45. For early American perceptions of Islam, see Allison, *Crescent Obscured*; Grimsted, "Early America Confronts Arabian Deys and Nights"; Carl T. Jackson, *Oriental Religions*; Thomas S. Kidd, *American Christians and Islam* and "'Is It Worse to Follow Mahomet?'"; Marr, *Cultural Roots*; McDermott, *Jonathan Edwards Confronts the Gods*, 166–75; and Sha'ban, *Islam and Arabs*.

46. For Islam among African American slaves, see Gomez, *Exchanging Our Country Marks*. For U.S. conflict with the Barbary states, see Allison, *Crescent Obscured*, 35–86, and Lambert, *Barbary Wars*.

47. For an extended account, see Fluhman, "'American Mahomet.'"

48. Allison, *Crescent Obscured*, 37–42.

49. Prideaux, *True Nature of Imposture*, 10–11.

50. For similar examples, see Adams, *Dictionary of All Religions*, 161; Benedict, *History of All Religions*, 31; Branagan, *Concise View*, 128; and Bush, *Life of Mohammed*, 17–18.

51. Prideaux, *True Nature of Imposture*, 12–13.

52. The author admitted a debt to Prideaux but adjusted his portrayal in various ways. *Life of Mahomet*, v, 21, 60–61. See also Allison, *Crescent Obscured*, 35–37; Bush, *Life of Mohammed*, 55; J. Newton Brown, *Encyclopedia of Religious Knowledge*, 826–831; Hayward, *Book of Religions*, 229–30; and Evans, *History of All Christian Sects*, 37–39.

53. *Life of Mahomet*, 68.

54. Ibid., 69–70.

55. Gibbon, *Life of Mahomet*, 9, 11–12, 14, 78–81. See also Branagan, *Concise View*, 125, 129, and Bush, *Life of Mohammed*, 46–47, 69.

56. Bush, *Life of Mohammed*, 12, 181. Bush acknowledged his reliance on Charles Forster's two-volume *Mahometanism Unveiled* (1829).

57. Bush, *Life of Mohammed*, 49–50, 136, 156.

58. Ibid., 17–18, 97. For a more moderate view, see Irving, *Mahomet and His Successors*, ix–x, 41, 43, 56–59, 61–62, 65–66, 333–37.

59. Miles, *Mohammed*. His effort was not novel—Voltaire, for instance, had written *Le Fanatisme ou Mahomet le Prophete* to decry religious intolerance in the mid-eighteenth century. English clergyman and playwright James Miller translated Voltaire's play into English, refashioning it into a meditation on the dangers that religious fanaticism held for political stability. Miller, *Mahomet*; Voltaire, *Le Fanatisme*. See also Allison, *Crescent Obscured*, 43–45, and Colas, *Civil Society and Fanaticism*, 88–91.

60. Miles, *Mohammed*, vii–viii.

61. Ibid., v–vii.

62. Ibid., 24–25, 34–35, 38.

63. By the 1850s, it was commonplace to narrate the Mormon prophet by invoking the Islamic one. See, e.g., Mackay, *The Mormons*, and "Yankee Mahomet."

64. See, e.g., "Was Mohammed an Imposter or an Enthusiast?"

65. Harris, *Mormonism Portrayed*, 14. Though William Harris was listed as author, prominent Illinois anti-Mormon Thomas Sharp took credit for much of the writing.

66. A memorable comparison of the two scriptures appears in "Editor's Table," 701.

67. Such a bifurcation reveals the fissures in Protestant thinking apparent by Smith's time. See Noll, *America's God*, 231.

68. J. Newton Brown (*Encyclopedia of Religious Knowledge*, 358), for instance, could not have been more characteristically Protestant when he defined Christianity itself in terms of belief in "the Scriptures . . . as the sole foundation of . . . faith and practice."

69. *Wayne Sentinel*, 26 June 1829.

70. "Mormonism," *Boston Recorder*, 10 October 1832, 161. Mormons could apparently feel as strongly about the book despite never having read it. Tyler Parsons (*Mormon Fanaticism Exposed*, 15) reported: "Mormons that have come to Boston, and with whom I have conversed, do not appear to be conversant with the Book of Mormon. One of them asserted in a public meeting, that he had never read it through, but he knew it was all true, by the power of God."

71. Bennett's articles are reproduced in Arrington, "Report on 'The Mormonites,'" 357, 362.

72. M'Chesney, *Antidote to Mormonism*, 19.

73. See also Benedict, *History of All Religions*, 32.

74. Irving, *Mahomet and His Successors*, 56, 78.

75. See, for instance, Mark Twain's quip that the Book of Mormon amounted to "chloroform in print." Clemens, *Roughing It*, 127. For another example, see Marks, *Life of David Marks*, 341–42.

76. Reprinted in Campbell, "Mormon Bible," 265. Edwin DeLeon ("Rise and Progress," 533) believed that it was "a book far beyond the powers of Smith to compose, and which as an imaginative fiction, will take a high rank in American literature, long after Mormonism."

77. My narrative here owes much to Richard Lyman Bushman, *Joseph Smith: Rough Stone Rolling*, 84–108. For quoted language, see Bushman, *Joseph Smith and the Beginnings*, 124.

78. Campbell, "Delusions." Campbell, and hosts of anti-Mormons after him, referred to the book as the "Bible of the Mormonites" (p. 91), despite the fact that Mormons rarely claimed the Book of Mormon replaced or superseded the Bible. Indeed, there is ample evidence that early Mormons (including Joseph Smith) never quite incorporated the book into their religious thinking as they had done with the Bible, relying instead on the Old and New Testaments for sermons, etc. See Barlow, *Mormons and the Bible*, 11–73; Givens, *By the Hand of Mormon*, 62–88; and Underwood, "Book of Mormon Usage."

79. Campbell, "Delusions," 91–95. For similar examples, see Barber, *Incidents in American History*, 284, and John A. Clark, *Gleanings*, 240.

80. Campbell, "Mormon Bible."

81. Eber D. Howe, *Mormonism Unvailed*, 279–91. For the claims of Spaulding's widow, see Campbell, "Mormon Bible."

82. Neither Hurlbut nor Howe thought they had the manuscript that family and friends described because of the dissimilarities between the Book of Mormon and what

Hurlbut had obtained from Spaulding's widow. The second manuscript never turned up, and the first vanished for a time as well. Rediscovered by L. L. Rice in Hawaii in 1884 among documents he had obtained from Howe after purchasing the *Painesville Telegraph*, it was published in full in 1996. See Spaulding, *Manuscript Found*.

83. Eber D. Howe, *Mormonism Unvailed*, 100; John A. Clark, *Gleanings*, 268.

84. The search turned out to be a brief one. Psychologist I. Woodbridge Riley rejected the Spaulding theory; he offered Ethan Smith's *View of the Hebrews* (1823) as a more plausible source for the Book of Mormon. Fawn M. Brodie brought Riley's argument into the historical mainstream in her 1945 biography of Joseph Smith. Terryl Givens notes the similarities between the two Smith works but adds that, since Joseph Smith called upon *View of the Hebrews* in his own newspaper to corroborate the Book of Mormon's authenticity, he "must be unique among frauds in providing the public with the source of his own plagiarism before anyone else had seen the connection." Ethan Smith, *View of the Hebrews*; Brodie, *No Man Knows My History*, 47; Riley, *Founder of Mormonism*, 124–26; Givens, *By the Hand of Mormon*, 161.

85. Wood, "Evangelical America," 381. Wood's point about timing has merit, but it fails to comprehend the book's thorough rejection in its own time, to say nothing of its appeal in later periods. Indeed, modern Mormons know the Book of Mormon better than their predecessors, use it in their preaching more than Joseph Smith ever did, and feature it in their missionary efforts more prominently than previously. Jon Butler's assertion that twentieth-century LDS missionaries favored Smith's "first vision" over the Book of Mormon is thus flawed when Mormon history is viewed at a wide angle. See Butler, *Awash in a Sea of Faith*, 247, and Givens, *By the Hand of Mormon*, 240–42.

86. M. S. C., "Mormonism," 1–2; Eber D. Howe, *Mormonism Unvailed*, 12, 112.

87. Eber D. Howe, *Mormonism Unvailed*, 138; Hunt, *Mormonism*, 127.

88. M'Chesney, *Antidote to Mormonism*, 17. See also William S. West, *A Few Interesting Facts*, 15.

89. Swartzell, *Mormonism Exposed*, iii.

90. Harris, *Mormonism Portrayed*, 44. See also John A. Clark, *Gleanings*, 311.

91. Jonathan B. Turner, *Mormonism in All Ages*, 71–72. See also Olney, *Absurdities of Mormonism Portrayed*, 30.

92. For examples, see Bunker and Bitton, *Mormon Graphic Image*, 26, 49.

93. Peterson, "Mormonism," 531.

94. "Editor's Table"; Stark, "Rise of a New World Faith." See also Stark, *Rise of Mormonism*.

95. For a denial of Mormonism's status as a world religion, see Davies, "World Religion."

96. "In obedience to our promise," 43.

97. D. Michael Quinn's (*Early Mormonism*) comprehensive treatment of the Smith family's folk magic was replicated but extended back in time by John Brooke (*Refiner's Fire*, xvii), who credits hermetic magic with providing Mormon theology's "inner logic."

98. Benton, "Mormonites." Benton claimed that Smith had confided in Addison Austin about his pretensions to seeric power: "To be candid, between you and me, I

cannot, any more than you or any body else; but any way to get a living." See also Vogel, *Early Mormon Documents*, 1:180.

99. Sellers, *Market Revolution*, 219–25. For an attempt to creatively straddle the historiographical divide between interpretations of Smith as either prophet or fraud, see Vogel, *Joseph Smith*. Vogel offers Smith as a "pious fraud" and seeks to "explore the inner moral conflicts of an individual who deceives in God's name while holding sincere religious beliefs" (pp. viii, x).

100. For the association of prophethood and theatricality, see Juster, *Doomsayers*, 30–31. For examples, see Coe, "Mormonism"; Eber D. Howe, *Mormonism Unvailed*, 12; Hunt, *Mormonism*, 10; Kidder, *Mormonism*, 11, 89; Lieber, "The Mormons"; Livesay, *Exposure of Mormonism*, 4; Peterson, "Mormonism"; Sunderland, *Mormonism Exposed and Refuted*, iv; and Samuel Williams, *Mormonism Exposed*, 4.

101. For Smith's early legal troubles, see Firmage and Mangrum, *Zion in the Courts*, 48–58.

102. Hurlbut's affidavits have generated scholarly debate. See Richard L. Anderson, "Smith's New York Reputation Reappraised," and Rodger I. Anderson, *Smith's New York Reputation Reexamined*.

103. Eber D. Howe, *Mormonism Unvailed*, 240–41.

104. Ibid., 237–39. Complicating the Stafford affidavit is the reminiscence of John Stafford, William's son, who denied a connection between his father and Smith. For debate over the account, see Richard L. Anderson, "Smith's New York Reputation Reappraised" and "Review of Rodger I. Anderson, *Smith's New York Reputation Reexamined*," 52–80; and Rodger I. Anderson, *Smith's New York Reputation Reexamined*, 48–55, 172–73.

105. For the pervasiveness of early American treasure hunting, see Alan Taylor, "Early Republic's Supernatural Economy."

106. Eber D. Howe, *Mormonism Unvailed*, 12.

107. Booth's description of his experience was originally published in Ravenna's *Ohio Star* and later reprinted in Eber D. Howe, *Mormonism Unvailed*, 175–221. For a similar account, see Hayward, *Book of Religions*, 271.

108. Jessee, *Papers of Joseph Smith*, 1:278. See also Givens, *By the Hand of Mormon*, 22–24, 83–84. David Hall (*Worlds of Wonder*, 75) has shown how the Bible similarly legitimized what some regarded as magical practice in early New England. Even so, anti-Mormons were typically unimpressed with Smith's biblical gloss on stone gazing. Charles Peterson ("Mormonism and the Mormons," 532), for one, referred to the Urim and Thummim as "a rude conjuror's weapon, such as low jugglers mystify gaping crowds with at a show."

109. Skousen, *Book of Mormon*, 216.

110. See Richard Lyman Bushman, *Joseph Smith: Rough Stone Rolling*, 120–21.

111. See Quinn, *Early Mormonism*.

112. *A Book of Commandments*, 19.

113. Jensen, Woodford, and Harper, *Manuscript Revelation Books*, 16–17, 19; *A Book of Commandments*, 20–21; Skousen, *Book of Mormon*, 216.

114. Brooke, *Refiner's Fire*, 7.

115. The characterization of magic as manipulative and religion as submissive goes back at least to the mid-nineteenth century. See Styers, *Making Magic*, 75.

116. Ibid., 5, 36–37. For related discussions, see Fitzgerald, *Ideology of Religious Studies*, 3–53, and Neusner, Frerichs, and Flesher, *Religion, Science, and Magic*.

117. See *Doctrine and Covenants*, 161–62, and Jensen, Woodford, and Harper, *Manuscript Revelation Books*, 16–17.

118. See Quinn, *Early Mormonism*, 242–47, 313–17.

119. Smith's case highlights the perils of invoking the terms "religion" and "magic" as if they have some transhistorical essence. Folklorists, anthropologists, and religionists have generally been more attuned to the arbitrary nature of these categories and the value judgments that typically inhere in them, but a growing number of historians resist uncritical characterizations. Alan Taylor ("Rediscovering the Context," 19) cautions against taking anti-Mormon descriptions of Smith's magic at face value. To read our "neat distinction between magic and religion" into an antebellum context, he concludes, perpetrates a glaring anachronism and a corresponding "value judgment that magic is superstitious, deluded, and irrational, if not downright evil, while religion is the lofty, abstract expression of our highest ideals." See also Eliason, Introduction to *Mormons*.

120. Styers, *Making Magic*, 9, 36–38.

121. Fleming, "Religious Heritage," 93–94.

122. Richard Lyman Bushman, *Joseph Smith and the Beginnings*, 6–7.

123. Franchot, *Roads to Rome*, 240.

124. James L. Baker (*Men and Things*, 131–33) linked Mormon "fanaticism" with other examples of "corrupted" Christianity, including the errant belief "in the actual presence of divinity in the consecrated wafer."

125. See Ben-Yehuda, "Witchcraft and the Occult."

126. Styers, *Making Magic*, 8–16, 34–38, 70–71.

127. See Eber D. Howe, *Mormonism Unvailed*, 17.

128. Bennett quoted in Arrington, "Report on 'The Mormonites,'" 361, 363. Unlike Shakers, early Latter-day Saints did not live communally (Smith disbanded an Ohio commune); rather, they donated property to the church and received back an "inheritance" or "stewardship" as personal property. (Attempts to secure permanent church ownership and use rights for individual stewards failed in court when ex-Mormons sued for their original holdings.) Surpluses were set aside in a "storehouse" for use by the poor, church publishers, or full-time church leaders. This system was modified after limited success in Ohio and Missouri. See Arrington, Fox, and May, *Building the City of God*, 15–40.

129. See Weiser, "Mormonism," 90; Eber D. Howe, *Mormonism Unvailed*, 129; Harris, *Mormonism Portrayed*, 44; Kidder, *Mormonism*, 181–82; Orr, *Mormonism Dissected*, 21; Sunderland, *Mormonism Exposed*, 18–21; and Wallace, *Confession of the Awful and Bloody Transactions*, 21.

130. Lee, *The Mormons*, 3.

131. For counterfeiting charges, see Joseph H. Jackson, *Narrative of the Adventures*, 14, and Kirk, *Mormons & Missouri*, 8.

132. Styers, *Making Magic*, 148–60.

133. Ibid., 28, 35, 71.

134. *Document Containing the Correspondence*, 58.

135. Juster, *Doomsayers*, 23.

136. Ford, *History of Illinois*, 360.

Chapter 2

1. *A Law Case*, 5.

2. Ibid., 6, 11–12.

3. Ibid., 21.

4. Ibid., 30.

5. See Holifield, *Theology in America*, 4–5.

6. Westergren, *From Historian to Dissident*, 42.

7. Peterson, "Mormonism." For other theories of Mormonism's success, see *Authentic History of Remarkable Persons*, 7; "Memoir of the Mormons"; Himes, *Mormon Delusions*, iv; and Lee, *The Mormons*, 5–6.

8. Kirk, *Mormons & Missouri*, 62–63.

9. See, e.g., Brooke, *Refiner's Fire*, and Butler, *Awash in a Sea of Faith*, 242–47.

10. What Susan Juster (*Doomsayers*, 28) has written of earlier polemical strategies remained true for anti-Mormonism: "Whatever the specific diagnosis, the thrust of critical commentary was to redefine the problem of religious enthusiasm in terms of individual pathology rather than supernatural agency."

11. Parsons, *Mormon Fanaticism Exposed*, 66.

12. Kidder, *Remarkable Delusions*, 8, 16, 46, 65, 102, 123, 131, 167, 189–207. For similar examples, see Emmons, *Spirit Land*, 3, and *Philosophy of Popular Superstitions*, 96–102.

13. The quotation, derived from Ecclesiastes 1:9, appears in a note appended to M. S. C., "Mormonism," 1–2. The author used it to summarize his comparison of Mormon religiosity with that of the French Prophets.

14. See, e.g., Spicer, *Autobiography*, 111–12; Eber D. Howe, "Beware of Impostors," 2; and "Mormorism [*sic*]," 358.

15. Towle, *Vicissitudes Illustrated*, 155.

16. See "Latest from the Mormonites."

17. See, e.g., Campbell, "Mormon Bible," 265–67, and *Delusions*, 3; and Bauder, *Kingdom and Gospel*, 36–38. Bauder's rare account can be found in Vogel, *Early Mormon Documents*, 1:16–18.

18. As reported in Joseph Smith, *History of the Church*, 1:395–99.

19. Phelps, "Free People of Color," 109. See also Roberts, *Comprehensive History*, 1:328, and Joseph Smith, *History of the Church*, 1:377–79.

20. Richard Lyman Bushman, "Mormon Persecutions."

21. See Winn, *Exiles*, and Givens, *Viper on the Hearth*. Whereas Givens casts the conflict as a profoundly religious struggle, Winn narrates it as a contest between competing versions of American republicanism.

22. Winn, *Exiles*, 89.

23. See Styers, *Making Magic*, 4–5, and Jonathan Z. Smith, "Religion, Religions, Religious."

24. Taves, *Fits, Trances, & Visions*, 16–18.

25. For Euro-American enthusiasm, see Garrett, *Spirit Possession*, and Lovejoy, *Religious Enthusiasm*.

26. Taves, *Fits, Trances, & Visions*, 3–5, 15, 19.

27. Whitman, "Book of Mormon," 46.

28. See Skousen, *Book of Mormon*, 669–72.

29. See Joseph Smith, *History of the Church*, 1:295–97; Whitmer, *Address to All Believers*, 33; Jessee, *Papers of Joseph Smith*, 1:242–43; Copeland, "Speaking in Tongues"; and Vogel and Dunn, "'Tongue of Angels.'"

30. See Richard Lyman Bushman, *Joseph Smith: Rough Stone Rolling*, 148–49.

31. Eber D. Howe, "Beware of Impostors," 2; Copeland, "Speaking in Tongues," 16–17. See also Corrill, *Brief History*, 9.

32. Woodruff quoted in Copeland, "Speaking in Tongues," 19. Joseph Smith, while never invalidating the practice, came to favor xenoglossia over glossolalia. Mormon vacillation on tongues was not lost on anti-Mormons. See Howe, *Mormonism Unvailed*, 132. In the end, Smith's awareness of the challenges posed by glossolalia eventually prompted firmer control. Vogel and Dunn ("'Tongue of Angels,'" 22–23) note that though glossolalia had flourished in every previous Mormon center, little evidence of it can be found for the Nauvoo period. Interestingly, while American Mormons were experiencing a lull in the early 1840s, British Mormon converts were experiencing an outburst of tongues. See Allen, Esplin, and Whittaker, *Men with a Mission*, 109, 116, 143–44, and Allen and Alexander, *Manchester Mormons*, 25, 95, 99, 157–58, 162, 164–65, 182, 199.

33. See, e.g., "The Mormons in Trouble," 148.

34. Joseph Smith, *History of the Church*, 1:374–76, 398.

35. Pettigrew, "A History," 15–17. For the high council's ruling, see Vogel and Dunn, "'Tongue of Angels,'" 15–17, and Cannon and Cook, *Far West Record*, 63.

36. For standard Protestant accounts of the practice, see Adams, *Dictionary of All Religions*, 84–85, 268–69; Amos Taylor, *Narrative of the Strange Principles*, 12–13; Branagan, *Concise View*, 45; Rathbun, *An Account of the Matter*, 4; and Benjamin West, *Scriptural Cautions*, 14. For the Irvingites, see Boyer, *When Time Shall Be No More*, 87. For American reactions to Pentecostal tongues, see Wacker, *Heaven Below*.

37. Kidder, *Mormonism*, 89, 223. Similarly, Jonathan Turner (*Mormonism in All Ages*, 40) wondered why Joseph Smith needed a Hebrew tutor for the Mormon brethren in Kirtland, Ohio. Had the "gift of the Spirit . . . withdrawn" and left the Mormons with the "vulgar necessity of grammars and lexicons"?

38. *Latter-Day Saints: The Dupes*, 9–11. For another example, see Hunt, *Mormonism*, 121–27.

39. See, e.g., 1 Corinthians 12–14.

40. See Parley P. Pratt, *Autobiography*, 61–62, and Corrill, *Brief History*, 17.

41. M. S. C., "Mormonism."

42. "Try the Spirits," 745. The editorial cited Buck's *Theological Dictionary*. See also Bowman and Brown, "Reverend Buck's *Theological Dictionary*."

43. Swartzell, *Mormonism Exposed*, 6. See also M. S. C., "Mormonism," and Spicer, *Autobiography*, 111.

44. "Mormonism," *Spirit of Practical Godliness*.

45. See Jensen, Woodford, and Harper, *Manuscript Revelation Books*, 100–101, 181–83. These directions revised earlier instructions. See ibid., 36–37.

46. Besides, Harris (*Mormonism Portrayed*, 8) wondered, if Smith could heal, why did he himself reportedly take "ordinary medicines?" See also Hunt, *Mormonism*, 279.

47. Backman, *The Heavens Resound*, 83.

48. Booth quoted in Howe, *Mormonism Unvailed*, 176.

49. Mary Smith quoted in Nelson Winch Green, *Fifteen Years*, 19, 52. Despite his alienation from the LDS Church, John Corrill (*Brief History*, 46) summed up Mormon healing matter-of-factly: "The Mormons believe in, and constantly practice the laying on of hands and praying for the healing of the sick; sometimes they have been healed, sometimes partly healed, and sometimes not benefitted at all."

50. *Latter-Day Saints: The Dupes*, 10.

51. Sunderland, *Mormonism Exposed and Refuted*, 11–12, 16. See also Himes, *Mormon Delusions*, v, and Taves, *Fits, Trances, & Visions*, 127–35, 179, 202–6.

52. Porterfield, *Healing*, 4, 6–12, 19.

53. Curtis, *Faith in the Great Physician*, 6–25.

54. For the context of Mormon visionary claims, see Richard Lyman Bushman, "Visionary World." See also Heyrman, *Southern Cross*, 28–76. For the transition to a less ecstatic revivalism in Methodism, see Butler, *Awash in a Sea of Faith*, 241.

55. Eber D. Howe, "'Golden Bible,'" 3.

56. "The Mormon Delusion," 44.

57. Lee, *The Mormons*, 8. Howe ("'Golden Bible,'" 3), borrowing from the *Palmyra Freeman*, reported that Smith had seen the spirit "in a dream." Smith could have saved himself considerable trouble with antebellum skeptics had he maintained that his angelic visitations were wholly visionary. See Park, "'A Uniformity So Complete.'" See also Spicer, *Autobiography*, 113.

58. Eber D. Howe, *Mormonism Unvailed*, 11.

59. Ibid., 37.

60. Taves, *Fits, Trances, & Visions*, 19.

61. For religious madness, see Goodheart, *Mad Yankees*; Schmidt, *Hearing Things*; Taves, *Fits, Trances, & Visions*; Rubin, *Religious Melancholy*; Numbers and Numbers, "Millerism and Madness"; Bainbridge, "Religious Insanity"; and Teresa Lynne Hill, "Religion, Madness."

62. Teresa Lynne Hill, "Religion, Madness," 1.

63. Ibid., 5–6.

64. Ibid., 14.

65. Brigham, *Observations*.

66. Ibid., xv–xxi.

67. Ibid., xxi, 170.

68. Ibid., 178, 259–62, 300.

69. For this study, I consulted the reports of the following institutions: Asylum for the Relief of Persons Deprived of the Use of Their Reason (Philadelphia), Boston Lunatic Hospital and McLean Hospital (Boston), Butler Hospital for the Insane (Providence, R.I.), Hartford Retreat for the Insane (Hartford, Conn.), Illinois State Hospital (Jacksonville), Indiana Hospital for the Insane (Indianapolis), Maine Insane Hospital (Augusta), New Hampshire Asylum for the Insane (Concord), Ohio Lunatic Asylum (Columbus), Pennsylvania Hospital for the Insane (Philadelphia), State Lunatic Asylum (Utica, N.Y.), State Lunatic Hospital (Worcester, Mass.), and Vermont Asylum for the Insane (Brattleboro). This set constitutes the major asylums of the antebellum North and West and those closest to Mormon centers.

70. Kirkbride, *Report of the Pennsylvania Hospital*, 15.

71. Ibid.

72. Ibid.

73. *Report of the Medical Visitors of the Connecticut Retreat*, 18.

74. *Seventh Report of the Medical Visitors of the Connecticut Retreat*, 8.

75. *Twentieth Annual Report on the State of the Asylum*, 7.

76. *Report of the Board of Visitors of the Boston Lunatic Hospital*, 18.

77. For examples, see *Report of the Board of Visitors and of the Superintendent of the Boston Lunatic Hospital*, 13, and *First Annual Report of the Commissioners and Medical Superintendent of the Hospital for the Insane*, 15.

78. Kirkbride, *Report of the Pennsylvania Hospital*, 15. The Indiana Hospital for the Insane intermittently tracked patients' religious affiliation. See *Annual Report of the Commissioners*, 33. For examples of "Mormonism" listed as the "cause" of a patient's insanity, see *Third Annual Report of the Managers of the State Lunatic Asylum*, 29; *Fourth Annual Report of the Managers of the State Lunatic Asylum*, 25; *Fifth Annual Report of the Managers of the State Lunatic Asylum*, 37; *Sixth Annual Report of the Managers of the State Lunatic Asylum*, 29. In the sample I analyzed, however, Mormonism appeared far less often than did Millerism or spiritualism. No doubt this was due in part to the fact that Mormon migrations had left the largest LDS communities far from most asylums by the time many institutions started listing "causes" in the mid-to-late 1840s.

79. *Twenty-Second Annual Report of the Officers of the Retreat for the Insane, at Hartford*, 49.

80. The table was included, he wrote, "in obedience to custom," and he hoped his explanation would prevent anyone from being "misled by it." *Annual Report of the Commissioners*, 23. See also *Report of the Superintendent of the Boston Lunatic Hospital*, 17; *Reports of the Trustees and Superintendent of the Maine Insane Hospital*, 15; *Report of the Superintendent of the Boston Lunatic Hospital*, 17; *Reports of the Illinois State Hospital for the Insane*, 199–200; *Annual Report of the Managers of the State Lunatic Asylum* [reprint of 1845 report], 25; *Report of the Superintendent of the Boston Lunatic Hospital*, 18–19; *Eighth Annual Report of the Trustees of the State Lunatic Hospital at Worcester*, 43; and *Annual Report, Pennsylvania Hospital for the Insane*, 40.

81. See *Annual Report of the Managers of the State Lunatic Asylum*, 25.

82. *Third Annual Report of the Superintendent of the Maine Insane Hospital*, 14–15, 17–20.

83. *Reports of the Trustees, Steward and Treasurer, and Superintendent of the Insane Hospital*, 47.

84. *Reports of the Illinois State Hospital*, 201–2.

85. See Taves, *Fits, Trances, & Visions*, 20–75.

86. See *Reports and Other Documents Relating to the State Lunatic Hospital at Worcester*, 160–61.

87. *Fifth Annual Report of the Trustees of the State Lunatic Hospital at Worcester*, 52. See also *Fourth Annual Report of the Directors and Superintendent of the Ohio Lunatic Asylum*, 51–52; *Reports of the Board of Visitors, of the Trustees, and of the Superintendent of the New Hampshire Asylum for the Insane*, 15–17; *Fifth Annual Report of the Directors and Superintendent of the Ohio Lunatic Asylum*, 47–48; and *Eleventh Annual Report of the Directors and Superintendent of the Ohio Lunatic Asylum*, 32.

88. See *Report of the Superintendent of the Boston Lunatic Hospital and Physician of the Public Institutions at South Boston* (1840), 100, and *Seventeenth Annual Report of the Board of Trustees for the Benevolent Institutions, and of the Officers of the Ohio Institution for the Ohio Lunatic Asylum*, 32.

89. *Third Annual Report of the Directors and Superintendent of the Ohio Lunatic Asylum*, 45.

90. *Sixth Annual Report of the Managers of the State Lunatic Asylum*, 20.

91. *Eighth Annual Report of the Managers of the State Lunatic Asylum*, 33.

92. Eber D. Howe, *Mormonism Unvailed*, 73–74; Hunt, *Mormonism*, 7–9; John A. Clark, *Gleanings*, 316. See also Juster, *Doomsayers*, 40–41.

93. Davison, A. C., and Scott, "The Mormon Bible." See also "Mormonism," *Gospel Messenger*, 1 June 1833, 67.

94. Parsons, *Mormon Fanaticism Exposed*, 52–53.

95. See Noll, *America's God*, 367–85. For Mormon uses of the Bible, see Barlow, *Mormons and the Bible*.

96. Jonathan B. Turner, *Mormonism in All Ages*, 141. See also Kidder, *Remarkable Delusions*, 201.

97. "The Spirit," *Christian Palladium*. See also a Quaker response in Griffen, "The Friends' Society."

98. Eber D. Howe, *Mormonism Unvailed*, 130–31.

99. Towle, *Vicissitudes Illustrated*, 152–53.

100. Ibid., 156–57.

101. Whitman, "Book of Mormon," 49.

102. Campbell, "Delusions," 95. See also Murray, *Parish and Other Pencilings*, 117–20.

103. Holifield, *Theology in America*, 5, 171–72, 189.

104. Ibid., 174–75, 186–87.

105. Ibid., 6, 159, 187.

106. Ibid., 74.

107. Ibid., 190, 333. Even so, Holifield's placement of Mormonism within the Baconian theological tradition is problematic. See Hughes, "Two Restoration Traditions," and Harper, "Infallible Proofs."

108. See Richard Lyman Bushman, *Joseph Smith: Rough Stone Rolling*, 63–64, and Kimball, "The Anthon Transcript."

109. Joseph Smith, *History of the Church*, 1:35. The revelation in question appeared in *A Book of Commandments*, 14–17.

110. Oliver Cowdery, "Dear Brother." See also Skousen, *Book of Mormon*, 139, 685; *A Book of Commandments*, 10–13; *Doctrine and Covenants*, 171; and Jensen, Woodford, and Harper, *Manuscript Revelation Books*, 654–57.

111. *Doctrine and Covenants*, 171. For the Book of Mormon "witnesses," see Richard L. Anderson, *Investigating the Book of Mormon Witnesses*; Vogel, *Joseph Smith*, 441–50; and Harper, "Evaluating the Book of Mormon Witnesses."

112. Marks, *Life of David Marks*, 340–41.

113. Ibid., 342. For a similar interpretation, see Livesay, *Exposure of Mormonism*, 4. For a Mormon response, see Parley P. Pratt, *Reply to Mr. Thomas Taylor's "Complete Failure."*

114. Harris, *Mormonism Portrayed*, 5–7. Harris viewed the witnesses' apostasy as a renunciation of their original "witness" experiences. This was not necessarily the case, however. See, e.g., Whitmer, *Address to All Believers*, 8–45. Harris's work was likely written by Thomas Sharp.

115. Harris, *Mormonism Portrayed*, 5–7. For a similar perspective, see Kidder, *Remarkable Delusions*, 194.

116. Sunderland, *Mormonism Exposed and Refuted*, 4. For a response, see Parley P. Pratt, *Mormonism Unveiled*.

117. Sunderland, *Mormonism Exposed and Refuted*, 14. For a similar view, see Hunt, *Mormonism*, 61–62.

118. Sunderland, *Mormonism Exposed and Refuted*, 14–18.

119. See also Bacheler, *Mormonism Exposed*, 28.

120. Guyatt, *Providence*, 56.

121. Campbell, "Delusions," 96. Mormons, too, could use the threat of atheism to their advantage. See, e.g., Hyde, *Modern Christianity*.

122. See James Turner, *Without God*, and Mathewes and Nichols, *Prophesies of Godlessness*.

123. Adams, *Dictionary of All Religions*, 63–65.

124. Hayward, *Book of Religions*, 217. See also Evans, *History of All Christian Sects*, 12.

125. Marks, *Life of David Marks*, 341.

126. Eber D. Howe, *Mormonism Unvailed*, 19.

127. Parrish, "Mormonism," 226–27.

128. Hunt, *Mormonism*, 14, 37. "Mormonism, in our view, is a dangerous *ism*— dangerous to the ignorant and unwary, being calculated to mislead them in matters where the eternal welfare of the soul is at stake . . . dangerous to the Christian religion, having made more than a hundred infidels to one *true* believer: hence the necessity for the present work must be apparent to every friend of truth" (p. iv).

129. See Branagan, *Concise View*, 116.

130. Ellis, "From Elder John Ellis." See also Reese, *Humbugs of New-York*, 265.

131. Jonathan B. Turner, *Mormonism in All Ages*, 3.

132. Ibid., 3–4.

133. Ibid., 8. See also David B. Davis, "Themes of Counter-Subversion."

134. Stone, *Matthias and His Impostures*.

135. Johnson and Wilentz, *Kingdom of Matthias*, 28–30, 154.

136. Stone (*Matthias and His Impostures*, 3, 5, 13–14) charged that the "ultraism" of the revivals' "new-measure men" was traceable to their "tampering with the sacred Scriptures" and "wresting [their] plain and obvious meaning."

137. Ibid., 16, 40, 42, 45.

138. Ibid., 16.

139. Ibid., 305, 308.

140. Ibid., 313.

141. Alexander Neibaur Journal, 24 May 1844, reprinted in Jessee, *Papers of Joseph Smith*, 1:461. Joseph Smith thus mirrors the Revolution-era prophets Susan Juster (*Doomsayers*, 5) describes as having both "fed on and repudiated the evangelical ethos."

142. See, e.g., Kent, *Wesley and the Wesleyans*, 95, 116–24, and Butler, *Awash in a Sea of Faith*, 241.

143. This point was made forcefully by Jonathan Turner, whose anti-Mormon title spoke volumes. His *Mormonism in All Ages* (1842) posited an extended history of deluded spirituality. Given the similarities he found between the pseudoreligions, Turner could even read religious history backwards, dubbing former religious impostors, for instance, "the Joe Smith of the day." Was the "Spirit of God responsible for the whole excitement, catterwaul, [and] nightmare" of the revivals? he asked. For Turner, the real culprit was "Mormonism, in all ages and all churches—*Mormonism*, whether found at Northampton, at Cambuslang, in Kentucky, or at Nauvoo" (pp. 76–89, 277; quotations, 85, 277). See also Cox, *Interviews*, 279–80, and Emmons, *Philosophy of Popular Superstitions*, 96–102.

Chapter 3

1. Jessee and Whittaker, "The Last Months of Mormonism in Missouri," 34. See also Leonard, *Nauvoo*, 41–42, 55, 74, 82.

2. George T. M. Davis, *Massacre of Joseph Smith*, 5–8.

3. For the concept of Zion in early Mormonism, see Richard Lyman Bushman, "Making Space"; Arrington, "Smith, Builder of Ideal Communities"; Olsen, "Smith's Concept of the City of Zion"; Hamilton, *Nineteenth-Century Mormon Architecture*, 13–32; Richard H. Jackson, "Mormon Village"; and Bradley, "Creating the Sacred Space."

4. Crabtree, "'A Beautiful and Practical Lesson,'" 51, 57.

5. Cohen, "Construction of the Mormon People."

6. Juster, *Doomsayers*, 46–47.

7. Hunt, *Mormonism*, iv.

8. *Doctrine and Covenants*, 252–54.

9. Jensen, Woodford, and Harper, *Manuscript Revelation Books*, 68–69.

10. Ibid., 42–45, 122–25.

11. Joseph Smith, "An Extract of Revelation."

12. Jensen, Woodford, and Harper, *Manuscript Revelation Books*, 204–7.

13. Skousen, *Book of Mormon*, 620, 625, 708.

14. Faulring, Jackson, and Matthews, *Joseph Smith's Translation*, 105. For a similar example, see Jensen, Woodford, and Harper, *Manuscript Revelation Books*, 318–21.

15. While the Saints often referred to Independence, Mo., alone as "Zion" in the 1830s, other gathering places were either denominated a "stake to Zion," "the land of Zion," "a corner stone of Zion," or some other variation. Jensen, Woodford, and Harper, *Manuscript Revelation Books*, 228–29; Joseph Smith, "An Extract of Revelation" and "Extracts From a Revelation," 424. In a famous 1844 statement, Smith preached that all of North and South America constituted Zion. See Ehat and Cook, *Words of Joseph Smith*, 362–63. Nothing symbolized Zion's promise more than the temples that functioned as its spiritual center. See Hamilton, *Nineteenth-Century Mormon Architecture*, 13–24, and Richard Lyman Bushman, "Making Space," 40–46.

16. See Pitzer, *America's Communal Utopias*.

17. See Stein, *The Shaker Experience*, 40–57.

18. See Delano, *Brook Farm*, and Francis, *Transcendental Utopias*.

19. Juster, *Doomsayers*, 8.

20. See Lieber, "The Mormons"; Weiser, "Mormonism," 82–83; Thompson, *Church and State*, 138–39; Sunderland, *Mormonism Exposed and Refuted*, 11; Parsons, *Mormon Fanaticism Exposed*, 5; Campbell, "Delusions"; Jonathan B. Turner, *Mormonism in All Ages*, 76–89; and John C. Bennett, *History of the Saints*, 304–7. Sigrun Haude (*In the Shadow of "Savage Wolves*," 1) writes that, for European Christians, a seamless narrative "from Thomas Müntzer to 'Münster,' from the Peasants' War to the Anabaptist reign ten years later, was self-evident." Modern historians who have associated Mormonism with Anabaptism include David B. Davis ("New England Origins"), Robert J. McCue ("Similarities and Differences"), Cornelius Krahn (*Dutch Anabaptism*, 144), William E. Juhnke ("Anabaptism and Mormonism"), D. Michael Quinn ("Socioreligious Radicalism"), and Steven C. Harper ("Thomas Müntzer and the Radical Reformation").

21. See Adams, *Dictionary of All Religions*, 23.

22. For republican thought and Christian theology, see Noll, *America's God*, 53–92.

23. Stone, *Matthias and His Impostures*, 293–94.

24. Parsons, *Mormon Fanaticism Exposed*, 5.

25. Colas, *Civil Society and Fanaticism*, xv–23.

26. Ibid., 107.

27. Ibid., 18.

28. Eber D. Howe, "The Book of Mormon," 3. See also Howe, "The Golden Bible," and Cole, "Book of Mormon."

29. See also "Mormorism [*sic*]," 353.

30. See, e.g., Campbell, *Delusions*, 4; Reed and Matheson, *Narrative of the Visit*,

105–6; "Latest from the Mormonites"; "Mormonism," *Spirit of Practical Godliness*; and Eber D. Howe, "Mormonism," 3.

31. See "The Mormonites," *Vermont Telegraph*.

32. For an overview of early anti-Mormon violence, see Arrington and Bitton, *Mormon Experience*, 44–64.

33. For the Ohio violence, see Backman, *The Heavens Resound*, 93–100.

34. Lucas, "Jackson County," 93–96.

35. Ibid.

36. Editor of *Missouri Republican* quoted in "'Regulating' the Mormonites," *Niles' Weekly Register*. See also "The Mormon Difficulties"; "The Mormons in Trouble," 148; "The Mormons and the Anti-Mormons"; and "The Mormon War."

37. Jensen, Woodford, and Harper, *Manuscript Revelation Books*, 342–55.

38. John Corril[l] to Oliver Cowdery, December 1833, as copied in "From Missouri," 126. Corrill was realistic in recognizing that, since the Missourians far outnumbered the Mormons, a self-defense plan might instigate more bloodshed.

39. See Backman, *The Heavens Resound*, 175–200; Crawley and Anderson, "Political and Social Realities"; "Miscellaneous Items"; and *Anti-Masonic Telegraph*, 9 July 1834.

40. See Daniel Dunklin to William W. Phelps and others, 4 February 1834, as quoted in Joseph Smith, *History of the Church*, 1:476–78.

41. Daniel Dunklin to Col. J. Thornton, 6 June 1834, as quoted in "Mormons in Missouri."

42. This version of the Jackson County trouble lacked the balance of Howe's own paper's denunciation of the mobbings from the year before. See *Painesville Telegraph*, 16 August 1833, 3.

43. Eber D. Howe, *Mormonism Unvailed*, 139–44.

44. Howe attributed to Sidney Rigdon the claim that, within three years, Mormons would win complete control of the political offices in Kirtland and, within five, seat their own congressman. Ibid., 145.

45. Ibid., 145–46.

46. See Marvin S. Hill, "Cultural Crisis"; Hill, Rooker, and Wimmer, "Kirtland Economy Revisited"; and Backman, *The Heavens Resound*, 310–41.

47. See Marvin S. Hill, "Cultural Crisis."

48. Warren Cowdery, "It is a Well Known and Established Fact," 535–41 (quotation, 538). See also Marvin S. Hill, "Cultural Crisis," 293–94.

49. For Brigham Young's perspective on the Kirtland crisis and the lessons it offered Mormons, see Young, "Discourse," 18:243. For an outsider's appraisal of Mormonism's political tyranny, see William S. West, *A Few Interesting Facts*, 3–6, 15.

50. See Joseph Smith, *History of the Church*, 2:449–51.

51. Rigdon, *Oration*, 12. The rare published account of Rigdon's address can be found in Crawley, "Two Rare Missouri Documents."

52. As reprinted in Joseph Smith, *History of the Church*, 3:175. For different views of the Missouri conflict, see Baugh, *A Call to Arms*; LeSueur, *1838 Mormon War*; and Gentry and Compton, *Fire and Sword*.

53. The statements of Marsh and Orson Hyde (below) appear in *Document Containing the Correspondence*, 57–59.

54. See also Parrish, "Mormonism," and Livesay, *Exposure of Mormonism*, 11.

55. For LDS accounts, see Johnson, *Mormon Redress Petitions*. For a sympathetic Missouri report, see "Letter From the Editor."

56. *Document Containing the Correspondence*, 9–10. The U.S. Senate also published the document; see U.S. Senate, *Document Showing the Testimony*.

57. A hint of the extent of LDS disaffection is found in a letter sent to Boggs in late October: "Mormon dissenters are daily flying to this county for refuge from the ferocity of the prophet Jo Smith, who, they say, threatens the lives of all Mormons who refuse to take up arms at his bidding or to do his commands." *Document Containing the Correspondence*, 50.

58. See ibid., 17, 55, 97, 99, 110–13, 116–29, 138–39; Corrill, *Brief History*, 31; Quinn, *Origins of Power*, 92–103; Whittaker, "Book of Daniel"; Gentry, "The Danite Band"; Baugh, *A Call to Arms*, 33–46; and Richard Lyman Bushman, *Joseph Smith: Rough Stone Rolling*, 349–55. For LDS responses, see Faulring, *An American Prophet's Record*, 198, and Jessee, *Papers of Joseph Smith*, 2:262, and *Personal Writings of Joseph Smith*, 415–22. Though the Danite organization never reappeared in Mormonism, former Danites comprised most of Smith's personal bodyguard detachment and, subsequently, the city police force in Illinois. See Quinn, *Origins of Power*, 102, 116–17.

59. See, e.g., "The Mormons," *Vermont Mercury*; Corrill, *Brief History*, 25, 30–32, 45, 47; and Swartzell, *Mormonism Exposed*, [iii], 9, 11–17, 20–23, 30, 33, 35.

60. "The Mormonites," *New York Times and Commercial Intelligencer*.

61. For the significance of Pratt's work, see Crawley, Foreword to *The Essential Parley P. Pratt*, xv–xxiv, and Whittaker, *Early Mormon Pamphleteering*, 18–19.

62. "A Voice of Warning and Instruction to All People . . . By P. P. Pratt"; Parley P. Pratt, *Voice of Warning*, 95–120, 174–76. See also Sunderland, *Mormonism Exposed and Refuted*, 5, 31–32, 42; Harris, *Mormonism Portrayed*, 22–23, 46; Bacheler, *Mormonism Exposed*, 8–11; and *Anti-Mormon Almanac*, [2]–3. Pratt responded to Sunderland in Pratt, *Mormonism Unveiled*.

63. Eber D. Howe, *Mormonism Unvailed*, 171. Owens got the chapter and verse wrong. In *A Book of Commandments*, the passage was found in chap. 64, verse 30 (see pp. 152–53). For the earliest extant manuscript, see Jensen, Woodford, and Harper, *Manuscript Revelation Books*, 184–85.

64. To be fair, anti-Mormons would have had a difficult time quoting *A Book of Commandments*, since few copies survived the 1833 mob action. Still, the more readily available *Doctrine and Covenants* (1835) made no substantive changes to the text: "Wherefore the land of Zion shall not be obtained but by purchase, or by blood, otherwise there is none inheritance for you. And if by purchase behold you are blessed; and if by blood, as you are forbidden to shed blood, lo, your enemies are upon you, and ye shall be scourged from city to city, and from synagogue to synagogue, and but few shall stand to receive an inheritance" (p. 143). Ironically, a similar, earlier passage from *A Book of Commandments* (p. 138) would have been easier to invoke for polemical purposes: "For

behold, verily I say unto you, the Lord willeth that the disciples, and the children of men, should open their hearts, even to purchase this whole region of country, as soon as time will permit. Behold here is wisdom; let them do this lest they receive none inheritance, save it be by the shedding of blood."

65. Sunderland, *Mormonism Exposed and Refuted*, 3–4.

66. Ibid., 5–8. For the political implications of Mormon notions of revelation, see Harper, "'Dictated by Christ.'"

67. Sunderland, *Mormonism Exposed and Refuted*, 14.

68. Ibid., 25.

69. Ibid., 25–26.

70. Sunderland, *Mormonism Exposed*, title page. Sunderland's note at the end of the introductory material is dated July 1841.

71. Ibid., iii–iv.

72. Ibid., iv–vi, 13, 24–46.

73. Ibid., 46–49, 63. See also M'Chesney, *Antidote to Mormonism*, iii, 5, 17, 52, 54–60.

74. See also Himes, *Mormon Delusions*, 89–90; Kidder, *Mormonism*, 73, 76–85, 104, 109–16, 141–43, 156, 228–29, 233, 238–41; Samuel Williams, *Mormonism Exposed*, 1–10, 13–15; and John A. Clark, *Gleanings*, 240–313.

75. *Anti-Mormon Almanac*, [2].

76. Jensen, Woodford, and Harper, *Manuscript Revelation Books*, 198–99; *Anti-Mormon Almanac*, [9–10].

77. Thomas Sharp ("Monsieur Violet and the Mormons") would claim that he had actually written *Mormonism Portrayed* based on materials Harris had provided.

78. See Jensen, Woodford, and Harper, *Manuscript Revelation Books*, 26–29. Sharp accurately understood that the *Doctrine and Covenants* was "regarded by the Mormons as equal, in point of authority and inspiration, to the Bible." Quoted in Harris, *Mormonism Portrayed*, 20.

79. Harris, *Mormonism Portrayed*, 9, 15.

80. Ibid., 34–36, 44–45.

81. Ibid., 34; Jonathan B. Turner, *Mormonism in All Ages*, 3.

82. Jonathan B. Turner, *Mormonism in All Ages*, 20.

83. See Andrew F. Smith, Introduction to *The History of the Saints*, xxi, xl–xli.

84. Jonathan B. Turner, *Mormonism in All Ages*, 225.

85. See Leonard, *Nauvoo*, 269–550, and Flanders, *Nauvoo*, 242–341. Some were skeptical of the Mormons' intentions from the start. See, e.g., "The Mormons," *Kendall's Expositor*.

86. See Flanders, *Nauvoo*, 211–41.

87. Quinn, *Origins of Power*, 105.

88. See Leonard, *Nauvoo*, 44. Lyman Wight fanned the partisan flames by writing critically of the Missouri Democrats to the *Quincy Whig*. Wanting to avoid alienating either party, the LDS First Presidency wrote that Wight's opinions were his own. "We disclaim any intention of making a political question of our difficulties with Missouri." Quoted in Leonard, *Nauvoo*, 45.

89. One newsman recorded his discomfort during an interview with Smith in which the prophet hinted at the Mormons' intent to "use" their "influence, as far as it goes" in politics. Bartlett, "A Glance at the Mormons."

90. See Hallwas and Launius, *Cultures in Conflict*, 83.

91. Ford, *History of Illinois*, 182. See also Ehat and Cook, *Words of Joseph Smith*, 228, 236–37; B., "Politics and Mormons," 2; and Hallwas and Launius, *Cultures in Conflict*, 85–87.

92. Leonard, *Nauvoo*, 92, 94; Flanders, *Nauvoo*, 92–114. Leonard demonstrates that, lacking legal status under state law, the high council's only recourse to enforcement of community rules was disfellowshipment from the church. With a state charter in place, the high council shifted back to its solely ecclesiastical functions in 1841 (p. 95).

93. Hallwas and Launius, *Cultures in Conflict*, 21; Leonard, *Nauvoo*, 108.

94. The charter appears in "An act to incorporate the City of Nauvoo," 281–86.

95. Joseph Smith, Sidney Rigdon, and Hyrum Smith, "A Proclamation, to the Saints Scattered Abroad."

96. Leonard, *Nauvoo*, 104–6, 115; Quinn, *Origins of Power*, 106; Bennett, Black, and Cannon, *Nauvoo Legion in Illinois*.

97. "Celebration of the aniversary [*sic*] of the church"; Hallwas and Launius, *Cultures in Conflict*, 55.

98. "Celebration of the aniversary [*sic*] of the church"; Hallwas and Launius, *Cultures in Conflict*, 55. See also Parsons, *Mormon Fanaticism Exposed*, 43, 81, and Kidder, *Mormonism*, 183.

99. Leonard, *Nauvoo*, 103.

100. Reprinted in Hallwas and Launius, *Cultures in Conflict*, 92–97.

101. *Chicago Democrat*, 26 June 1843. See also Leonard, *Nauvoo*, 284–85.

102. Other charges, including allegations of Mormon theft and counterfeiting, are detailed in Hallwas and Launius, *Cultures in Conflict*, 67, 70, 206, 212, 267.

103. On the beginnings of Mormon polygamy, see Hardy, *Doing the Works of Abraham*, 33–72; Richard Lyman Bushman, *Joseph Smith: Rough Stone Rolling*, 437–46; Daynes, *More Wives Than One*, 17–35; Van Wagoner, *Mormon Polygamy*, 1–81; Compton, *In Sacred Loneliness*; and George D. Smith, *Nauvoo Polygamy*.

104. See Andrew F. Smith, *Saintly Scoundrel*.

105. One paper called it "a collection of all newspaper trash about the Mormons." See Andrew F. Smith, Introduction to *The History of the Saints*, xxx–xxxii, and John C. Bennett, *History of the Saints*, 159.

106. John C. Bennett, *History of the Saints*, 218, 220–23, 226–29, 236–45, 254. Much of what Bennett described could not be corroborated by any contemporary source, Mormon or not, but he did secure convincing evidence of Smith's polygamy. For the Smith-Bennett controversy, see Richard Lyman Bushman, *Joseph Smith: Rough Stone Rolling*, 436–525; Andrew F. Smith, *Saintly Scoundrel*, 51–128; Van Wagoner, *Mormon Polygamy*, 29–62; and Wyl, *Joseph Smith the Prophet*, 60–63.

107. John C. Bennett, *History of the Saints*, 192.

108. Andrew F. Smith, Introduction to *The History of the Saints*, xxxiv.

109. See John C. Bennett, *History of the Saints*, 286.

110. Ibid., 293–307 (quotations, 302, 304–7).

111. For an example of Smith's own perspective on the political and spiritual unity of God's kingdom, see an editorial likely penned by him (as the paper's editor at the time) in "The Government of God."

112. The substance of the revelation is unknown, but the revelation is referred to in several period documents. See George D. Smith, *Intimate Chronicle*, 153–54.

113. For the "Anointed Quorum," see Anderson and Bergera, *Smith's Quorum of the Anointed*; Quinn, *Origins of Power*, 113–20; Allen, *No Toil Nor Labor Fear*, 122–25, 130; and Richard Lyman Bushman, *Joseph Smith: Rough Stone Rolling*, 497. The Council of Fifty, established in March 1844, took over much of the political strategizing from the Anointed Quorum. For the Council of Fifty, see Richard Lyman Bushman, *Joseph Smith: Rough Stone Rolling*, 519–25; Hansen, *Quest for Empire*; and Quinn, "Council of Fifty" and *Origins of Power*, 111–41.

114. See John C. Bennett, *History of the Saints*, 272–76. The term "theo-democracy" appears in Joseph Smith to *Daily Globe*, 14 March 1844; it is reprinted in "History of Joseph Smith," 391.

115. Allen, *No Toil Nor Labor Fear*, 131–32.

116. See Partridge, "Death of a Mormon Dictator," and Hallwas and Launius, *Cultures in Conflict*, 169–72.

117. The news of Smith's plural marriages had been crushing to Law, who had publicly defended him in the wake of Bennett's accusations. See Cook, "William Law, Nauvoo Dissenter"; Cook, *William Law*; and Law, "[Letter to the Editors]," 1. See also Hallwas and Launius, *Cultures in Conflict*, 164–65.

118. Hallwas and Launius, *Cultures in Conflict*, 143–48.

119. Sharp, "Unparralleled [*sic*] Outrage."

120. For an overview of the hostilities of 1845–46 with supporting documents, see Hallwas and Launius, *Cultures in Conflict*, 243–349.

121. *Proceedings of a Convention*, 18–19, quoted in Hallwas and Launius, *Cultures in Conflict*, 305–9. The same year a citizens' convention in Lee County, Iowa (directly across the Mississippi from Nauvoo), published a broadside with similar resolutions. See Guthrie, *Lee County Anti-Mormon Meeting*.

122. Conyers, *A Brief History of the Leading Causes*, 9–10, 28, 32–33, 81–83. For another moderate plea, see *To the Anti-Mormon Citizens of Hancock*. For a more hostile account, see Bonney, *Banditti of the Prairies*, 13–16, 20–21. As one of a very few non-Mormons to participate in Smith's Council of Fifty, Bonney had not always been so negative. It was only after Brigham Young summarily dropped him from the council in February 1845 that he took a more stridently anti-Mormon stance. See Quinn, *Extensions of Power*, 228–29.

123. Massey, *James's Traveler's Companion*, 21–22.

124. The letter is reprinted in part in Roberts, *Comprehensive History*, 2:522–23. See also Joseph Smith, *History of the Church*, 6:188, 7:449; Van Wagenen, *Texas Republic*,

45; Christian, "Mormon Knowledge of the American Far West," 89; and Pykles, "'Look Well to the West.'"

125. See Leonard, *Nauvoo*, 511–12.

126. Thomas Drew to Brigham Young et al., 27 May 1845, reproduced in Roberts, *Comprehensive History*, 2:525–26.

127. Thomas Ford to Jacob Backenstos, 29 December 1845, reprinted in Joseph Smith, *History of the Church*, 7:562–64. Mormons were clearly aware of the letter. See, e.g., George D. Smith, *Intimate Chronicle*, 255. Ford had been urging the Saints to leave since April 1845. See Joseph Smith, *History of the Church*, 7:398.

128. As reported in William Clayton, Journal, 11 December 1845, in George D. Smith, *Intimate Chronicle*, 208.

129. Samuel Brannan to Brigham Young, 26 January 1846, in Joseph Smith, *History of the Church*, 7:588–89.

130. See Isaac C. Haight, Journal, 16 September 1846, quoted in Richard E. Bennett, *We'll Find the Place*, 25. For the uncertainties facing the Mormon pioneer company, see Bennett, *We'll Find the Place*, 8–10; Esplin, "'A Place Prepared'"; and Leonard, *Nauvoo*, 512–20. Young would later report "that we had come here [to Utah] according to the direction & council of Br Joseph Smith before his death." Kenney, *Wilford Woodruff's Journal*, 3:240.

131. For Sharp's perspective after the murders, see Launius, "Anti-Mormonism in Illinois."

132. Sharp, "To the Public." See also Marie H. Nelson, "Anti-Mormon Mob Violence."

133. The report of the anti-Mormon convention appeared in a 10,000-word historical broadside published by Hancock County newsman and self-appointed historian Thomas Gregg in 1846. It can be found in Hallwas and Launius, *Cultures in Conflict*, 82 (emphasis added).

134. Quinn, *Origins of Power*, 107–8.

135. Gilje, *Rioting in America*, 184, 231 fn5.

136. David Grimsted's (*American Mobbing*, viii) study of antebellum mob violence similarly portrays an American society unsuited for the faint of heart.

137. Oaks and Hill, *Carthage Conspiracy*, 163–90.

138. *Proceedings of a Convention*, 19; Jonathan B. Turner, *Mormonism in All Ages*, 3.

Chapter 4

1. *Reynolds v. United States*, 162–63. James Madison had feared that the Constitution's vagueness on the definition of religion would leave the provision fatally weak. See Sehat, *Myth of American Religious Freedom*, 48–50.

2. Gordon, *Mormon Question*, 121.

3. Thomas A. R. Nelson, *Polygamy in the Territorites [sic]*, 2.

4. Colin Kidd (*Forging of Races*, 3) uses the screen metaphor to describe the Bible's function in Protestant theorizing about race.

5. See Gaines M. Foster, *Moral Reconstruction*, 27–46, 81–90, 133–39.

6. Gunnison, *The Mormons* (1856), 154. Non-Mormons adopted "colonization" language, too. U.S. Indian agent Garland Hurt, for one, referred to the "delicate relations that exist between the United States and the little colony of Utah." Quoted in Bigler, *Forgotten Kingdom*, 101. Colonization talk proved durable in Utah and became important in the West generally. See Rogers, "Volatile Sagebrush Rebellion," 379–80, and Worster, *Rivers of Empire*, 14.

7. Bushnell, *Barbarism the First Danger*, 16. On Bushnell's thought, see Holifield, *Theology in America*, 452–66. For similar views on the West from other major religious figures, see Beecher, *A Plea for the West*, and Dwight, *Travels*, 2:459. The classic study of the West as a construct is Henry Nash Smith, *Virgin Land*.

8. Bushnell, *Barbarism the First Danger*, 4–5, 24.

9. Ibid., 25.

10. Shipps, *Sojourner*, 19. Shipps writes: "Historians of the West shape the western story like a doughnut, circling all around the Great Basin" (p. 21). This perspective is echoed in Farmer, *On Zion's Mount*, 14. For a nineteenth-century example, see "Yankee Mahomet," whose author wrote that his history of Mormonism was important precisely because "public attention is so generally turned towards the . . . western limits of our country" (p. 554).

11. Bushnell, *Barbarism the First Danger*, 32. The term "theo-democracy" is Joseph Smith's; see Smith to *Daily Globe*, 14 March 1844, quoted in "History of Joseph Smith," 391. The term caught on with some later LDS leaders, though they would eventually use the term to describe LDS ecclesiology exclusively. See, e.g., Orson F. Whitney, "Elder Orson F. Whitney," 94.

12. Sarah Gordon (*Mormon Question*, 57, 60) finds this to be true by 1860. David Bigler (*Forgotten Kingdom*, 16–17) is right that the 1850s were "especially significant in shaping Utah's history and culture" and that the period receives arguably "the least attention from most historians."

13. Gordon, *Mormon Question*, 60.

14. Ibid., 55.

15. Clayton, *Speech of John M. Clayton*, 17–18.

16. His earlier praise appears in Truman Smith, *Speech of Mr. Smith*.

17. Truman Smith, *Speech of Truman Smith*, 17–18.

18. Norris, *Speech of the Hon. M. Norris*, 7.

19. Dodge, *Nebraska and Kansas*, 3, 6.

20. Caleb Lyon, *No Government Bounty to Polygamy*, 1–2.

21. For a sampling, see Lieber, "The Mormons"; Peterson, "Mormonism"; and Jonathan B. Turner, *Mormonism in All Ages*. The *Reynolds* opinion, in fact, cited Lieber by name. See *Reynolds v. United States*, 166.

22. Morrill, *Speech of Hon. Justin S. Morrill*, 3–5.

23. Ibid., 4–12 (quotation, 9).

24. Ibid., 10, 12–14.

25. For Know-Nothing ideology, see Anbinder, *Nativism and Slavery*, xiii–xiv, 23, 104–5, 115, 120–21.

26. Douglas, *Kansas, Utah*, 6–8. Government fears of Mormon influence with Native Americans persisted after the Utah War. See, e.g., Browne, *Indian War*, 12, and Lander, *Practicability of Railroads*, 8.

27. Shipps, "Difference and Otherness."

28. On the significance of antipolygamy in the postbellum South, see Mason, "Opposition to Polygamy" and *Mormon Menace*. Notions of Mormon difference partly mirrored perceptions of a Jewish "race." As Eric Goldstein (*Price of Whiteness*, 1) argues, Jews constituted a racial "conundrum" because they could not be easily characterized given prevailing categories.

29. *Reynolds v. United States*, 164.

30. Colin Kidd, *Forging of Races*, 21–25. Kidd writes that the decline of scriptural authority in the late nineteenth century was integral to the "intellectual respectability" of "scientific" racism (p. 81).

31. On Mormon conceptions of race, see Mauss, *All Abraham's Children*.

32. Skousen, *Book of Mormon*, 137. Other Book of Mormon passages, however, reflect racialized language. See, e.g., ibid., p. 90. See also Colin Kidd, *Forging of Races*, 226–34, and Mauss, *All Abraham's Children*, 48–56.

33. *Doctrine and Covenants*, 254.

34. Colin Kidd, *Forging of Races*, 226–37; Mauss, *All Abraham's Children*, 212–21.

35. *Western Monitor*, 2 August 1833, reprinted in Joseph Smith, *History of the Church*, 1:396.

36. Parley P. Pratt, *History of the Late Persecution*, 28.

37. *Times and Seasons*, 1 November 1845, 1012. I am indebted to David Grua for this reference.

38. "The Mormon Prophet."

39. Moore, *Religious Outsiders*, 25–47.

40. Givens, *Viper on the Hearth*, 14–18; Limerick, "Peace Initiative."

41. Bartholow quoted in Coolidge, *Statistical Report*, 301–2. Mormons were clearly aware of such characterizations and contested them in various ways. See, e.g., Simpson, "Mormons Study 'Abroad,'" 791.

42. U.S. Congress, House Committee on the Territories, *Condition of Utah*, 3. See also Billings, *Circular No. 4*, 366, and Cragin, *Execution of Laws in Utah*, 18.

43. Draper, *Thoughts on . . . Civil Policy*, iv, 9, 11, 16.

44. European homogeneity was allegedly "proved by the affinities of . . . various languages to the Sanscrit." Ibid., 25, 40–41. For the significance of language study for modern theories of race, religion, and history, see Masuzawa, *Invention of World Religions*, xii–xv.

45. Draper, *Thoughts on . . . Civil Policy*, 53–58.

46. Ibid., 91, 172–73.

47. Masuzawa, *Invention of World Religions*, xi–xiii, 3.

48. Draper, *Thoughts on . . . Civil Policy*, 172–77.

49. In Orientalist discourse, Asia could simply equate to Islam, too.

50. Draper, *Thoughts on . . . Civil Policy*, 174.

51. Fitch, *The Utah Bill*, 1.

52. John C. Bennett, *History of the Saints*, 304; Parsons, *Mormon Fanaticism Exposed*, 5.

53. Gordon, *Mormon Question*, 28–63.

54. Oman, "Natural Law."

55. See, e.g., Blum, *Reforging the White Republic*.

56. Hooper, *The Utah Bill*, 7, 13–14, 25–26. See also John Taylor in Colfax, *Mormon Question*, 7.

57. Blair, *Polygamous Marriages*, 2–4.

58. Oman, "Natural Law," 688–89.

59. Claudia L. Bushman, "Mormon Domestic Life," 92.

60. Bederman, *Manliness & Civilization*.

61. Snow and Others, "Great Indignation Meeting."

62. "Woman Suffrage"; Talbot, "Mormonism and the Woman Question."

63. For Mormon polygamy and American reactions to it, see, respectively, Lawrence Foster, *Religion and Sexuality*, 123–225; Hardy, *Doing the Works of Abraham*; Daynes, *More Wives Than One*; and Gordon, *Mormon Question*.

64. Orson Pratt, "Celestial Marriage," 54.

65. Jones, *Performing American Identity*, 6.

66. Givens, *Viper on the Hearth*, 4, 6, 97–152 (quotation, 6).

67. Moore, *Selling God*, 128–29, 133–36 (quotation, 129). See also Goetzmann, *Beyond the Revolution*, 109–10.

68. Walker, Whittaker, and Allen, *Mormon History*, 12–13; Belisle, *The Prophets*.

69. See Walker, Whittaker, and Allen, *Mormon History*, 13.

70. Chidester, *Authentic Fakes*, 193.

71. See Lyman, *Political Deliverance*, 4; Gordon, *Mormon Question*, 260–61 fn6; and Hansen, *Quest for Empire*, preface, xvii–xviii, 170. Whereas Hansen views theocracy as the animating anxiety behind late-century anti-Mormonism, Lyman sees polygamy mattering more. Gordon writes: "Polygamy was the true center of national anti-Mormonism in the latter half of the nineteenth century . . . antipolygamists were committed to the idea that polygamy and church authority were mutually dependent" (p. 261).

72. Carvalho, *Incidents of Travel*, vii, 137–41, 143, 145, 150–54, 189 (quotations, 143, 154, 189).

73. Kane, *Twelve Mormon Homes*, 65. See also Claudia L. Bushman, "Mormon Domestic Life," 98.

74. Stenhouse, *Exposé of Polygamy*, 11; Burton, *City of the Saints*, 224.

75. See Stenhouse, *Exposé of Polygamy*, 12–15.

76. Ibid., 51, 54–55, 58.

77. Ibid., 35.

78. Stenhouse, *"Tell It All,"* 31, and *Exposé of Polygamy*, 170. See also Walker, "The Stenhouses."

79. Ann Eliza Young, *Wife No. 19*, 7.

80. Richards, "Inner Facts of Social Life in Utah," in Hardy, *Doing the Works of Abraham*, 146–51 (quotation, 151).

81. Helen Mar Kimball Whitney, *Plural Marriage*, 11–12, 15, 28.

82. Ibid., 27, 46; Helen Mar Kimball Whitney, *Why We Practice Plural Marriage*, 65.

83. Laurie, "First Senator Among Women," in Hardy, *Doing the Works of Abraham*, 151–52.

84. Hardy, *Doing the Works of Abraham*, 150–51. See also Compton, *In Sacred Loneliness*, 486–534.

85. Napheys, *Physical Life of Woman*, 64; Hardy, *Doing the Works of Abraham*, 245–46.

86. For examples, see Bunker and Bitton, *Mormon Graphic Image*, 18, 21–22, 24, 26.

87. Foote, *Plain Home Talk*, 657–59, 869.

88. See Hardy, *Doing the Works of Abraham*, 298, and Bederman, *Manliness and Civilization*, 15, 22–30.

89. Bederman, *Manliness and Civilization*, 25.

90. As quoted in Talbot, "'Turkey Is in Our Midst,'" 386.

91. Ibid. 364, 379, 382.

92. Colfax, *Mormon Question*, 4, 6 (pagination restarts in Taylor's response).

93. Wade, *In the Senate*, 2.

94. U.S. War Department, *Military Posts*, 7. An American travel guide offered that polygamy "more especially distinguished" the Mormons "from those of all other parts of the Republic." Richards, *Appletons' Illustrated Handbook*, 395. Similarly, one English lexicon defined the LDS Church itself as simply "a sect whose leading tenet or practice is a plurality of wives." Jenkins, *Vest-Pocket Lexicon*, 315, as quoted in Hardy, *Solemn Covenant*, 82 fn148.

95. Blair, *Polygamous Marriages*, 4.

Chapter 5

1. See Mazur, *Americanization of Religious Minorities*, 20.

2. Masuzawa, *Invention of World Religions*, 64–65. See also Jonathan Z. Smith, "Religion, Religions, Religious."

3. The phraseology "less theological" is purposeful because, as Jonathan Z. Smith and others have detailed, the "history of the history of religions is *not* best conceived as a liberation from the hegemony of theology." Smith, *Relating Religion*, 362–63 (emphasis added). See also Styers, *Making Magic*, 4–5.

4. Fitzgerald, *Ideology of Religious Studies*, ix–x.

5. Once the LDS social structure was whittled back from real and perceived peculiarity, Mormons were left to experiment with theological radicalism as a possible marker of communal identity. Their late-century theological experimentation developed in fits and starts until the mounting calculus of costs and rewards spawned a late

twentieth-century strategy of selective "neo-orthodoxy." This move toward theological orthodoxy developed in tandem with pervasive emphasis on moral rigor, religious practice, and institutional efficiency over overt theologizing. See White, *Mormon Neo-Orthodoxy*. Neo-orthodoxy in the case of twentieth-century Mormonism entails emphasis on traditional Christian themes such as sin, human depravity, salvation through Christ's grace, etc. These subjects had long been part of the Mormon theological inventory, so any late-century emphasis amounts to recovery rather than invention. Unlike Protestant neo-orthodoxy, however, the Mormon neo-orthodox strain did not develop exclusively within its liberal wing.

6. M. S. C., "Mormonism," 1–2.

7. Goetzmann, *Beyond the Revolution*, 399; Burris, *Exhibiting Religion*, xiii–xiv.

8. Masuzawa, *Invention of World Religions*, 266.

9. Quoted material in Hutchison, *Religious Pluralism*, 132, 170–95; Burris, *Exhibiting Religion*, xviii, 123–25; Bederman, *Manliness & Civilization*, 31; Chidester, *Savage Systems*, xiii.

10. Konden R. Smith, "Appropriating the Secular"; Neilson, *Exhibiting Mormonism*; Bitton, "B. H. Roberts."

11. Neilson, *Exhibiting Mormonism*, 141–75; Konden R. Smith, "Appropriating the Secular," 163–64; Roberts, "Elder B. H. Roberts Arraignes the Religious Congress for its Slight," reprinted in Roberts, *The Essential B. H. Roberts*, 49–57 (quotations, 49). For other Mormon reactions to the parliament, see sermons of George Q. Cannon and B. H. Roberts in *Collected Discourses*, 3:349–56, 5:154–62.

12. Konden R. Smith, "Appropriating the Secular," 169.

13. Mormons and antipolygamists each backed into secular models by century's end. As Sarah Gordon (*Mormon Question*, 82, 222) writes, the most poignant of the antipolygamy crusade's paradoxes was its "dismantling of public religious power to protect private Christian faith." She argues that by checking Mormon control through federalization of American marriage laws, antipolygamists precipitated a "second disestablishment."

14. Ibid., xi, 46–47, 58.

15. Masuzawa, *Invention of World Religions*, 12.

16. Burris, *Exhibiting Religion*, xviii, 64–80.

17. Masuzawa, *Invention of World Religions*, 79–84; Jacobson, *Barbarian Virtues*, 139–48 (quotation, 141).

18. Jacobson, *Barbarian Virtues*, 151–53; Burris, *Exhibiting Religion*, xix. Frazer is quoted in Kuper, *Invention of Primitive Society*, 105.

19. Bowman, "Crisis of Mormon Christology"; Mauss, *The Angel and the Beehive*, 33–195; Quinn, *Elder Statesman*; White, *Mormon Neo-Orthodoxy*.

20. Roberts, *Mormon Doctrine of Deity*, 18–19.

21. Widtsoe, *Joseph Smith as Scientist* and *Rational Theology*.

22. Schleiermacher's *On Religion* (1799) was translated into English in the year of the Chicago parliament.

23. Fitzgerald, *Ideology of Religious Studies*, ix–x, 8–9, 15–20. See also Masuzawa, *Invention of World Religions*, 20, and McCutcheon, *Manufacturing Religion*, 3, 35.

24. One recalls the main thrust of Sarah Gordon's (*Mormon Question*, 221–38) argument: antipolygamists won the battle but secularists won the war.

25. Novick, *That Noble Dream*, 62. In Richard Bushman's words, Mormons gave up on their "radicalism because the United States government beat it out of them. . . . As a result, everything became secular. Mormons, in reaction to this treatment, turned to laissez faire liberalism, having no confidence in the government" ("Mormonism and Politics").

26. For memorable examples, see *The True Lamplighter*, 24, and Bonney, *Banditti of the Prairies*, 24–25.

27. *Authentic History of Remarkable Persons*, 3. Similarly, Charles Peterson wrote that Mormonism "received new vitality from his martyrdom." Peterson found Smith's death to be advantageous to the Saints in another sense as well: "Though a man peculiarly fitted to originate and even organize such a movement, he was not so capable of controlling it. . . . Impetuosity, and even recklessness, may assist the founder of a sect; but prudence, even to extreme caution, best befits the successor" ("Mormonism," 535).

28. Johnston, "Joe Smith and the Mormons." For other examples, see Gunnison, *The Mormons* (1856), 127; Lee, *The Mormons*, 7; Kirk, *Mormons & Missouri*, 3; Kidder, *Remarkable Delusions*, 201–2; Cleaveland, *An Address*, xxvi; and DeLeon, "Rise and Progress," 526–38. See also Farmer, *On Zion's Mount*, 96.

29. Hardy, *Doing the Works of Abraham*, 251 fn74.

30. *Latter-Day Saints: The Dupes*, 3.

31. "Yankee Mahomet," 60. The Joseph Smith story garnered attention in the 1850s well beyond the immediate proximity of Mormon communities or snippets in the national press. Indicative of Mormonism's widespread appeal as a popular topic was the fact that noted British author Charles Mackay's *The Mormons* (1851) went through five London editions, six in the United States, and others in France, Germany, and Sweden. Not only did the work signal Mormonism's graduation as a topic of interest to an international educated class, Mackay cast a long shadow over later treatments. Walker, Whittaker, and Allen, *Mormon History*, 9–10; Mackay, *History of the Mormons*, iv, 18, 67–68, 398–99.

32. "Editor's Table," 701.

33. Breisach, *Historiography*, 256.

34. Masuzawa, *Invention of World Religions*, 15.

35. Burris, *Exhibiting Religion*, xvi; Novick, *That Noble Dream*, 4, 21–27, 37–43, 85–87; Elizabeth A. Clark, *History, Theory, Text*, 9–10.

36. Riley, *Founder of Mormonism*, x–xi, 3–4.

37. Robert Baird had penned just such a master text (*Religion in America*) in 1844, at the same time that Mormonism's founding epic came to a bloody end. Baird, a prominent Presbyterian, made his narrative priorities clear in the work's subtitle (*An Account of the Origin, Progress, Relation to the State, and Present Condition of the Evangelical*

Churches in the United States. With Notices of the Unevangelical Denominations). He would document the "Evangelical Churches" and leave to the "Unevangelical Denominations" brief "notices" only. *Religion in America* grouped Baird's allies into a unified "Anglo-Saxon" body and linked it firmly to America's "national character." His paean cast the United States as "a Christian empire" offering religious liberty that was "in every respect perfect." Even as he made the babble of antebellum religion seem harmonious, at least for evangelicals, Baird set forth a hierarchy that systematically weighed American religion against Protestant orthodoxy. Baird could summarize: "It is not difficult to draw a line between the various unevangelical sects on the one hand, and those that may be classed . . . as evangelical denominations on the other. The chief of the former . . . are the Roman Catholics, Unitarians, Christ-ians, Universalists, Hicksite Quakers, Swedenborgians, Tunkers or Dunkers, Jews, Shakers, and so on down to the Mormons, beginning with the sect that has buried the truth amid a heap of corruptions of heathenish origin, and ending with the grossest of all the delusions that Satanic malignity or human ambition ever sought to propagate." Baird, *Religion in America*, 25–26, 32–33, 84, 106, 110–11, 214, 270, 288. See also Baird, *Progress and Prospects*, and *Christian Retrospect*.

38. Schaff, *America*, 198.

39. Schaff, *Church and State*, 9, 15, 35–37. See also Graham, *Cosmos in the Chaos*, 130–34.

40. Dorchester, *Christianity*, 3–4, 538–42, 646–48, 780. For an example of Dorchester's influence on later narratives, see Goucher, *Christianity*.

41. Carroll's book answered Schaff's call for a modern American church history, and Schaff himself served on the general editorial board for the "American Church History Series" that Carroll's volume inaugurated. Carroll, *Religious Forces*, ix, xiv, xvii, xxix–xxx, xxiv, 165–74.

42. Bacon, *History of American Christianity*, 1, 335. Bacon noted his reliance on Dorchester and Carroll for information on Mormonism.

43. William H. Lyon, *A Study of the Sects*, vii, 188.

44. Carroll, *Religious Forces*, 167–68; Bacon, *History of American Christianity*, 355.

45. Gregg, *Prophet of Palmyra*, 2. See also Walker, Whittaker, and Allen, *Mormon History*, 19.

46. Bancroft's neutrality came with a price, however, as his access to the rich LDS archives provided Mormon leaders a prepublication review of his text. Walker, Whittaker, and Allen, *Mormon History*, 20–21; Bancroft, *History of Utah*, ix, 40.

47. David B. Davis, "New England Origins."

48. Ely and Ericksen quoted in Walker, Whittaker, and Allen, *Mormon History*, 39–40.

49. Alexander, *Things in Heaven and Earth*, 261–87.

50. Larson, *"Americanization" of Utah*; Mauss, *The Angel and the Beehive*, 21–32; Yorgason, *Transformation*, 2–3; Underwood, "Re-visioning Mormon History," 405–6.

51. Yorgason, *Transformation*, 194 fn5.

52. Bloom, *The American Religion*, 77–128; Wood, "Evangelical America"; Hatch, *Democratization*, 113–22.

53. Shipps, *Sojourner*, 51–97.

54. Hardy, *Solemn Covenant*, 298–99.

55. Quinn, "LDS Church Authority"; Alexander, *Mormonism in Transition*, 60–73; Hardy, *Solemn Covenant*, 127–335.

56. Strong, *Our Country*, 118.

57. See Flake, *Politics*.

58. Alexander, *Mormonism in Transition*, 6–15.

59. Quinn, *Extensions of Power*, 325–56; Alexander, *Mormonism in Transition*, 8–10.

60. A century after the Thatcher episode, Utah was more Mormon, more politically unified, and more in lock-step with LDS leaders than at any point in its history. Based on early twenty-first-century voter self-identification, Utah was also more ideologically conservative and more Republican than any state in the nation. When Utah is viewed in tandem with other pockets of Mormon strength (southern Idaho, north-central Arizona, southern California), the "Book of Mormon belt" emerges as the least politically diverse region in America and the one tied most directly to the influence of a single church. See Hinton and Roberds, "Public Opinion, Culture," and Flake, "Mormon Corridor."

61. Rutherford B. Hayes Diary, 13 January 1880, as quoted in T. Harry Williams, *Hayes*, 258–59.

62. Quinn, *Extensions of Power*, 198–225; Alexander, *Mormonism in Transition*, 4–6. The classic study of Mormon economic history remains Arrington, *Great Basin Kingdom*. See also Arrington, Fox, and May, *Building the City of God*.

63. Prince and Wright, *David O. Mckay*, 199–226; Poll, *Working the Divine Miracle*, 186–219; Quinn, *Extensions of Power*, 219–20.

64. Quinn, *Extensions of Power*, 225.

65. Tanner, *A Mormon Mother*, 129–30; Yorgason, *Transformation*, 33–42 (quotation, 33).

66. Quinn, *Extensions of Power*, 373–402.

67. Gunnison, *The Mormons* (1856), 36–37, 164.

68. Powell, *Report on the Lands of the Arid Region*, vii, 8, 11; Worster, *A River Running West*, 353–54.

69. Worster, *A River Running West*, 264.

70. "Meddling With The Mormons," reprinted in Hardy, *Doing the Works of Abraham*, 250–51. For similar rhetoric, see Cleaveland, *An Address*, xxvi.

71. See Larson, *"Americanization" of Utah*, 65–72, and Hardy, *Doing the Works of Abraham*, 246.

72. For an example of a favorable mining report, see Murphy, *Mineral Resources*.

73. See Hardy, *Solemn Covenant*, 285.

74. Union Pacific Railroad Company, *Sights and Scenes in Utah*, 6–7, 11–13.

75. Rio Grande Western Railway Company, *Valleys of the Great Salt Lake*, 6, 13, 26.

76. Wenger, *History Lessons*.

77. Shipps, "From Peoplehood to Church Membership."

BIBLIOGRAPHY

Newspapers

Alexandria Gazette (Alexandria, Va.)

Anti-Masonic Telegraph (Norwich, N.Y.)

Boston Recorder

Chicago Democrat

Christian Examiner and Religious Miscellany (Boston)

Christian Palladium (Rochester, N.Y.)

Church News (Salt Lake City)

Daily Graphic (New York)

Deseret Evening News (Salt Lake City)

Elders' Journal of the Church of Jesus Christ of Latter Day Saints
    (Kirtland, Ohio, and Far West, Mo.)

The Evangelist (Carthage, Ohio)

Evening and the Morning Star (Independence, Mo.)

Gospel Messenger (Auburn, N.Y.)

The Journal (Logan, Utah)

Latter Day Saints' Messenger and Advocate (Kirtland, Ohio)

Latter-day Saints' Millennial Star (Manchester, England)

Macomb Journal (Macomb, Ill.)

Millennial Harbinger (Bethany, Va.)

Morning Courier and Enquirer (New York)

Nauvoo Expositor (Nauvoo, Ill.)

New York American

New York Herald

New York Observer

New York Times and Commercial Intelligencer

New York Tribune

Niles' Weekly Register (Baltimore)

Ohio Observer (Hudson, Ohio)

Ohio Star (Ravenna, Ohio)

Painesville Republican (Painesville, Ohio)

Painesville Telegraph (Painesville, Ohio)

Palmyra Freeman (Palmyra, N.Y.)

Reflector (Palmyra, N.Y.)

Times and Seasons (Nauvoo, Ill.)

Upper Mississippian (Rock Island, Ill.)

Vermont Mercury (Woodstock, Vt.)

Vermont Telegraph (Brandon, Vt.)
Warsaw Signal (Warsaw, Ill.)
Wayne Sentinel (Palmyra, N.Y.)
Western Courier (Ravenna, Ohio)
Western Monitor (Fayette, Mo.)

Primary Sources

"An act to incorporate the City of Nauvoo." *Times and Seasons*, 15 January 1841, 281–87.

Adams, Hannah. *A Dictionary of All Religions and Religious Denominations, Jewish, Heathen, Mahometan, and Christian, Ancient and Modern.* 4th ed. New York: James Eastburn and Co., 1817.

Allen, James B., and Thomas G. Alexander, eds. *Manchester Mormons: The Journal of William Clayton, 1840 to 1842.* Classic Mormon Diary Series, vol. 1. Santa Barbara, Calif.; Salt Lake City: Peregrine Smith, 1974.

An Authentic History of Remarkable Persons, Who Have Attracted Public Attention in Various Parts of the World; Including a Full Exposure of the Iniquities of the Pretended Prophet Joe Smith, and of the Seven Degrees of the Mormon Temple; Also an Account of the Frauds Practised by Matthias the Prophet, and Other Religious Impostors. New York: Wilson and Co., Brother Jonathan Press, 1849.

Annual Report of the Commissioners, Treasurer, and Medical Superintendent of the Indiana Hospital for the Insane, to the General Assembly of the State of Indiana. Indianapolis: J. P. Chapman, State Printer, 1851.

Annual Report of the Managers of the State Lunatic Asylum. 1845. Reprint, State Hospital, Utica, N.Y., July 1890.

Annual Report, Pennsylvania Hospital for the Insane. Philadelphia: N.p., 1841.

Anti-Mormon Almanac, for 1842. Containing, Besides the Usual Astronomical Calculations, a Variety of Interesting and Important Facts, Showing the Treasonable Tendency, and the Wicked Imposture of That Great Delusion, Advocated by a Sect, Lately Risen up, in the United States, Calling Themselves Mormons, or Latter Day Saints; with Quotations from Their Writings and from Public Document No. 189, Published by Order of Congress, February 15, 1841, Showing That Mormonism Authorizes the Crimes of Theft, Robbery, High Treason, and Murder . . . New York: N.p., 1841.

Arrington, Leonard J. "James Gordon Bennett's 1831 Report on 'The Mormonites.'" *Brigham Young University Studies* 10, no. 3 (Spring 1970): 353–64.

B. "Politics and Mormons." *Macomb Journal*, 25 January 1877, 2.

Bacheler, Origen. *Mormonism Exposed, Internally and Externally.* New York: Published at 162 Nassau-St., 1838.

Bacon, Leonard W. *A History of American Christianity.* New York: Christian Literature Co., 1897.

Badger, Joseph. "Matthias the Prophet." *Christian Palladium*, 1 December 1834, 235–39.

Bailey, Rev. A. S. "Anti-American Influences in Utah." In *Christian Progress in Utah.*

The Discussions of the Christian Convention Held in Salt Lake City, April 3rd, 4th and 5th, 1888, 18–23. Salt Lake City: Frank H. Nelden and Co., 1888.

Baird, Robert. *The Christian Retrospect and Register: A Summary of the Scientific, Moral and Religious Progress of the First Half of the Xixth Century.* New York: M. W. Dodd, 1851.

———. *The Progress and Prospects of Christianity in the United States of America; with Remarks on the Subject of Slavery in America; and on the Intercourse Between British and American Churches.* London: Partridge and Oakey, 1851.

———. *Religion in America; or, An Account of the Origin, Progress, Relation to the State, and Present Condition of the Evangelical Churches in the United States. With Notices of the Unevangelical Denominations.* New York: Harper and Brothers, 1844.

Baker, James L. *Men and Things; or, Short Essays on Various Subjects, Including Free Trade.* Boston: Crosby, Nichols and Co., 1858.

Bancroft, Hubert Howe. *History of Utah, 1540–1886.* The Works of Hubert Howe Bancroft, vol. 26. San Francisco: History Co., 1889.

Barber, John Warner. *Incidents in American History; Being a Selection of the Most Important and Interesting Events Which Have Transpired since the Discovery of America, to the Present Time.* 3rd ed. New York: Geo. F. Cooledge and Brother, 1847.

Bartlett, Sylvester M. "A Glance at the Mormons." *Quincy Whig*, 17 October 1840, 1.

Bauder, Peter. *The Kingdom and Gospel of Jesus Christ: Contrasted with That of Anti-Christ. A Brief Review of Some of the Most Interesting Circumstances, Which Have Transpired Since the Institution of the Gospel of Christ, from the Days of the Apostles.* Canajoharie, N.Y.: Printed by A. H. Calhoun, 1834.

Beecher, Lyman. *A Plea for the West.* 2nd ed. Cincinnati: Truman and Smith, 1835.

Belisle, Orvilla S. *The Prophets; or, Mormonism Unveiled.* Philadelphia: Wm. White Smith, 1855.

Benedict, David. *History of All Religions, as Divided into Paganism, Mahometism, Judaism, and Christianity.* Providence, R.I.: John Miller, Printer, 1824.

Bennett, James G. "Mormon Religion—Clerical Ambition—Western New York—the Mormonites Gone to Ohio." *Morning Courier and Enquirer*, 1 September 1831.

———. "Mormonism—Religious Fanaticism—Church and State Party." *Morning Courier and Enquirer*, 31 August 1831.

Bennett, John C. *The History of the Saints; or, An Expose of Joe Smith and Mormonism.* 3rd ed. Boston: Leland and Whiting, 1842.

Benton, Abram W. "Mormonites." *Evangelical Magazine and Gospel Advocate*, 9 April 1831, 120.

Billings, John Shaw. *Circular No. 4. War Department, Surgeon General's Office, Washington, December 5, 1870. A Report on Barracks and Hospitals, with Descriptions of Military Posts.* Washington: Government Printing Office, 1870.

Blair, James Gorrall. *Polygamous Marriages in Utah. Speech of Hon. James G. Blair, of Missouri, in the House of Representatives, February 17, 1872.* [Washington]: [Printed at the Congressional Globe Office], 1872.

Bonney, Edward. *The Banditti of the Prairies; or, The Murderer's Doom!! A Tale of the*

Mississippi Valley. 1850. Western Frontier Library. Reprint, Norman: University of Oklahoma Press, 1963.

A Book of Commandments, for the Government of the Church of Christ, Organized According to Law, on the 6th of April, 1830. Zion [Independence, Mo.]: W. W. Phelps and Co., 1833.

Branagan, Thomas. *A Concise View, of the Principal Religious Denominations, in the United States of America, Comprehending a General Account of Their Doctrines, Ceremonies, and Modes of Worship.* Philadelphia: Printed by John Cline, 1811.

Brigham, Amariah. *Observations on the Influence of Religion Upon the Health and Physical Welfare of Mankind.* Boston: Marsh, Capen and Lyon, 1835.

Brown, Henry. *The History of Illinois, From Its First Discovery and Settlement, to the Present Time.* New York: J. Winchester, New World Press, 1844.

Brown, J. Newton. *Fessenden & Co.'s Encyclopedia of Religious Knowledge; or, Dictionary of the Bible, Theology, Religious Biography, All Religions, Ecclesiastical History, and Missions . . .* Brattleboro, Vt.: Fessenden and Co., 1835.

———. *The Encyclopedia of Religious Knowledge; or, Dictionary of the Bible, Theology, Religious Biography, All Religions, Ecclesiastical History, and Missions; Containing Definitions of All Religious Terms . . .* Brattleboro, Vt.: Fessenden and Co., 1836.

Browne, John Ross. *Indian War in Oregon and Washington Territories. Letter from the Secretary of the Interior, Transmitting, in Compliance with the Resolution of the House of 15th Instant, the Report of J. Ross Browne, on the Subject of the Indian War in Oregon and Washington Territories.* Washington: James B. Steedman, Printer, 1858.

Buck, Charles. *A Theological Dictionary: Containing Definitions of All Religious Terms; a Comprehensive View of Every Article in the System of Divinity; an Impartial Account of All the Principle Denominations Which Have Subsisted in the Religious World, from the Birth of Christ to the Present Day.* 2 vols. Whitehall [Philadelphia]: Printed for W. W. Woodward, 1807.

Burton, Richard Francis. *The City of the Saints, and Across the Rocky Mountains to California.* New York: Harper and Brothers, Publishers, 1862.

Bush, George. *The Life of Mohammed; Founder of the Religion of Islam, and of the Empire of the Saracens.* Harper's Family Library. New York: J. and J. Harper, 1832.

Bushnell, Horace. *Barbarism the First Danger. A Discourse for Home Missions.* New York: Printed for the American Home Missionary Society, 1847.

Campbell, Alexander. "Delusions." *Millennial Harbinger,* 7 February 1831, 85–96.

———. *Delusions: An Analysis of the Book of Mormon; with an Examination of Its Internal and External Evidences, and a Refutation of Its Pretences to Divine Authority.* Boston: Benjamin H. Greene, 1832.

———. "The Mormon Bible." *Millennial Harbinger,* June 1839.

Cannon, Donald Q., and Lyndon W. Cook, eds. *Far West Record: Minutes of the Church of Jesus Christ of Latter-Day Saints, 1830–1844.* Salt Lake City: Deseret Book Co., 1983.

Carroll, Henry K. *The Religious Forces of the United States Enumerated, Classified, and Described on the Basis of the Government Census of 1890; With an Introduction on*

the Condition and Character of American Christianity. American Church History
Series, vol. 1. Edited by Philip Schaff et al. New York: Christian Literature Co., 1893.

Cartwright, Peter. *Autobiography of Peter Cartwright, the Backwoods Preacher.* Edited
by W. P. Strickland. New York: Published by Carlton and Porter, 1857.

Carvalho, Solomon Nunes. *Incidents of Travel and Adventure in the Far West; with
Col. Fremont's Last Expedition Across the Rock Mountains: Including Three Months'
Residence in Utah, and a Perilous Trip Across the Great American Desert, to the
Pacific. By S. N. Carvalho, Artist to the Expedition.* New York: Derby and Jackson,
1860.

"Celebration of the aniversary [sic] of the church—Military parade—Prest. Rigdon's
address—Laying the corner stones of the Temple." *Times and Seasons,* 15 April
1841, 375–77.

Clark, John A. *Gleanings by the Way.* Philadelphia: W. J. and J. K. Simon, 1842.

Clayton, John Middleton. *Speech of John M. Clayton, of Delaware, on the Bill to
Organize the Territorial Governments in Nebraska and Kansas . . .* Washington:
Congressional Globe Office, 1854.

Cleaveland, Nehemiah. *An Address, Delivered at Topsfield in Massachusetts, August 28,
1850: The Two Hundredth Anniversary of the Incorporation of the Town.* New York:
Pudney and Russell, Printers, 1851.

Clemens, Samuel L. *Roughing It, by Mark Twain. (Samuel L. Clemens.) Fully Illustrated
by Eminent Artists.* Hartford, Conn.: American Publishing Co., 1872.

Coe, Truman. "Mormonism." *Ohio Observer,* 11 August 1836.

Cole, Abner. "Book of Mormon." *Reflector,* 14 February 1831, 102.

Colfax, Schuyler. *The Mormon Question. Being a Speech of Vice-President Schuyler
Colfax, at Salt Lake City. A Reply Thereto by Elder John Taylor; and a Letter of Vice-
President Colfax Published in the "New York Independent," with Elder Taylor's Reply.*
Salt Lake City: Deseret News Office, 1870.

*Collected Discourses Delivered by President Wilford Woodruff, His Two Counselors,
the Twelve Apostles, and Others.* Edited by Brian H. Stuy. 5 vols. Burbank, Calif.:
B. H. S. Publishing, 1989.

Conyers, Josiah B. *A Brief History of the Leading Causes of the Hancock Mob in the Year
1846.* St. Louis: Cathcart and Prescott, 1846.

Coolidge, Richard H. *Statistical Report on the Sickness and Mortality in the Army
of the United States, Compiled from the Records of the Surgeon General's Office;
Embracing a Period of Five Years, from January, 1855, to January, 1860. Prepared
under the Direction of Brevet Brigadier General Thomas Lawson, Surgeon General of
the United States Army, by Richard H. Coolidge, M.D., Assistant Surgeon U.S. Army.*
Washington: George W. Bowman, 1860.

Corrill, John. *A Brief History of the Church of Christ of Latter Day Saints, (Commonly
Called Mormons;).* St. Louis: Printed for the Author, 1839.

Cowdery, Oliver. "Dear Brother." *Messenger and Advocate,* October 1834, 14–16.

Cowdery, Warren A. "It is a Well Known and Established Fact." *Messenger and
Advocate,* July 1837, 535–43.

Cox, Samuel H. *Interviews: Memorable and Useful; from Diary and Memory Reproduced. By Samuel Hanson Cox, D.D. Pastor of the First Presbyterian Church, Brooklyn, New York.* New York: Harper and Brothers, 1853.

Cragin, Aaron H. *Execution of Laws in Utah. Speech of Hon. Aaron H. Cragin, of New Hampshire, Delivered in the Senate of the United States, May 18, 1870.* Washington: F. and J. Rives and Geo. A. Bailey, Reporters and printers of the debates of Congress, 1870.

Crawley, Peter L. "Two Rare Missouri Documents." *Brigham Young University Studies* 14, no. 4 (Summer 1974): 517–27.

Davis, George T. M. *An Authentic Account of the Massacre of Joseph Smith, the Mormon Prophet, and Hyrum Smith, His Brother, Together with a Brief History of the Rise and Progress of Mormonism, and All the Circumstances Which Led to Their Death.* St. Louis: Chambers and Knapp, 1844.

Davison, Matilda, A. C., and W. Scott. "The Mormon Bible." *The Evangelist*, 1 July 1839, 158–60.

DeLeon, Edwin. "The Rise and Progress of the Mormon Faith and People." *Southern Literary Messenger*, September 1844, 526–38.

Document Containing the Correspondence, Orders, &C. In Relation to the Disturbance with the Mormons . . . Fayette, Mo.: Printed at the Office of the Boon's Lick Democrat, 1841.

Doctrine and Covenants of the Church of the Latter Day Saints: Carefully Selected from the Revelations of God, and Compiled by Joseph Smith, Junior, Oliver Cowdery, Sidney Rigdon, Frederick G. Williams, [Presiding Elders of Said Church]. Kirtland, Ohio: Printed by F. G. Williams and Co. for the Proprietors, 1835.

Dodge, Augustus Caesar. *Nebraska and Kansas. Speech of Mr. Dodge, of Iowa, in the Senate of the United States, Feb. 25, 1854, the Senate Having under Consideration the Bill to Organize the Territories of Nebraska and Kansas.* Washington: Printed at the Congressional Globe Office, [1854?].

Dorchester, Daniel. *Christianity in the United States from the First Settlement Down to the Present Time.* New York: Phillips and Hunt, 1888.

Douglas, Stephen A. *Kansas, Utah, and the Dred Scott Decision. Remarks of Hon. Stephen A. Douglass, Delivered in the State House at Springfield, Illinois, on 12th June, 1857.* Springfield, Ill.: N.p., 1857.

Draper, John W. *Thoughts on the Future Civil Policy of America.* New York: Harper and Brothers, Publishers, 1865.

Dwight, Timothy. *Travels in New-England and New York.* 4 vols. New Haven: Timothy Dwight, 1821–22.

Eastman, Hubbard. *Noyesism Unveiled: A History of the Sect Self-Styled Perfectionists; with a Summary View of Their Leading Doctrines.* Brattleboro, Vt.: By the Author, 1849.

"Editor's Table." *Harper's New Monthly Magazine*, October 1851, 701–2.

Ehat, Andrew F., and Lyndon W. Cook, eds. *The Words of Joseph Smith: The Contemporary Accounts of the Nauvoo Discourses of the Prophet Joseph.* Religious

Studies Monograph Series, vol. 6. Provo: Religious Studies Center, Brigham Young University, 1980.

Eighth Annual Report of the Managers of the State Lunatic Asylum. 1851. Reprint, Utica, N.Y.: Utica State Hospital Press, 1895.

Eighth Annual Report of the Trustees of the State Lunatic Hospital at Worcester. December, 1840. Boston: Dutton and Wentworth, State Printers, 1841.

Eleventh Annual Report of the Directors and Superintendent of the Ohio Lunatic Asylum, to the Forty-Eighth General Assembly of the State of Ohio. For the Year 1849. Columbus: S. Medary, Printer, 1850.

Ellis, John. "From Elder John Ellis, Salem, Pa. August 7, 1835." *Christian Palladium,* 1 October 1835, 174.

Emmons, Samuel B. *Philosophy of Popular Superstitions and the Effects of Credulity and Imagination Upon the Moral, Social, and Intellectual Condition of the Human Race.* Boston: L. P. Crown and Co., 1853.

———. *The Spirit Land.* Boston: Crown and Co., 1858.

Evans, John. *History of All Christian Sects and Denominations; Their Origin, Peculiar Tenets, and Present Condition.* 2nd ed. New York: James Mowatt, 1844.

Faulring, Scott H., ed. *An American Prophet's Record: The Diaries and Journals of Joseph Smith.* Salt Lake City: Signature Books, 1989.

Faulring, Scott H., Kent P. Jackson, and Robert J. Matthews, eds. *Joseph Smith's New Translation of the Bible: Original Manuscripts.* Provo: Religious Studies Center, Brigham Young University, 2004.

Fifth Annual Report of the Directors and Superintendent of the Ohio Lunatic Asylum, to the Forty Second General Assembly. December 13, 1843. Columbus: Samuel Medary, State Printer, 1843.

Fifth Annual Report of the Managers of the State Lunatic Asylum. Albany: Charles Van Benthuysen, Public Printer, 1848.

Fifth Annual Report of the Trustees of the State Lunatic Hospital at Worcester. December, 1837. Boston: Dutton and Wentworth, 1838.

First Annual Report of the Commissioners and Medical Superintendent of the Hospital for the Insane, to the General Assembly, of the State of Indiana. Indianapolis: John D. Defrees, State Printer, 1849.

Fitch, Thomas. *The Utah Bill. Speeches of Hon. Thos. Fitch, of Nevada, and Hon. A. A. Sargent, of California. Delivered in the House of Representatives.* [Washington?]: [Cunningham and McIntosh, Printers], 1870.

Foote, Edward Bliss. *Plain Home Talk About the Human System—the Habits of Men and Women—the Causes and Prevention of Disease—Our Sexual Relations and Social Natures. Embracing Medical Common Sense Applied to Causes, Prevention, and Cure of Chronic Diseases—the Natural Relations of Men and Women to Each Other—Society—Love—Marriage—Parentage—Etc.* New York: Wells and Coffin, 1870.

Ford, Thomas. *A History of Illinois: From Its Commencement as a State in 1818 to 1847.* 1854. Reprint, Urbana: University of Illinois Press, 1995.

Forster, Charles. *Mahometanism Unveiled: An Inquiry, in Which that Arch-Heresy, Its Diffusion and Continuance, Are Examined on a New Principle, Tending to Confirm the Evidences, and Aid the Propagation, of the Christian Faith.* 2 vols. London: Printed for J. Duncan, 37. Paternoster-Row; and J. Cochran, 108. Strand, 1829.

Fourth Annual Report of the Directors and Superintendent of the Ohio Lunatic Asylum, to the Forty First General Assembly, December 9, 1842. Columbus: Samuel Medary, State Printer, 1842.

Fourth Annual Report of the Managers of the State Lunatic Asylum. 1847. Reprint, Utica, N.Y.: State Hospital, 1890.

"From Missouri." *Evening and the Morning Star*, January 1834, 124–26.

Gibbon, Edward. *The Life of Mahomet.* Leominster, Mass.: Printed by Salmon Wilder for John Whiting, 1805.

Goodrich, Charles A. *A History of the Church from the Birth of Christ to the Present Time . . .* New York: Justin Carpenter, 1834.

———. *Pictorial and Descriptive View of All Religions; Embracing the Forms of Worship, Practised by the Several Nations of the Known World from the Earliest Records to the Present Time. To Which Is Added a Brief View of the Minor Sects; on the Basis of the Celebrated and Splendid Work of Bernard Picart. Also a History of the Jews and Life of Mahommed.* Toronto: L. D. Ellis, 1848.

———. *Religious Ceremonies and Customs or the Forms of Worship Practised by the Several Nations of the Known World, from the Earliest Records to the Present Times . . .* Hartford, Conn.: Hutchison and Dwier, 1836.

Goucher, John Franklin. *Christianity and the United States.* New York: Eaton and Mains, 1908.

"The Government of God." *Times and Seasons*, 15 July 1842, 855–58.

Grant, Miles. *Spiritualism Unveiled: And Shown to Be the Work of Demons; an Examination of Its Origin, Morals, and Politics.* Boston: The "Crisis" office, 1866.

Green, Nelson Winch. *Fifteen Years Among the Mormons: Being the Narrative of Mrs. Mary Ettie V. Smith, Late of Great Salt Lake City: A Sister of One of the Mormon High Priests, She Having Been Personally Acquainted with Most of the Mormon Leaders, and Long in the Confidence of The "Prophet," Brigham Young.* New York: Charles Scribner, 1858.

Gregg, Thomas. *The Prophet of Palmyra: Mormonism Reviewed and Examined in the Life, Character, and Career of Its Founder, From "Cumorah Hill" To Carthage Jail and the Desert, Together with a Complete History of the Mormon Era in Illinois, an Exhaustive Investigation of The "Spalding [sic] Manuscript" Theory of the Origin of the Book of Mormon.* New York: John B. Alden, 1890.

Griffen, Joseph. "The Friend's Society." *Christian Palladium*, 15 December 1834, 249–51.

Gunnison, John W. *The Mormons; or, Latter-Day Saints, in the Valley of the Great Salt Lake: A History of Their Rise and Progress, Peculiar Doctrines, Present Condition, and Prospects, Derived From Personal Observation, During a Residence Among Them.* Philadelphia: Lippincott, Grambo and Co., 1852.

———. *The Mormons, or, Latter-Day Saints, in the Valley of the Great Salt Lake:*

A History of Their Rise and Progress, Peculiar Doctrines, Present Condition, and Prospects, Derived from Personal Observation During a Residence Among Them. Philadelphia: J. B. Lippincott and Co., 1856.

Guthrie, Edwin. *Lee County Anti-Mormon Meeting.* N.p., 1845.

Harris, William. *Mormonism Portrayed; Its Errors and Absurdities Exposed, and the Spirit and Designs of Its Authors Made Manifest.* Warsaw, Ill.: Sharp and Gamble, Publishers, 1841.

Hayward, John. *The Book of Religions: Comprising the Views, Creeds, Sentiments, or Opinions, of All the Principal Religious Sects in the World, Particularly of All Christian Denominations in Europe and America, to Which Are Added Church and Missionary Statistics, Together with Biographical Sketches.* Concord, N.H.: I. S. Boyd and E. W. Buswell, 1843.

———. *The Religious Creeds and Statistics of Every Christian Denomination in the United States and British Provinces; with Some Account of the Religious Sentiments of the Jews, American Indians, Deists, Mahometans, &C., Alphabetically Arranged.* Boston: John Hayward, 1836.

Himes, Joshua V. *Mormon Delusions and Monstrosities, a Review of the Book of Mormon, and An Illustration of Mormon Principles and Practices.* Boston: Joshua V. Himes, 1842.

Hinckley, Gordon B., and Mike Wallace. "An Interview with Gordon Hinckley: A Look Back at Mike Wallace's 1996 Interview with the President of the Mormon Church," Segment Transcript, "60 Minutes," CBS News, 7 April 1996, http://www .cbsnews.com/stories/2008/01/31/60minutes/main3775068.shtml?tag=contentMain ;contentBody. 18 November 2010.

"History of Joseph Smith." *Latter-Day Saints' Millennial Star,* 22 June 1861, 389–92.

Hooper, William H. *The Utah Bill. Plea for Religious Liberty. Speech of Hon. W. H. Hooper of Utah, Delivered in the House of Representatives, March 23, 1870.* Washington: Gibson Brothers, Printers, 1870.

Howe, Eber D. "Beware of Impostors." *Painesville Telegraph,* 14 December 1830.

———. "The Book of Mormon." *Painesville Telegraph,* 30 November 1830.

———. "'Golden Bible.'" *Painesville Telegraph,* 22 September 1829.

———. "The Golden Bible." *Painesville Telegraph,* 16 November 1830.

———. "Mormonism." *Painesville Telegraph,* 18 January 1831.

———. *Mormonism Unvailed [sic]; or, A Faithful Account of That Singular Imposition and Delusion, from Its Rise to the Present Time. With Sketches of the Characters of Its Propagators, and a Full Detail of the Manner in Which the Famous Golden Bible Was Brought before the World. To Which Are Added, Inquiries into the Probability That the Historical Part of the Said Bible Was Written by One Solomon Spalding [sic], More Than Twenty Years Ago, and by Him Intended to Have Been Published as a Romance.* Painesville, Ohio: E. D. Howe, 1834.

Hunt, James Henry. *Mormonism: Embracing the Origin, Rise and Progress of the Sect, with an Examination of the Book of Mormon; Also, Their Troubles in Missouri, and Final Expulsion from the State. With an Appendix, Giving an Account of the Late*

Disturbances in Illinois, Which Resulted in the Death of Joseph and Hyrum Smith.
By G. W. Westbook. St. Louis: Printed by Ustick and Davies, 1844.

Hyde, John. *Modern Christianity. A Dialogue between a Baptist and an Infidel.*
Cleveland: Smead and Cowles, Job Printers, n.d.

"In obedience to our promise." *Elders' Journal of the Church of Jesus Christ of Latter
Day Saints*, July 1838, 43–44.

Irving, Washington. *Mahomet and His Successors.* Revised ed. [New York?]: Putnam,
1849.

Jackson, Joseph H. *A Narrative of the Adventures and Experience of Joseph H. Jackson,
in Nauvoo. Disclosing the Depths of Mormon Villany.* 1844. Reprint, Morrison, Ill.:
News-Sentinel Publishers, 1960.

Jenkins, Jabez. *Jenkin's Vest-Pocket Lexicon . . .* Philadelphia: Lippincott, 1862.

Jensen, Robin S., Robert J. Woodford, and Steven C. Harper, eds. *Manuscript
Revelation Books.* Facsimile ed. Vol. 1 of the Revelations and Translations Series of
The Joseph Smith Papers. Edited by Dean C. Jessee, Ronald K. Esplin, and Richard
Lyman Bushman. Salt Lake City: Church Historian's Press, 2009.

Jessee, Dean C., comp. and ed. *The Papers of Joseph Smith: Volume 1, Autobiographical
and Historical Writings.* Salt Lake City: Deseret Book Co., 1989.

———. *The Papers of Joseph Smith: Volume 2, Journal, 1832–1842.* Salt Lake City:
Deseret Book Co., 1992.

———. *Personal Writings of Joseph Smith.* Revised ed. Salt Lake City and Provo:
Deseret Book Co. and Brigham Young University Press, 2002.

Jessee, Dean C., and David J. Whittaker. "The Last Months of Mormonism in
Missouri: The Albert Perry Rockwood Journal." *Brigham Young University Studies*
28, no. 1 (Winter 1988): 5–41.

Jessee, Dean C., Mark Ashurst-McGee, and Richard L. Jensen, eds. *Journals: Volume 1,
1832–1839.* Vol. 1 of the Journals Series of *The Joseph Smith Papers.* Edited by
Dean C. Jessee, Ronald K. Esplin, and Richard Lyman Bushman. Salt Lake City:
Church Historian's Press, 2008.

Johnson, Clark V., ed. *Mormon Redress Petitions: Documents of the 1833–1838 Missouri
Conflict.* Religious Studies Monograph Series. Provo: Religious Studies Center,
Brigham Young University, 1992.

Johnston, James F. W. "Joe Smith and the Mormons." *Harper's New Monthly Magazine*,
June 1851, 64–66.

*Journal of Discourses by Brigham Young, President of the Church of Jesus Christ of
Latter-Day Saints, His Two Counsellors, the Twelve Apostles, and Others.* 26 vols.
Liverpool: F. D. and S. W. Richards, 1854–86.

Kane, Elizabeth Wood. *Twelve Mormon Homes Visited in Succession on a Journey
Through Utah to Arizona.* Philadelphia: William Wood, 1874.

Kenney, Scott G., ed. *Wilford Woodruff's Journal, 1833–1898 Typescript.* 9 vols. Midvale,
Ut.: Signature Books, 1983–84.

Kidder, Daniel P. *Mormonism and the Mormons: A Historical View of the Rise and
Progress of the Sect Self-Styled Latter-Day Saints.* New York: G. Lane and P. P.

Sandford, for the Methodist Episcopal Church, at the Conference Office, 200 Mulberry-Street, 1842.

———. *Remarkable Delusions: or, Illustrations of Popular Errors*. New York: Lane and Scott, 1852.

Kirk, Thomas J. *The Mormons & Missouri: A General Outline of the History of the Mormons, from Their Origin to the Present, (Including the Late Disturbance in Illinois;) and a Particular Account of the Last Mormon Disturbance in Missouri, or the Mormon War: With an Appendix, Contaiaing* [sic] *an Epitome of the Book of Mormon, with Remarks on the Nature and Tendency of Mormon Faith*. Chillicothe: J. H. Darlington, Printer, 1844.

Kirkbride, Thomas S. *Report of the Pennsylvania Hospital for the Insane, for the Year 1844*. Philadelphia: Published by Order of the Board of Managers, 1845.

Kitchell, Ashbel. "A Mormon Interview. Copied from Brother Ashbel Kitchell's Pocket Journal." 1831. Photocopy, Small Manuscript Collections, L. Tom Perry Special Collections, Harold B. Lee Library, Brigham Young University, Provo.

Land, Richard, and Robert Siegel. "Glenn Beck and Obama's Christianity." Interview transcript, *All Things Considered*, National Public Radio, aired 30 August 2010, http://www.npr.org/templates/story/story.php?storyId=129535008. 18 November 2010.

Lander, Frederick West. *Practicability of Railroads through the South Pass. Letter from the Secretary of the Interior, Transmitting a Report from F. W. Lander, Esq., Relative to the Practicability of a Railroad through the South Pass*. Washington: James B. Steedman, 1858.

"Latest from the Mormonites." *New York American*, 10 June 1831.

Latter-Day Saints: The Dupes of a Foolish and Wicked Imposture. New York: Tract Society, [1849?].

A Law Case Exhibiting the Most Extraordinary Developments Peculiar to Modern Times Arising from an Implicit Obedience to the Dictates of Mesmeric Clairvoyance, as Related by a Mormon Prophet. Also—the Speeches of Counsel in the Case Reported by Mr. Webster the Phonographic Writer. By a Member of the Cincinnati Bar. Cincinnati: Printed at the Daily Atlas Office, 1848.

Law, William. "[Letter to the Editors]." *Upper Mississippian*, 7 September 1844.

Lee, E. G. *The Mormons; or, Knavery Exposed. Giving An Account of the Discovery of the Golden Plates* . . . Philadelphia: E. G. Lee, Frankford, Pa., 1841.

"Letter From the Editor." *St. Louis Republican*, 12, 13 December 1838.

Lieber, Francis. "The Mormons: Shall Utah Be Admitted to the Union?" *Putnam's Monthly*, March 1855, 225–36.

The Life of Mahomet; or, The History of That Imposture Which Was Begun, Carried on, and Finally Established by Him in Arabia; and Which Has Subjugated a Larger Portion of the Globe, Than the Religion of Jesus Has yet Set at Liberty. Worcester: Printed by Isaiah Thomas, June 1802.

Livesay, Richard. *An Exposure of Mormonism, Being a Statement of Facts Relating to the Self-Styled "Latter Day Saints," And the Origin of the Book of Mormon, by Richard*

Livesay, of Winchendon, Massachusetts, America, Minister of the Methodist Episcopal Church. Manchester, England: Wm. Shackleton and Son, Printers, Ducie Place, 1838, 1840.

Lucas, Samuel. "Jackson County." In *Gazetteer of the State of Missouri*, edited by Alphonso Wetmore, 92–99. St. Louis: C. Keemle, 1837.

Lyon, Caleb. *No Government Bounty to Polygamy. Speech of Hon. Caleb Lyon, of Lyonsdale, New York, in the House of Representatives, May 4, 1854*. Washington: Printed at the Congressional Globe Office, [1854?].

Lyon, William H. *A Study of the Sects*. Boston: Unitarian Sunday-School Society, 1891.

Mackay, Charles. *History of the Mormons; or, Latter-Day Saints. With Memoirs of the Life and Death of Joseph Smith, The "American Mahomet."* Auburn and Buffalo: Miller, Orton and Mulligan, 1854.

———. *The Mormons; or, Latter-Day Saints. With Memoirs of the Life and Death of Joseph Smith, The "American Mahomet."* London: Office of the National Illustrated Library, 1851.

Marks, David. *The Life of David Marks, to the 26th Year of His Age. Including the Particulars of His Conversion, Call to the Ministry, and Labours in Itinerant Preaching for Nearly Eleven Years*. Limerick, Maine: Printed at the office of the Morning Star, 1831.

Massey, Stephen L. *James's Traveler's Companion. Being a Complete Guide Through the Western States, to the Gulf of Mexico and the Pacific, Via the Great Lakes, Rivers, Canals, Etc. Giving Full and Accurate Descriptions of All Places on, and in the Vicinity of, the Western Waters*. Cincinnati: Published by J. A. and U. P. James, 1851.

Matthews, Margaret. *Matthias. By His Wife*. New York, 1835.

Mattison, Hiram. *A Scriptural Defence of the Doctrine of the Trinity; or, A Check to Modern Arianism as Taught by Campbellites, Hicksites, New Lights, Universalists and Mormons, and Especially by a Sect Calling Themselves "Christians."* New York: L. Colby, 1846.

Mazzuchelli, Samuel. *The Memoirs of Father Samuel Mazzuchelli*. Chicago: Priory Press, 1967.

M'Chesney, James. *An Antidote to Mormonism: A Warning Voice to the Church and Nation; the Purity of Christian Principles Defended; and Truth Disentangled from Error and Delusion*. New York: Published by the author at the book store of Burnett and Pollard, 1838.

"Meddling With The Mormons." *Daily Graphic*, 9 December 1873, 3:239, 250/2–3.

"Memoir of the Mormons." *Southern Literary Messenger*, November 1848, 641–55.

Memoirs of Matthias the Prophet, with a Full Exposure of His Atrocious Impositions, and of the Degrading Delusions of His Followers. New York: Office of the Sun, 1835.

Miles, George H. *Mohammed, the Arabian Prophet: A Tragedy in Five Acts*. Boston: Phillips, Sampson and Co., 1850.

Miller, James. *Mahomet, the Imposter*. London: Printed for and sold by J. Watts . . . and by B. Dod, 1744.

Millet, Robert L. *After All We Can Do, Grace Works*. Salt Lake City: Deseret Book Co., 2003.

Milner, Vincent. *Religious Denominations of the World: Comprising a General View of the Origin, History, and Condition of the Various Sects of Christians, the Jews, the Mahometans, as Well as the Pagan Forms of Religion Existing in the Different Countries of the Earth*. Philadelphia: J. W. Bradley, 1860.

"Miscellaneous Items." *Niles' Weekly Register*, 7 June 1834, 255.

"More Mormon Trouble." *Anti-Masonic Telegraph*, 18 December 1833.

"The Mormon Delusion." *Vermont Telegraph*, 6 December 1831, 44.

"The Mormon Difficulties." *St. Louis Republican*, 10 March 1834.

"The Mormon Prophet." *North American Miscellany*, 31 May 1851, 204–6.

"The Mormon War." *Anti-Masonic Telegraph*, 1 January 1834.

"Mormonism." *Boston Recorder*, 10 October 1832, 161.

"Mormonism." *The Spirit of Practical Godliness, Devoted to the Present and Future Happiness of Mankind*, May 1832, 95–96.

"Mormonism." *Gospel Messenger*, 1 June 1833, 67.

"The Mormonites." *Vermont Telegraph*, 4 October 1831, 7.

"The Mormonites." *New York Times and Commercial Intelligencer*, 27 November 1838.

"The Mormons." *Vermont Mercury*, 7 December 1838.

"The Mormons." *Kendall's Expositor*, 30 June 1841, 208.

"The Mormons and the Anti-Mormons." *Anti-Masonic Telegraph*, 18 December 1833.

"Mormons in Missouri." *Niles' Weekly Register*, 26 July 1834, 368.

"The Mormons in Trouble." *Boston Recorder*, 11 September 1833, 145–48.

"Mormorism [*sic*]." *Niles' Weekly Register*, 16 July 1831, 353.

Morrill, Justin S. *Speech of Hon. Justin S. Morrill, of Vermont, on Utah Territory and Its Law-Polygamy and Its License; Delivered in the House of Representatives, February 23, 1857*. Washington: Printed at the office of the Congressional Globe, 1857.

M. S. C. "Mormonism." *Painesville Telegraph*, 15 February 1831.

Murphy, John R. *The Mineral Resources of the Territory of Utah, with Mining Statistics and Maps*. San Francisco: A. L. Bancroft and Co., 1872.

Murray, Nicholas. *Parish and Other Pencilings; by Kirwan [Pseud.]*. New York: Harper and Bros., 1854.

Napheys, George H. *The Physical Life of Woman: Advice to the Maiden, Wife, and Mother*. New stereotype ed. Philadelphia: J. F. Fergus and Co., 1873.

"Nauvoo." *Sangamo Journal*, 9 February 1841.

Nelson, Thomas A. R. *Polygamy in the Territorities [sic] of the United States, [To accompany Bill H. R. No 7], March 14, 1860*. Washington: N.p., 1860.

Norris, Moses. *Speech of the Hon. M. Norris of New Hampshire, in the United States Senate, March 3, 1845 on Nebraska and Kansas*. Washington: Printed at the Sentinel Office, 1854.

Olney, Oliver H. *The Absurdities of Mormonism Portrayed; Its Errors and Absurdities Exposed*. Hancock County, Ill.: N.p., 1843.

Orr, Adrian Van Brocklin. *Mormonism Dissected; or, Knavery "On Two Sticks" Exposed.* Bethania, Pa.: Printed by Reuben Chambers, 1841.

Parkman, Francis. "Religious Denominations in the United States." *Christian Examiner and Religious Miscellany*, September 1844, 235–47.

Parrish, Warren. "Mormonism." *The Evangelist*, 1 October 1838, 226–27.

Parsons, Tyler. *Mormon Fanaticism Exposed. A Compendium of the Book of Mormon, or Joseph Smith's Golden Bible.* Boston: Printed for the Author, 1841.

Partridge, George F., ed. "The Death of a Mormon Dictator: Letters of Massachusetts Mormons, 1843–1848." *New England Quarterly* 9 (December 1936): 583–617.

Paulos, Michael H., ed. *The Mormon Church on Trial: Transcripts of the Reed Smoot Hearings.* Salt Lake City: Signature Books, 2008.

Peterson, Charles J. "Mormonism and the Mormons." *Graham's Magazine*, May 1853, 531–40.

Pettigrew, David. "A History of David Pettigrew." David Pettigrew Papers, 1840–57, microfilm, Historical Department Archives, Church of Jesus Christ of Latter-day Saints, Salt Lake City.

Phelps, William W. "Free People of Color." *Evening and the Morning Star*, July 1833, 109.

Powell, John Wesley. *Report on the Lands of the Arid Region of the United States, With a More Detailed Account of the Lands of Utah. With Maps.* 2nd ed. Washington: Government Printing Office, 1879.

Pratt, Orson. "Celestial Marriage." In *Journal of Discourses by Brigham Young, President of the Church of Jesus Christ of Latter-Day Saints, His Two Counsellors, the Twelve Apostles, and Others.* 26 vols, 1:53–66. Liverpool: F. D. and S. W. Richards, 1854–86.

Pratt, Parley P. *Autobiography of Parley P. Pratt.* Edited by Parley P. Pratt. 3rd ed. Salt Lake City: Deseret Book Co., 1938.

———. *History of the Late Persecution Inflicted by the State of Missouri Upon the Mormons, in Which Ten Thousand American Citizens Were Robbed, Plundered, and Driven from the State, and Many Others Murdered, Martyred, &C. For Their Religion, and All This by Military Force, by Order of the Executive.* Detroit: Dawson and Bates, 1839.

———. *Mormonism Unveiled: Zion's Watchman Unmasked, and Its Editor, Mr. L. R. Sunderland, Exposed; Truth Vindicated; the Devil Mad, and Priestcraft in Danger.* New York: Printed for the Publisher, 1838.

———. *A Reply to Mr. Thomas Taylor's "Complete Failure," &C., and Mr. Richard Livesay's "Mormonism Exposed"* . . . Manchester, England: W. R. Thomas, 1840.

———. *A Voice of Warning and Instruction to All People, Containing a Declaration of the Faith and Doctrine of the Church of the Latter Day Saints, Commonly Called Mormons.* New York: Printed by W. Sandford, 1837.

Prideaux, Humphrey. *The True Nature of Imposture, Fully Displayed in the Life of Mahomet.* Fair Haven, Vt.: James Lyon, 1798.

The Proceedings of a Convention, Held at Carthage, in Hancock County, Ill., on Tuesday and Wednesday, October 1st and 2nd, 1845. Quincy, Ill.: Printed at the Quincy Whig Book and Job Office, 1845.

Rathbun, Valentine. *An Account of the Matter, Form, and Manner of a New and Strange Religion, Taught and Propagated by a Number of Europeans, Living in a Place Called Nisqueunia, in the State of New-York.* Providence, R.I.: Bennett Wheeler, 1781.

Reed, Andrew, and James Matheson. *A Narrative of the Visit to the American Churches, by the Deputation from the Congregational Union of England and Wales.* New York: Harper and Brothers, 1835.

Reese, David Meredith. *Humbugs of New-York: Being a Remonstrance Against Popular Delusion; Whether in Science, Philosophy, or Religion.* New York: John S. Taylor, 1838.

"'Regulating' the Mormonites." *Niles' Weekly Register,* 14 September 1833, 47–48.

Report of the Board of Visitors of the Boston Lunatic Hospital Containing a Statement of the Condition of That Institution, and Transmitting the Annual Report of the Superintendent, for 1849. Boston: J. H. Eastburn, City Printer, 1849.

Report of the Board of Visitors and of the Superintendent of the Boston Lunatic Hospital, for 1848. Boston: J. H. Eastburn, City Printer, 1849.

Report of the Medical Visitors of the Connecticut Retreat for the Insane, Presented to the Society May 13, 1830. Hartford: Hudson and Skinner, Printers, 1830.

Report of the Superintendent of the Boston Lunatic Hospital and Physician of the Public Institutions at South Boston. Boston: John H. Eastburn, City Printer, 1840.

Report of the Superintendent of the Boston Lunatic Hospital and Physician of the Public Institutions at South Boston. Boston: John H. Eastburn, City Printer, 1844.

Report of the Superintendent of the Boston Lunatic Hospital and Physician of the Public Institutions at South Boston. Boston: John H. Eastburn, City Printer, 1845.

Reports of the Board of Visitors, of the Trustees, and of the Superintendent of the New Hampshire Asylum for the Insane. Concord: Carroll and Baker, State Printers, 1843.

Reports of the Illinois State Hospital for the Insane. 1847–1862. Chicago: F. Fulton and Co., Book and Job Printers, 1863.

Reports and Other Documents Relating to the State Lunatic Hospital at Worcester, Mass. Boston: Dutton and Wentworth, Printers to the State, 1837.

Reports of the Trustees, Steward and Treasurer, and Superintendent of the Insane Hospital. Augusta, Maine: William T. Johnson, Printer to the State, 1851.

Reports of the Trustees and Superintendent of the Maine Insane Hospital. Augusta: Stevens and Sayward, Printers to the State, 1858.

Reynolds v. United States. 98 U.S. 145 (1879).

Richards, T. Addison. *Appleton's Illustrated Handbook of American Travel.* New York: D. Appleton and Co., 1857.

Rigdon, Sidney. *Oration Delivered by Mr. S. Rigdon, on the 4th of July, 1838, at Far West, Caldwell Country, Missouri.* Far West: Printed at the Journal Office, 1838.

Riley, I. Woodbridge. *The Founder of Mormonism: A Psychological Study of Joseph Smith, Jr.* New York: Dodd, Mead and Co., 1902.

Rio Grande Western Railway Company. *Valleys of the Great Salt Lake. Describing the Garden of Utah and the Two Great Cities of Salt Lake and Ogden. Issued under the*

Auspices of the Passenger Department of the Denver & Rio Grande and Rio Grande
    Western Railroads. Chicago: R. R. Donnelley and Sons Co., 1890.
Roberts, Brigham H. A Comprehensive History of the Church of Jesus Christ of Latter-
    Day Saints. 6 vols. 1930. Reprint, Provo: The Church of Jesus Christ of Latter-day
    Saints and Brigham Young University Press, 1965.
————. The Essential B. H. Roberts. Edited by Brigham D. Madsen. Classics in
    Mormon Thought, No. 6. Salt Lake City: Signature Books, 1999.
————. The Mormon Doctrine of Deity: The Roberts-Van Der Donckt Discussion, to
    Which Is Added a Discourse, Jesus Christ: The Revelation of God, Also a Collection
    of Authoritative Mormon Utterances on the Being and Nature of God. 1903. Reprint,
    Signature Mormon Classics. Salt Lake City: Signature Books, 1998.
Robinson, Stephen E. Are Mormons Christians? Salt Lake City: Bookcraft, 1991.
————. Believing Christ: The Parable of the Bicycle and Other Good News. Salt Lake
    City: Deseret Book Co., 1992.
Rupp, I. Daniel. He Pasa Ekklesia: An Original History of the Religious Denominations
    at Present Existing in the United States. Containing Authentic Accounts of
    Their Rise, Progress, Statistics and Doctrines. Written Expressly for the Work by
    Eminent Theological Professors, Ministers, and Lay-Members, of the Respective
    Denominations. Philadelphia: J. Y. Humphreys, 1844.
————. Religious Denominations in the United States: Their Past History, Present
    Condition, and Doctrines, Accurately Set Forth in Fifty-Three Carefully-Prepared
    Articles, Written by Eminent Clerical and Lay Authors Connected with the Respective
    Persuasions . . . Philadelphia: C. Desilver, 1861.
Schaff, Philip. America: A Sketch of Its Political, Social, and Religious Character. Edited
    by Perry Miller. The John Harvard Library. Cambridge: Harvard University Press,
    1961.
————. Church and State in the United States; or, The American Idea of Religious
    Liberty and Its Practical Effects. New York: Charles Scribner's Sons, 1888.
Schleiermacher, Friedrich. On Religion: Speeches to Its Cultured Despisers. 1799.
    Translated by John Oman. London: Kegan Paul, Trench, Trübner and Co., Ltd.,
    1893.
Seventeenth Annual Report of the Board of Trustees for the Benevolent Institutions, and
    of the Officers of the Ohio Institution for the Ohio Lunatic Asylum, to the Governor of
    Ohio. Columbus: Statesman Steam Press, 1856.
Seventh Report of the Medical Visitors of the Connecticut Retreat for the Insane,
    Presented to the Society May 1831. Hartford, Conn.: Hudson and Skinner, Printers,
    1831.
Sharp, Thomas. "Monsieur Violet and the Mormons." Warsaw Signal, 11 September
    1844.
————. "To the Public. Mormon Difficulties in Illinois." Warsaw Signal, 10 July 1844.
————. "Unparralleled [sic] Outrage at Nauvoo." Warsaw Signal, 12 June 1844.
Sixth Annual Report of the Managers of the State Lunatic Asylum. Albany: Weed,
    Parsons and Co., Public Printers, 1849.

Skinner, Dolphus. "Changes of Mormonism." *Evangelical Magazine and Gospel Advocate*, 17 March 1832, 87.

Skousen, Royal, ed. *The Book of Mormon: The Earliest Text*. New Haven: Yale University Press, 2009.

Smith, Ethan. *View of the Hebrews: 1825, 2nd Edition*. Edited by Charles D. Tate. Religious Studies Center Specialized Monograph Series. Provo: Religious Studies Center, Brigham Young University, 1996.

Smith, George D., ed. *An Intimate Chronicle: The Journals of William Clayton*. Trade ed. Salt Lake City: Signature Books, 1995.

Smith, Joseph, Jr. "An Extract of Revelation." *Elders' Journal of the Church of Jesus Christ of Latter Day Saints*, August 1838, 52–53.

———. "Extracts From a Revelation given to Joseph Smith, jr., Jan. 19th 1841." *Times and Seasons*, 1 June 1841, 424–29.

———. *History of the Church of Jesus Christ of Latter-Day Saints*. Edited by Brigham H. Roberts. 7 vols. Salt Lake City: Church of Jesus Christ of Latter-day Saints, 1902.

Smith, Joseph, Jr., Sidney Rigdon, and Hyrum Smith. "A Proclamation, to the Saints Scattered Abroad." *Times and Seasons*, 15 January 1841, 273–77.

Smith, Lucy Mack. *Biographical Sketches of Joseph Smith, the Prophet, and His Progenitors for Many Generations*. Liverpool: Published for Orson Pratt by S. W. Richards, 1853.

Smith, Truman. *Speech of Mr. Smith, of Conn., on the Bill "To Admit California into the Union—to Establish Territorial Governments for Utah and New Mexico, Making Proposals to Texas for the Establishment of the Western and Northern Boundaries." Delivered in the Senate of the United States, July 8, 1850*. Washington: Gideon and Co., Printers, 1850.

———. *Speech of Truman Smith, of Connecticut, on the Nebraska Question. Delivered in the Senate of the United States, February 10 and 11, 1854*. Washington: Printed by John T. and Lem. Towers, 1854.

Snow, Eliza R., and Others. "Great Indignation Meeting of the Ladies of Salt Lake City, to Protest Against the Passage of Cullom's Bill." *Deseret Evening News*, 19 January 1870.

Spaulding, Solomon. *Manuscript Found: The Complete Original "Spaulding Manuscript."* Edited by Kent P. Jackson. Religious Studies Center Specialized Monograph Series. Provo: Religious Studies Center, Brigham Young University, 1996.

Spicer, Tobias. *Autobiography of Rev. Tobias Spicer: Containing Incidents and Observations; Also Some Account of His Visit to England*. Boston: C. H. Peirce and Co., 1851.

"The Spirit." *Christian Palladium*, 1 September 1834, 148–49.

Stahle, Shaun D. "Pres. Hinckley Addresses Journalists." *Church News*, 20 September 1997, http://www.ldschurchnews.com/articles/29684/Pres-Hinckley-addresses-journalists.html. 6 December 2010.

Stenhouse, Fanny. *Exposé of Polygamy: A Lady's Life among the Mormons*. Edited by

Linda Wilcox DeSimone. Life Writings of Frontier Women, vol. 10. Logan: Utah State University Press, 2008.

———. *"Tell It All." The Story of a Life's Experience in Mormonism. An Autobiography: By Mrs. T. B. H. Stenhouse of Salt Lake City, for More Than Twenty Years the Wife of a Mormon Missionary and Elder. With Introductory Preface by Mrs. Harriet Beecher Stowe.* Hartford, Conn.: A. D. Worthington and Co., 1874.

Stone, William L. *Matthias and His Impostures; or, The Progress of Fanaticism. Illustrated in the Extraordinary Case of Robert Matthews, and Some of His Forerunners and Disciples.* New York: Harper and Brothers, 1835.

Strong, Josiah. *Our Country: Its Possible Future and Its Present Crisis.* Rev. ed. New York: Baker and Taylor Co., For the American Home Missionary Society, 1891.

Sunderland, La Roy. *Mormonism Exposed and Refuted.* New York: Piercy and Reed, Printers, 1838.

———. *Mormonism Exposed: In Which Is Shown the Monstrous Imposture, the Blasphemy, and the Wicked Tendency, of the Enormous Delusion, Advocated by a Professedly Religious Sect, Calling Themselves "Latter Day Saints."* New York: Printed and Published at the Office of the N. Y. Watchman, 1842.

Swartzell, William. *Mormonism Exposed, Being a Journal of a Residence in Missouri from the 28th of May to the 20th of August, 1838, Together with an Appendix, Containing the Revelations Concerning the Golden Bible, with Numerous Extracts from the 'Book of Covenants,' &C., &C.* Pittsburgh: O. Pekin, Published by the Author. A. Ingram Jr., Printer, 1840.

Tanner, Annie Clark. *A Mormon Mother: An Autobiography.* 3rd ed. Salt Lake City: Tanner Trust Fund, University of Utah Library, 1991.

Taylor, Amos. *A Narrative of the Strange Principles, Conduct and Character of the People Known by the Name of Shakers: Whose Errors Have Spread in Several Parts of North-America, but Are Beginning to Diminish, and Ought to Be Guarded Against.* Worcester, Mass.: Printed for the Author, 1782.

Third Annual Report of the Directors and Superintendent of the Ohio Lunatic Asylum, to the Fortieth General Assembly. December 13, 1841. Columbus: Samuel Medary, Printer to the State, 1841.

Third Annual Report of the Managers of the State Lunatic Asylum. Utica, N.Y.: N.p., 1846.

Third Annual Report of the Superintendent of the Maine Insane Hospital. Augusta: Severance and Dorr, Printers to the State, 1842.

Thompson, Joseph P. *Church and State in the United States.* Boston: James R. Osgood, 1873.

To the Anti-Mormon Citizens of Hancock and the Surrounding Counties . . . Warsaw, Ill.: Warsaw Signal Print, 1845.

Towle, Nancy. *Vicissitudes Illustrated, in the Experience of Nancy Towle, in Europe and America.* 2nd ed. Portsmouth, N.H.: Printed for the Authoress, by John Caldwell, 1833.

The True Lamplighter, and Aunt Mary's Cabin. Sketches of Franklin Gray, Queen

Victoria, Joe Smith and the Mormons, P. T. Barnum, Ward Trial in Kentucky, Wooden
   Nutmegs, John Burrill, Jona. Whilson. Boston: Published by Cushing, Perkins and
   Fay, 1854.

"Try the Spirits." *Times and Seasons*, 1 April 1842, 743–48.

Turner, Jonathan B. *Mormonism in All Ages; or, The Rise, Progress, and Causes of
   Mormonism; with the Biography of Its Author and Founder, Joseph Smith, Junior.*
   New York: Platt and Peters, 1842.

*Twentieth Annual Report of the State of the Asylum for the Relief of Persons Deprived of
   the Use of Their Reason.* Philadelphia: Brown and Sinquet, Printers, 1837.

*Twenty-Second Annual Report of the Officers of the Retreat for the Insane, at Hartford,
   Conn. May, 1846.* Hartford: Printed by Case, Tiffany and Burnham, 1846.

U.S. Congress. House Committee on the Territories. *The Condition of Utah. July 23,
   1866. Mr. James M. Ashley, from the Committee on the Territories, Made the Following
   Report. The Committee on the Territories to Whom Were Referred the Subjoined
   Resolutions, Have Had the Subject Matter Therein Named under Consideration, and
   Herewith Submit the Testimony of Such Witnesses as They Have Been Able to Bring
   before Them.* [Washington]: [Government Printing Office], 1866.

U.S. Senate. 26th Congress. 2nd Session. *Document Showing the Testimony Given
   Before the Judge of the Fifth Judicial Circuit of the State of Missouri, on the Trial of
   Joseph Smith, Jr., and Others, for High Treason, and Other Crimes Against That State,
   26th Cong., 2d Sess., Ordered to be Printed February 15, 1841.* Washington: Blair and
   Rives, Printers, 1841.

Union Pacific Railroad Company. *Sights and Scenes in Utah for Tourists. Compliments
   of the Passenger Department, Union Pacific System*, 2nd ed. Omaha, Neb.: E. L.
   Lomax, General Passenger Agent, Rand, McNally and Co., Printer, Chicago, 1890.

U.S. War Department. *Military Posts. Letter from the Secretary of War, in Answer to a
   Resolution of the House of the 5th December, Transmitting a Report of Inspection of
   Military Posts.* [Washington]: [Government Printing Office], 1867.

Vale, Gilbert. *Fanaticism; Its Source and Influence, Illustrated by the Simple Narrative of
   Isabella, in the Case of Matthias . . .* 2 vols. New York: G. Vale, 1835.

Vogel, Dan, ed. *Early Mormon Documents.* 5 vols. Salt Lake City: Signature Books,
   1996–2003.

"A Voice of Warning and Instruction to All People . . . By P. P. Pratt [book review]."
   Christian Examiner and General Review, November 1838, 270–72.

Voltaire (François-Marie Arouet). *Le Fanatisme Ou Mahomet Le Prophete.*
   Amsterdam: Jacques Desbordes, 1743.

Wade, Benjamin F. *In the Senate of the United States. February 15, 1863.—Ordered to
   Be Printed. Mr. Wade, from the Committee on Territories, Submitted the Following
   Report. The Committee on Territories, to Whom Was Referred the Resolution of
   the Senate of the 16th of January in Regard to the Suppression of the Publication
   of the Message of the Governor of the Territory of Utah, Have Had the Same under
   Consideration and Beg Leave to Report.* [Washington]: [Government Printing
   Office], 1863.

Wallace, Charles. *A Confession of the Awful and Bloody Transactions in the Life of Charles Wallace, the Fiend-Like Murderer of Miss Mary Rogers, the Beautiful Cigar Girl of Broadway, New York, Whose Fate Has for Several Years Been Wrapt in the Most Profound Mystery*. New Orleans: Published by E. E. Barclay and Co., 1851.

Ward, Austin N. (pseud.). *Male Life among the Mormons; or, The Husband in Utah: Detailing Sights and Scenes among the Mormons; with Remarks on Their Moral and Social Economy. By Austin N. Ward. Edited by Maria Ward. . . .* New York: Derby and Jackson, 1859.

Ward, Maria N. (pseud.). *Female Life among the Mormons. A Narrative of Many Years' Personal Experience. By the Wife of a Mormon Elder, Recently from Utah.* New York: J. C. Derby, 1855.

"Was Mohammed an Imposter or an Enthusiast?" *North American Review*, October 1846, 496–513.

Watson, Richard. *A Biblical and Theological Dictionary: Explanatory of the History, Manners, and Customs of the Jews, and Neighbouring Nations. With an Account of the Most Remarkable Places and Persons Mentioned in Sacred Scripture; an Exposition of the Principle Doctrines of Christianity; and Notices of Jewish and Christian Sects and Heresies.* New York: Published by B. Waugh and T. Mason for the Methodist Episcopal Church, 1832.

Weiser, R. "Mormonism the great Crater for the Fanaticism of all ages . . ." *Evangelical Review* 10 (1859): 80–100.

West, Benjamin. *Scriptural Cautions against Embracing a Religious Scheme, Taught by a Number of Europeans, Who Came from England to America, in the Year 1776, and Stile Themselves the Church, &C. &C.* Hartford, Conn.: Bavil Webster, 1783.

West, William S. *A Few Interesting Facts, Respecting the Rise Progress and Pretensions of the Mormons.* [Warren, Ohio?]: N.p., 1837.

Westergren, Bruce N., ed. *From Historian to Dissident: The Book of John Whitmer.* Salt Lake City: Signature Books, 1995.

Whitman, Jason. "The Book of Mormon." *The Unitarian*, January 1834, 40–50.

Whitmer, David. *An Address to All Believers in Christ.* Richmond, Mo.: David Whitmer, 1887.

Whitney, Helen Mar Kimball. *Plural Marriage, as Taught by the Prophet Joseph: A Reply to Joseph Smith, Editor of the Lamoni (Iowa) "Herald."* Salt Lake City: Printed at the Juvenile Instructor Office, 1882.

———. *Why We Practice Plural Marriage: By a "Mormon" Wife and Mother–Helen Mar Whitney.* Salt Lake City: Published at the Juvenile Instructor Office, 1884.

Whitney, Orson F. "Elder Orson F. Whitney." In *Conference Report* (October), 91–97. Salt Lake City: Church of Jesus Christ of Latter-day Saints, 1926.

Widtsoe, John A. *Joseph Smith as Scientist: A Contribution to Mormon Philosophy.* Salt Lake City: The General Board, Young Men's Mutual Improvement Associations, 1908.

———. *Rational Theology: As Taught by the Church of Jesus Christ of Latter-Day*

Saints. 1915. Reprint, Signature Mormon Classics. Salt Lake City: Signature Books, 1997.

Williams, Samuel. *Mormonism Exposed*. [Pittsburgh?]: N.p., 1842.

Williams, T. Harry, ed. *Hayes: The Diary of a President, 1875–1881. Covering the Disputed Election, the End of Reconstruction, and the Beginning of Civil Service*. New York: David McKay Co., Inc., 1964.

"Woman Suffrage." *Congressional Globe*, 17 February 1973, 1428.

Woodruff, Wilford. "Fulfillment of God's Word." In *Collected Discourses Delivered by President Wilford Woodruff, His Two Counselors, the Twelve Apostles, and Others*. Edited by Brian H. Stuy. 5 vols, 3:60–63. Burbank, Calif.: B. H. S. Publishing, 1989.

Wyl, Wilhelm. *Joseph Smith the Prophet, His Family and His Friends*. Salt Lake City: Tribune Pub. Co., 1886.

"The Yankee Mahomet." *American Whig Review*, June 1851, 554–64.

Young, Ann Eliza (Webb). *Wife No. 19; or, The Story of a Life in Bondage, Being a Complete Exposé of Mormonism, and Revealing the Sorrows, Sacrifices and Sufferings of Women in Polygamy, by Ann Eliza Young, Brigham Young's Apostate Wife. With Introductory Notes by John B. Gough and Mary A. Livermore*. Hartford, Conn., Chicago, Ill., Cincinnati: Dustin, Gilman and Co., 1875.

Young, Brigham. "Discourse by President Brigham Young." In *Journal of Discourses by Brigham Young, President of the Church of Jesus Christ of Latter-Day Saints, His Two Counsellors, the Twelve Apostles, and Others*. 26 vols, 18:235–49. Liverpool: F. D. and S. W. Richards, 1854–86.

Young, Joseph. "Remarks on Behalf of the Indians." In *Journal of Discourses by Brigham Young, President of the Church of Jesus Christ of Latter-Day Saints, His Two Counsellors, the Twelve Apostles, and Others*, 26 vols, 9:229–33. Liverpool: F. D. and S. W. Richards, 1854–86.

Secondary Sources

Alexander, Thomas G. *Mormonism in Transition: A History of the Latter-Day Saints, 1890–1930*. Illini Books ed. Urbana: University of Illinois, 1996.

———. Review of Will Bagley, *Blood of the Prophets. Brigham Young University Studies* 42, no. 1 (2003): 167–74.

———. *Things in Heaven and Earth: The Life and Times of Wilford Woodruff, a Mormon Prophet*. Salt Lake City: Signature Books, 1991.

Allen, James B. *No Toil Nor Labor Fear: The Story of William Clayton*. Biographies in Latter-day Saint History. Provo: Brigham Young University Press, 2002.

Allen, James B., Ronald K. Esplin, and David J. Whittaker. *Men with a Mission, 1837–1841: The Quorum of the Twelve Apostles in the British Isles*. Salt Lake City: Deseret Book Co., 1992.

Allen, James B., Ronald W. Walker, and David J. Whittaker. *Studies in Mormon History, 1830–1997: An Indexed Bibliography*. Urbana: University of Illinois Press, 2000.

Allison, Robert J. *The Crescent Obscured: The United States and the Muslim World, 1776–1815*. New York: Oxford University Press, 1995.

Anbinder, Tyler. *Nativism and Slavery: The Northern Know Nothings and the Politics of the 1850s*. New York: Oxford University Press, 1992.

Anderson, Devery S., and Gary J. Bergera, eds. *Joseph Smith's Quorum of the Anointed, 1842–1845: A Documentary History*. Salt Lake City: Signature Books, 2005.

Anderson, Richard L. *Investigating the Book of Mormon Witnesses*. Salt Lake City: Deseret Book Co., 1981.

———. "Joseph Smith's New York Reputation Reappraised." *Brigham Young University Studies* 10, no. 3 (Spring 1970): 283–314.

Anderson, Rodger I. *Joseph Smith's New York Reputation Reexamined*. Salt Lake City: Signature Books, 1990.

Arrington, Leonard J. *Great Basin Kingdom: An Economic History of the Latter-Day Saints, 1830–1900*. Cambridge: Harvard University Press, 1958.

———. "Joseph Smith, Builder of Ideal Communities." In *The Prophet Joseph: Essays on the Life and Mission of Joseph Smith*, edited by Larry C. Porter and Susan E. Black, 115–37. Salt Lake City: Deseret Book Co., 1988.

Arrington, Leonard J., and Davis Bitton. *The Mormon Experience: A History of the Latter-Day Saints*. 2nd ed. Urbana: University of Illinois Press, 1992.

Arrington, Leonard J., Feramorz Y. Fox, and Dean L. May. *Building the City of God: Community and Cooperation among the Mormons*. 2nd ed. Urbana: University of Illinois Press, 1992.

Arthur, David T. "Joshua V. Himes and the Cause of Adventism." In *The Disappointed: Millerism and Millenarianism in the Nineteenth Century*, edited by Ronald L. Numbers and Jonathan L. Butler, 36–58. Knoxville: University of Tennessee Press, 1993.

Asad, Talal. *Genealogies of Religion: Discipline and Reasons of Power in Christianity and Islam*. Baltimore: Johns Hopkins University Press, 1993.

Backman, Milton V. *The Heavens Resound: A History of the Latter-Day Saints in Ohio, 1830–1838*. Salt Lake City: Deseret Book Co., 1983.

Bagley, Will. *Blood of the Prophets: Brigham Young and the Massacre at Mountain Meadows*. Norman: University of Oklahoma Press, 2002.

Bainbridge, William Sims. "Religious Insanity in America: The Official Nineteenth-Century Theory." *Sociological Analysis* 45, no. 3 (Fall 1984): 223–39.

Barlow, Philip. *Mormons and the Bible: The Place of the Latter-Day Saints in American Religion*. Religion in America. New York: Oxford University Press, 1991.

Baugh, Alexander L. *A Call to Arms: The 1838 Mormon Defense of Northern Missouri*, Dissertations in Latter-Day Saint History. Provo: Joseph Fielding Smith Institute of Latter-day Saint History, Brigham Young University Studies, 2000.

Bederman, Gail. *Manliness & Civilization: A Cultural History of Gender and Race in the United States, 1880–1917*. Women in Culture and Society. Chicago: University of Chicago Press, 1995.

Ben-Yehuda, Nachman. "Witchcraft and the Occult as Boundary Maintenance Devices." In *Religion, Science, and Magic: In Concert and in Conflict*, edited by Jacob Neusner, Ernest S. Frerichs, and Paul Virgil McCracken Flesher, 229–60. New York: Oxford University Press, 1989.

Bennett, Richard E. *We'll Find the Place: The Mormon Exodus, 1846–1948*. Salt Lake City: Deseret Book Co., 1997.

Bennett, Richard E., Susan Easton Black, and Donald Q. Cannon. *The Nauvoo Legion in Illinois: A History of the Mormon Militia, 1841–1846*. Norman, Okla.: Arthur H. Clark Co., 2010.

Bigler, David L. *Forgotten Kingdom: The Mormon Theocracy in the American West, 1847–1896*. Kingdom in the West: The Mormons and the American Frontier, vol. 2. Edited by Will Bagley. Spokane, Wash.: Arthur H. Clark Co., 1998.

Bitton, Davis. "B. H. Roberts at the World Parliament of Religion, 1893 Chicago." *Sunstone* 7, no. 1 (January-February 1982): 46–51.

Blomberg, Craig, and Stephen E. Robinson. *How Wide the Divide?: A Mormon & an Evangelical in Conversation*. Downers Grove, Ill.: InterVarsity Press, 1997.

Bloom, Harold. *The American Religion: The Emergence of the Post-Christian Nation*. New York: Simon and Schuster, 1992.

Blum, Edward J. *Reforging the White Republic: Race, Religion, and American Nationalism, 1865–1898*. Conflicting Worlds: New Dimensions of the American Civil War. Edited by T. Michael Parrish. Baton Rouge: Louisiana State University Press, 2005.

Bowman, Matthew. "The Crisis of Mormon Christology: History Progress, and Protestantism, 1880–1930." *Fides et Historia: Journal of the Conference on Faith and History* 40, no. 2 (Summer-Fall 2008): 1–25.

Bowman, Matthew, and Samuel Brown. "Reverend Buck's *Theological Dictionary* and the Struggle to Define American Evangelicalism, 1802–1851." *Journal of the Early Republic* 29, no. 3 (Fall 2009): 441–73.

Boyer, Paul. *When Time Shall Be No More: Prophecy Belief in Modern American Culture*. Studies in Cultural History. Cambridge: Belknap Press of Harvard University Press, 1992.

Bradley, Martha Sonntag. "Creating the Sacred Space of Zion." *Journal of Mormon History* 31, no. 1 (Spring 2005): 1–30.

Breisach, Ernst. *Historiography: Ancient, Medieval, and Modern*. 3rd ed. Chicago: University of Chicago Press, 2007.

Brodie, Fawn M. *No Man Knows My History: The Life of Joseph Smith*. New York: Alfred A. Knopf, 1945.

Brooke, John L. *The Refiner's Fire: The Making of Mormon Cosmology, 1644–1844*. New York: Cambridge University Press, 1994.

Buckley, Thomas E. *Church and State in Revolutionary Virginia, 1776–1787*. Charlottesville: University Press of Virginia, 1977.

Bunker, Gary L., and Davis Bitton. *The Mormon Graphic Image, 1834–1914: Cartoons,*

Caricatures, and Illustrations. University of Utah Publications in the American West. Salt Lake City: University of Utah Press, 1983.

Burris, John P. *Exhibiting Religion: Colonialism and Spectacle at International Expositions, 1851–1893.* Studies in Religion and Culture. Edited by Frank Burch Brown, Gary L. Ebersole, and Edith Wyschogrod. Charlottesville: University Press of Virginia, 2001.

Bushman, Claudia L. "Mormon Domestic Life in the 1870s: Pandemonium or Arcadia?" In *The Collected Leonard J. Arrington Mormon History Lectures,* 91–118. Logan: Special Collections and Archives, University Libraries, Utah State University, 2005.

Bushman, Richard Lyman. *Joseph Smith and the Beginnings of Mormonism.* Urbana: University of Illinois Press, 1984.

———. "A Joseph Smith for the Twenty-first Century." *Brigham Young University Studies* 40, no. 3 (2001): 155–71.

———. *Joseph Smith: Rough Stone Rolling.* New York: Alfred A. Knopf, 2005.

———. "Making Space for the Mormons." In *The Collected Leonard J. Arrington Mormon History Lectures,* 30–53. Logan: Special Collections and Archives, Utah State University Libraries, 2004.

———. "Mormon Persecutions in Missouri, 1833." *Brigham Young University Studies* 3, no. 1 (Autumn 1960): 11–20.

———. "Mormonism and Politics: Are They Compatible?" Session Comments, The Pew Forum on Religion and Public Life, event transcript, 14 May 2007, http://pewforum.org/events/?EventID=148. 22 January 2008.

———. "The Visionary World of Joseph Smith." *Brigham Young University Studies* 37, no. 1 (1997–98): 183–204.

Butler, Jon. *Awash in a Sea of Faith: Christianizing the American People.* Studies in Cultural History. Cambridge: Harvard University Press, 1992.

———. "Historiographical Heresy: Catholicism as a Model for American Religious History." In *Belief in History: Innovative Approaches to European and American Religion,* edited by Thomas Kselman, 286–309. Notre Dame, Ind.: University of Notre Dame Press, 1991.

Carwardine, Richard. "Religion and National Construction in the Age of Lincoln." *Journal of Mormon History* 36, no. 2 (Spring 2010): 29–53.

Chidester, David. *Authentic Fakes: Religion and American Popular Culture.* Berkeley, Calif.: University of California Press, 2005.

———. *Savage Systems: Colonialism and Comparative Religion in Southern Africa.* Studies in Religion and Culture. Charlottesville: University Press of Virginia, 1996.

Christian, Lewis Clark. "A Study of Mormon Knowledge of the American Far West Prior to the Exodus, 1830–February 1846." M.A. thesis, Brigham Young University, 1972.

Clark, Elizabeth A. *History, Theory, Text: Historians and the Linguistic Turn.* Cambridge: Harvard University Press, 2004.

Coates, Lawrence. Review of Will Bagley, *Blood of the Prophets*. *Brigham Young University Studies* 42, no. 1 (2003): 153–58.

Cohen, Charles L. "The Construction of the Mormon People." *Journal of Mormon History* 32, no. 1 (Spring 2006): 25–64.

Colas, Dominique. *Civil Society and Fanaticism: Conjoined Histories*. Translated by Amy Jacobs. Mestizo Spaces. Edited by V. Y. Mudimbe. Stanford, Calif.: Stanford University Press, 1997.

Compton, Todd. *In Sacred Loneliness: The Plural Wives of Joseph Smith*. Salt Lake City: Signature Books, 1997.

Conkin, Paul K. *American Originals: Homemade Varieties of Christianity*. Chapel Hill: University of North Carolina Press, 1997.

Cook, Lyndon W. *William Law: Biographical Essay, Nauvoo Diary, Correspondence, Interview*. Orem, Utah: Grandin Book Co., 1994.

———. "William Law, Nauvoo Dissenter." *Brigham Young University Studies* 22, no. 1 (Winter 1982): 47–72.

Copeland, Lee. "Speaking in Tongues in the Restoration Churches." *Dialogue: A Journal of Mormon Thought* 24, no. 1 (Spring 1991): 13–33.

Corrigan, John, and Lynn S. Neal, eds. *Religious Intolerance in America: A Documentary History*. Chapel Hill: University of North Carolina Press, 2010.

Crabtree, Sarah. "'A Beautiful and Practical Lesson of Jurisprudence': The Transatlantic Quaker Ministry in an Age of Revolution." *Radical History Review* 99 (Fall 2007): 51–79.

Crawley, Peter L. Foreword to *The Essential Parley P. Pratt*. Classics in Mormon Thought, No. 1. Salt Lake City: Signature Books, 1990.

Crawley, Peter L., and Richard L. Anderson. "The Political and Social Realities of Zion's Camp." *Brigham Young University Studies* 14, no. 4 (Summer 1974): 406–20.

Curry, Thomas J. *The First Freedoms: Church and State in America to the Passage of the First Amendment*. New York: Oxford University Press, 1986.

Curtis, Heather D. *Faith in the Great Physician: Suffering and Divine Healing in American Culture, 1860–1900*. Baltimore: Johns Hopkins University Press, 2007.

Davies, Douglas J. *An Introduction to Mormonism*. Cambridge: Cambridge University Press, 2003.

———. "World Religion: Dynamics and Constraints." *Brigham Young University Studies* 44, no. 4 (2005): 253–70.

Davis, David B. "The New England Origins of Mormonism." *New England Quarterly* 26, no. 2 (June 1953): 147–68.

———. "Some Themes of Counter-Subversion: An Analysis of Anti-Masonic, Anti-Catholic, and Anti-Mormon Literature." *Mississippi Valley Historical Review* 47, no. 2 (September 1960): 205–24.

Daynes, Kathryn M. *More Wives Than One: Transformation of the Mormon Marriage System, 1840–1910*. Urbana: University of Illinois Press, 2001.

Delano, Sterling F. *Brook Farm: The Dark Side of Utopia*. Cambridge: Belknap Press, 2004.

Eliason, Eric A. Introduction to *Mormons and Mormonism: An Introduction to an American World Religion*, edited by Eric A. Eliason, 1–21. Urbana: University of Illinois Press, 2001.

Epperson, Steven. *Mormons and Jews: Early Mormon Theologies of Israel*. Salt Lake City: Signature Books, 1992.

Esplin, Ronald K. "'A Place Prepared': Joseph, Brigham and the Quest for Promised Refuge in the West." *Journal of Mormon History* 9 (1982): 85–111.

Fales, Susan L., and Chad J. Flake, comps. *Mormons and Mormonism in U.S. Government Documents: A Bibliography*. Salt Lake City: University of Utah Press, 1989.

Farmer, Jared. *On Zion's Mount: Mormons, Indians, and the American Landscape*. Cambridge: Harvard University Press, 2008.

Feldman, Noah. "What Is It about Mormonism?" *New York Times Magazine*, 6 January 2008, http://www.nytimes.com/2008/01/06/magazine/06mormonism-t.html. 18 November 2010.

Firmage, Edwin B., and Richard C. Mangrum. *Zion in the Courts: A Legal History of the Church of Jesus Christ of Latter-Day Saints, 1830–1900*. Urbana: University of Illinois Press, 1988.

Fitzgerald, Timothy. *The Ideology of Religious Studies*. New York: Oxford University Press, 2000.

Flake, Chad J., and Larry W. Draper, eds. *A Mormon Bibliography, 1830–1930: Books, Pamphlets, Periodicals, and Broadsides relating to the First Century of Mormonism*. 2nd ed. 2 vols. Provo: Religious Studies Center, Brigham Young University, 2004.

Flake, Kathleen. "The Mormon Corridor: Utah and Idaho." In *Religion and Public Life in the Mountain West: Sacred Landscapes in Transition*, edited by Jan Shipps and Mark Silk, 91–114. Religion by Region. Walnut Creek, Calif.: AltaMira Press, 2004.

———. *The Politics of American Religious Identity: The Seating of Senator Reed Smoot, Mormon Apostle*. Chapel Hill: University of North Carolina Press, 2004.

Flanders, Robert Bruce. *Nauvoo: Kingdom on the Mississippi*. Urbana: University of Illinois Press, 1965.

Fleming, Stephen J. "The Religious Heritage of the British Northwest and the Rise of Mormonism." *Church History: Studies in Christianity and Culture* 77, no. 1 (March 2008): 73–104.

Fluhman, J. Spencer. "An 'American Mahomet': Joseph Smith, Muhammad, and the Problem of Prophets in Antebellum America." *Journal of Mormon History* 34, no. 3 (Summer 2008): 23–45.

Foster, Craig L. *Penny Tracts and Polemics: A Critical Analysis of Anti-Mormon Pamphleteering in Great Britain, 1837–1860*. Salt Lake City: Greg Kofford Books, 2002.

Foster, Gaines M. *Moral Reconstruction: Christian Lobbyists and the Federal Legislation of Morality, 1865–1920*. Chapel Hill: University of North Carolina Press, 2002.

Foster, Lawrence. "Career Apostates: Reflections on the Works of Jerald and Sandra Tanner." *Dialogue: A Journal of Mormon Thought* 17, no. 2 (Summer 1984): 35–60.

———. *Religion and Sexuality: The Shakers, the Mormons, and the Oneida Community*. Illini Books ed. Urbana: University of Illinois Press, 1984.

Franchot, Jenny. *Roads to Rome: The Antebellum Protestant Encounter with Catholicism*. The New Historicism: Studies in Cultural Poetics, vol. 28. Berkeley: University of California Press, 1994.

Francis, Richard. *Transcendental Utopias: Individual and Community at Brook Farm, Fruitlands, and Walden*. Ithaca: Cornell University Press, 1997.

Garrett, Clarke. *Spirit Possession and Popular Religion: From the Camisards to the Shakers*. Baltimore: Johns Hopkins University Press, 1987.

Gentry, Leland H. "The Danite Band of 1838." *Brigham Young University Studies* 14, no. 4 (Summer 1974): 421–50.

Gentry, Leland H., and Todd M. Compton. *Fire and Sword: A History of the Latter-day Saints in Northern Missouri, 1836–39*. Salt Lake City: Greg Kofford Books, 2011.

Gilje, Paul A. *Rioting in America*. Interdisciplinary Studies in History. Bloomington: Indiana University Press, 1996.

Givens, Terryl L. *By the Hand of Mormon: The American Scripture That Launched a New World Religion*. Religion in America. New York: Oxford University Press, 2002.

———. *The Viper on the Hearth: Mormons, Myths, and the Construction of Heresy*. New York: Oxford University Press, 1997.

Goetzmann, William H. *Beyond the Revolution: A History of American Thought from Paine to Pragmatism*. New York: Basic Books, 2009.

Goldstein, Eric L. *The Price of Whiteness: Jews, Race, and American Identity*. Princeton: Princeton University Press, 2006.

Gomez, Michael A. *Exchanging Our Country Marks: The Transformation of African Identities in the Colonial and Antebellum South*. Chapel Hill: University of North Carolina Press, 1998.

Goodheart, Lawrence B. *Mad Yankees: The Hartford Retreat for the Insane and Nineteenth-Century Psychiatry*. Amherst: University of Massachusetts Press, 2003.

Goodstein, Laurie. "Huckabee Is Not Alone in Ignorance on Mormonism." *New York Times*, 14 December 2007, http://www.nytimes.com/2007/12/14/us/politics/14mormon.html. 18 November 2010.

Gordon, Sarah Barringer. *The Mormon Question: Polygamy and Constitutional Conflict in Nineteenth-Century America*. Studies in Legal History. Chapel Hill: University of North Carolina Press, 2002.

Graham, Stephen R. *Cosmos in the Chaos: Philip Schaff's Interpretation of Nineteenth-Century American Religion*. Grand Rapids, Mich.: Wm. B. Eerdmans, 1995.

Green, Arnold H. "Mormonism and Islam: From Polemics to Mutual Respect and Cooperation." *Brigham Young University Studies* 40, no. 4 (2001): 199–220.

———. "The Muhammad–Joseph Smith Comparison: Subjective Metaphor or a Sociology of Prophethood." In *Mormons and Muslims: Spiritual Foundations and Modern Manifestations*, edited by Spencer J. Palmer, 63–84. Religious Studies Monograph Series, vol. 8. Provo: Religious Studies Center, Brigham Young University, 1983.

Green, Arnold H., and Lawrence P. Goldrup. "Joseph Smith, an American Muhammad? An Essay on the Perils of Historical Analogy." *Dialogue: A Journal of Mormon Thought* 6, no. 1 (Spring 1971): 46–58.

Green, Steven K. *The Second Disestablishment: Church and State in Nineteenth-Century America.* New York: Oxford University Press, 2010.

Grimsted, David. *American Mobbing, 1828–1861: Toward Civil War.* New York: Oxford University Press, 1998.

———. "Early America Confronts Arabian Deys and Nights." *Reviews in American History* 24, no. 2 (1996): 226–31.

Grow, Matthew J. "The Whore of Babylon and the Abomination of Abominations: Nineteenth-Century Catholic and Mormon Mutual Perceptions and Religious Identity." *Church History: Studies in Christianity and Culture* 73, no. 1 (March 2004): 139–67.

Guyatt, Nicholas. *Providence and the Invention of the United States, 1607–1876.* New York: Cambridge University Press, 2007.

Hall, David D. *Worlds of Wonder, Days of Judgment: Popular Religious Belief in Early New England.* Cambridge: Harvard University Press, 1989.

Hallwas, John E., and Roger D. Launius, eds. *Cultures in Conflict: A Documentary History of the Mormon War in Illinois.* Logan: Utah State University Press, 1995.

Halttunen, Karen. *Confidence Men and Painted Women: A Study of Middle-Class Culture in America, 1830–1870.* Yale Historical Publications. New Haven: Yale University Press, 1982.

Hamburger, Philip. *Separation of Church and State.* Cambridge: Harvard University Press, 2002.

Hamilton, C. Mark. *Nineteenth-Century Mormon Architecture and City Planning.* New York: Oxford University Press, 1995.

Hansen, Klaus J. *Quest for Empire: The Political Kingdom of God and the Council of Fifty in Mormon History.* East Lansing: Michigan State University Press, 1967.

Hardy, B. Carmon. *Solemn Covenant: The Mormon Polygamous Passage.* Urbana: University of Illinois Press, 1992.

———, ed. *Doing the Works of Abraham: Mormon Polygamy, Its Origin, Practice, and Demise.* Kingdom in the West: The Mormons and the American Frontier, vol. 9. Edited by Will Bagley. Norman, Okla.: Arthur H. Clark Co., 2007.

Harper, Steven C. "'Dictated by Christ': Joseph Smith and the Politics of Revelation." *Journal of the Early Republic* 26, no. 2 (Summer 2006): 275–304.

———. "Evaluating the Book of Mormon Witnesses." *Religious Educator* 11, no. 2 (2010): 37–49.

———. "Infallible Proofs, Both Human and Divine: The Persuasiveness of Mormonism for Early Converts." *Religion and American Culture* 10, no. 1 (Winter 2000): 99–118.

———. "Thomas Müntzer and the Radical Reformation." In *Prelude to the Restoration: From Apostasy to the Restored Church,* 59–69. The 33rd Annual

Sidney B. Sperry Symposium. Salt Lake City and Provo: Deseret Book Co. and
Religious Studies Center, Brigham Young University, 2004.

Harrison, Peter. *"Religion" and the Religions in the English Enlightenment*. Cambridge:
Cambridge University Press, 1990.

Hatch, Nathan O. *The Democratization of American Christianity*. New Haven: Yale
University Press, 1989.

Haude, Sigrun. *In the Shadow of "Savage Wolves": Anabaptist Münster and the German
Reformation during the 1530's*. Studies in Central European Histories. Boston:
Humanities Press International, 2000.

Hedges, Andrew H. "The Refractory Abner Cole." In *Revelation, Reason, and Faith:
Essays in Honor of Truman G. Madsen*, edited by Donald W. Parry, Daniel C.
Peterson, and Stephen D. Ricks, 447–75. Provo: Foundation for Ancient Research
and Mormon Studies, 2002.

Heyrman, Christine Leigh. *Southern Cross: The Beginnings of the Bible Belt*. New York:
Alfred A. Knopf, 1997.

Hill, Marvin S. "Cultural Crisis in the Mormon Kingdom: A Reconsideration of the
Causes of Kirtland Dissent." *Church History* 49, no. 3 (September 1980): 286–97.

Hill, Marvin S., C. Keith Rooker, and Larry T. Wimmer. "The Kirtland Economy
Revisited: A Market Critique of Sectarian Economics." *Brigham Young University
Studies* 17, no. 4 (Summer 1977): 391–475.

Hill, Teresa Lynne. "Religion, Madness and the Asylum: A Study of Medicine and
Culture in New England, 1820–1840." Ph.D. diss., Brown University, 1991.

Hinton, Wayne K., and Stephen Roberds. "Public Opinion, Culture, and Religion in
Utah." In *Utah in the Twentieth Century*, edited by Brian Q. Cannon and Jessie L.
Embry, 227–44. Logan: Utah State University Press, 2009.

Holifield, E. Brooks. *Theology in America: Christian Thought from the Age of the
Puritans to the Civil War*. New Haven: Yale University Press, 2003.

Howe, Daniel W. *What Hath God Wrought: The Transformation of America, 1815–1848*.
Oxford History of the United States. Edited by David M. Kennedy. New York:
Oxford University Press, 2007.

Hughes, Richard T. "Two Restoration Traditions: Mormons and the Churches of
Christ in the Nineteenth Century." In *The Mormon History Association's Tanner
Lectures: The First Twenty Years*, edited by Dean L. May and Reid L. Neilson, 29–44.
Urbana: University of Illinois Press, 2006.

Hunt, Lynn, Margaret C. Jacob, and W. W. Mijnhardt. *The Book That Changed Europe:
Picart and Bernard's Religious Ceremonies of the World*. Cambridge: Belknap Press
of Harvard University Press, 2010.

Hutchison, William R. *Religious Pluralism in America: The Contentious History of a
Founding Ideal*. New Haven: Yale University Press, 2003.

Introvigne, Massimo. "Old Wine in New Bottles: The Story behind Fundamentalist
Anti-Mormonism." *Brigham Young University Studies* 35, no. 3 (1995–96): 45–73.

———. "The Devil Makers: Contemporary Evangelical Fundamentalist Anti-

Mormonism." *Dialogue: A Journal of Mormon Thought* 27, no. 1 (Spring 1994): 153–69.

Jackson, Carl T. *The Oriental Religions and American Thought.* No. 55, Contributions in American Studies. Westport, Conn.: Greenwood Press, 1981.

Jackson, Richard H. "The Mormon Village: Genesis and Antecedents of the City of Zion Plan." *Brigham Young University Studies* 17, no. 2 (Winter 1977): 223–40.

Jacobson, Matthew Frye. *Barbarian Virtues: The United States Encounters Foreign Peoples at Home and Abroad, 1876–1917.* New York: Hill and Wang, 2000.

Johnson, Paul E., and Sean Wilentz. *The Kingdom of Matthias: A Story of Sex and Salvation in 19th-Century America.* New York: Oxford University Press, 1994.

Jones, Megan Sanborn. *Performing American Identity in Anti-Mormon Melodrama.* American Popular History and Culture. New York: Routledge, 2009.

Juhnke, William E. "Anabaptism and Mormonism: A Study in Comparative History." *John Whitmer Historical Association Journal* 2 (1982): 38–46.

Juster, Susan. *Doomsayers: Anglo-American Prophecy in the Age of Revolution.* Early American Studies. Philadelphia: University of Pennsylvania Press, 2003.

Kent, John. *Wesley and the Wesleyans.* Cambridge: Cambridge University Press, 2002.

Kerber, Linda K. *Women of the Republic: Intellect and Ideology in Revolutionary America.* Chapel Hill: University of North Carolina Press, 1980.

Kidd, Colin. *The Forging of Races: Race and Scripture in the Protestant Atlantic World, 1600–2000.* New York: Cambridge University Press, 2006.

Kidd, Thomas S. *American Christians and Islam.* Princeton: Princeton University Press, 2009.

———. "'Is It Worse to Follow Mahomet Than the Devil?': Early American Uses of Islam." *Church History: Studies in Christianity and Culture* 72, no. 4 (December 2003): 766–90.

Kimball, Stanley B. "The Anthon Transcript: People, Primary Sources, and Problems." *Brigham Young University Studies* 10, no. 3 (Spring 1970): 325–52.

Krahn, Cornelius. *Dutch Anabaptism: Origin, Spread, Life and Thought (1450–1600).* The Hague: Martinus Nijhoff, 1968.

Kuper, Adam. *The Invention of Primitive Society: Transformations of an Illusion.* London: Routledge, 1988.

Lambert, Frank. *The Barbary Wars: American Independence in the Atlantic World.* New York: Hill and Wang, 2005.

———. *The Founding Fathers and the Place of Religion in America.* Princeton: Princeton University Press, 2003.

Larson, Gustive O. *The "Americanization" of Utah for Statehood.* San Marino, Calif.: Huntington Library, 1971.

Launius, Roger D. "Anti-Mormonism in Illinois: Thomas C. Sharp's Unfinished History of the Mormon War, 1845." *Journal of Mormon History* 15 (1989): 27–45.

Leonard, Glen M. *Nauvoo: A Place of Peace, a People of Promise.* Salt Lake City and Provo: Deseret Book Co. and Brigham Young University Press, 2002.

Leone, Mark P. "Mormon 'Peculiarity': Recapitulation of Subordination." In *Persistent*

Peoples: Cultural Enclaves in Perspective, edited by George Pierre Castile and Gilbert Kushner, 78–85. Tucson: University of Arizona Press, 1981.

LeSueur, Stephen C. *The 1838 Mormon War in Missouri*. Columbia: University of Missouri Press, 1987.

Limerick, Patricia N. "Peace Initiative: Using the Mormons to Rethink Ethnicity in American Life." *Journal of Mormon History* 21, no. 2 (Fall 1995): 1–30.

Linker, Damon. "The Big Test: Taking Mormonism Seriously." *New Republic*, 15 January 2007, http://www.tnr.com/article/politics/the-big-test. 18 November 2010.

Lovejoy, David S. *Religious Enthusiasm in the New World: Heresy to Revolution*. Cambridge: Harvard University Press, 1985.

Lyman, Edward L. *Political Deliverance: The Mormon Quest for Utah Statehood*. Urbana: University of Illinois Press, 1986.

Lyon, James K. "Mormonism and Islam through the Eyes of a 'Universal Historian.'" *Brigham Young University Studies* 40, no. 4 (2001): 221–36.

Madsen, Gordon A. "Joseph Smith and the Missouri Court of Inquiry: Austin A. King's Quest for Hostages." *Brigham Young University Studies* 43, no. 4 (2004): 92–136.

Manuel, Frank E. *The Eighteenth Century Confronts the Gods*. Cambridge: Harvard University Press, 1959.

Marini, Stephen A. *Radical Sects of Revolutionary New England*. Cambridge: Harvard University Press, 1982.

Marr, Timothy. *The Cultural Roots of American Islamicism*. New York: Cambridge University Press, 2006.

Mason, Patrick Q. *The Mormon Menace: Violence and Anti-Mormonism in the Postbellum South*. New York: Oxford University Press, 2011.

———. "Opposition to Polygamy in the Postbellum South." *Journal of Southern History* 76, no. 3 (August 2010): 541–78.

Masuzawa, Tomoko. *The Invention of World Religions; or, How European Universalism Was Preserved in the Language of Pluralism*. Chicago: University of Chicago Press, 2005.

Mathewes, Charles, and Christopher McKnight Nichols, eds. *Prophesies of Godlessness: Predictions of America's Imminent Secularization from the Puritans to the Present Day*. New York: Oxford University Press, 2008.

Mauss, Armand L. *All Abraham's Children: Changing Mormon Conceptions of Race and Lineage*. Urbana: University of Illinois Press, 2003.

———. *The Angel and the Beehive: The Mormon Struggle with Assimilation*. Urbana: University of Illinois Press, 1994.

Mazur, Eric Michael. *The Americanization of Religious Minorities: Confronting the Constitutional Order*. Baltimore: Johns Hopkins University Press, 1999.

McCue, Robert J. "Similarities and Differences in the Anabaptist Restitution and the Mormon Restoration." M.A. thesis, Brigham Young University, 1959.

McCutcheon, Russell T. *Manufacturing Religion: The Discourse on Sui Generis Religion and the Politics of Nostalgia*. New York: Oxford University Press, 1997.

McDermott, Gerald R. *Jonathan Edwards Confronts the Gods: Christian Theology, Enlightenment Religion, and Non-Christian Faiths*. New York: Oxford University Press, 1999.

Millet, Robert L., and Gerald R. McDermott. *Claiming Christ: A Mormon-Evangelical Debate*. Grand Rapids, Mich.: Brazos Press, 2007.

Moore, R. Laurence. *Religious Outsiders and the Making of Americans*. New York: Oxford University Press, 1986.

———. *Selling God: American Religion in the Marketplace of Culture*. New York: Oxford University Press, 1994.

Neilson, Reid L. *Exhibiting Mormonism: Latter-day Saints and the 1893 Chicago World's Fair*. Religion in America. New York: Oxford University Press, 2011.

Nelson, Marie H. "Anti-Mormon Mob Violence and the Rhetoric of Law and Order in Early Mormon History." *Legal Studies Forum* 21, no. 2 (1997): 353–88.

Nelson, William O. "Anti-Mormon Publications." In *Encyclopedia of Mormonism*, edited by Daniel H. Ludlow, 1:45–52. New York: Macmillan, 1992.

Neusner, Jacob, Ernest S. Frerichs, and Paul Virgil McCracken Flesher, eds. *Religion, Science, and Magic: In Concert and in Conflict*. New York: Oxford University Press, 1989.

Noll, Mark A. *America's God: From Jonathan Edwards to Abraham Lincoln*. New York: Oxford University Press, 2002.

———. "A Jesuit Interpretation of Mid-Nineteenth-Century America: 'Mormonism in Connection with Modern Protestantism.'" *Brigham Young University Studies* 45, no. 3 (2006): 39–74.

Novick, Peter. *That Noble Dream: The "Objectivity Question" and the American Historical Profession*. Ideas in Context. Edited by Richard Rorty, J. B. Schneewind, Quentin Skinner, and Wolf Lepenies. Cambridge: Cambridge University Press, 1988.

Numbers, Ronald L., and Janet S. Numbers. "Millerism and Madness: A Study of 'Religious Insanity' in Nineteenth-Century America." In *The Disappointed: Millerism and Millenarianism in the Nineteenth Century*, edited by Ronald L. Numbers and Jonathan M. Butler, 92–118. Knoxville: University of Tennessee Press, 1993.

Oaks, Dallin H., and Marvin S. Hill. *Carthage Conspiracy: The Trial of the Accused Assassins of Joseph Smith*. Urbana: University of Illinois Press, 1975.

Olsen, Steven L. "Joseph Smith's Concept of the City of Zion." In *Joseph Smith: The Prophet, the Man*, edited by Susan E. Black and Charles D. Tate, 203–12. Religious Studies Center Monograph Series, vol. 17. Provo: Religious Studies Center, Brigham Young University, 1993.

Oman, Nathan B. "Natural Law and the Rhetoric of Empire: *Reynolds v. United States*, Polygamy, and Imperialism." *Washington University Law Review* 88, no. 3 (2011): 661–706.

Orsi, Robert A. "A 'Bit of Judgment.'" *Harvard Divinity Bulletin* 32, vol. 3 (Summer 2004), http://www.hds.harvard.edu/news/bulletin/articles/orsi_et_al.html. 19 April 2010.

Palmer, Grant H. *An Insider's View of Mormon Origins*. Salt Lake City: Signature Books, 2002.

Park, Benjamin E. "'A Uniformity So Complete': Early Mormon Angelology." *Intermountain West Journal of Religious Studies* 2, no. 1 (Summer 2010): 1–37.

Patterson, Sara M. "'A P.O. Box and a Desire to Witness For Jesus': Identity and Mission in the Ex-Mormons for Jesus/Saints Alive in Jesus, 1975–90." *Journal of Mormon History* 36, no. 3 (Summer 2010): 54–81.

Paulsen, David L. "Are Christians Mormon? Reassessing Joseph Smith's Theology in His Bicentennial." *Brigham Young University Studies* 45, no. 1 (2006): 35–128.

Perciaccante, Marianne. "The Mormon-Muslim Comparison." *Muslim World* 82, nos. 3–4 (October 1992): 296–314.

Pitzer, Donald E., ed. *America's Communal Utopias*. Chapel Hill: University of North Carolina Press, 1997.

Poll, Richard D. *Working the Divine Miracle: The Life of Apostle Henry D. Moyle*. Edited by Stan Larson. Salt Lake City: Signature Books, 1999.

Porterfield, Amanda. *Healing in the History of Christianity*. New York: Oxford University Press, 2005.

Prince, Gregory A., and Wm. Robert Wright. *David O. Mckay and the Rise of Modern Mormonism*. Salt Lake City: University of Utah Press, 2005.

Pykles, Benjamin C. "'Look Well to the West': Anti-Mormon Rhetoric and Nineteenth-Century Views of the American West." In *Archive of Restoration Culture: Summer Fellows' Papers, 2000–2002*, edited by Richard Lyman Bushman, 187–95. Provo: Joseph Fielding Smith Institute for Latter-day Saint History, 2005.

Quinn, D. Michael. "The Council of Fifty and Its Members, 1844 to 1945." *Brigham Young University Studies* 20, no. 2 (Winter 1980): 163–97.

———. *Early Mormonism and the Magic World View*. Salt Lake City: Signature Books, 1987.

———. *Early Mormonism and the Magic World View*. 2nd ed. Salt Lake City: Signature Books, 1998.

———. *Elder Statesman: A Biography of J. Reuben Clark*. Salt Lake City: Signature Books, 2002.

———. "LDS Church Authority and New Plural Marriages, 1890–1904." *Dialogue: A Journal of Mormon Thought* 18, no. 1 (Spring 1985): 9–105.

———. *The Mormon Hierarchy: Extensions of Power*. Salt Lake City: Signature Books, 1997.

———. *The Mormon Hierarchy: Origins of Power*. Salt Lake City: Signature Books, 1994.

———. "Socioreligious Radicalism of the Mormon Church: A Parallel to the Anabaptists." In *New Views of Mormon History: A Collection of Essays in Honor of Leonard J. Arrington*, edited by Davis Bitton and Maureen Ursenbach Beecher, 363–86. Salt Lake City: University of Utah Press, 1987.

Reeve, W. Paul, and Ardis E. Parshall. Review of Will Bagley, *Blood of the Prophets*. *Mormon Historical Studies* 4, no. 1 (Spring 2003): 149–57.

Remini, Robert V. *Joseph Smith*. Penguin Lives. Edited by James Atlas. New York: Viking, 2002.

Rogers, Jedediah S. "The Volatile Sagebrush Rebellion." In *Utah in the Twentieth Century*, edited by Brian Q. Cannon and Jessie L. Embry, 367–84. Logan: Utah State University Press, 2009.

Rubin, Julius H. *Religious Melancholy and Protestant Experience in America*. Religion in America. New York: Oxford University Press, 1994.

Schmidt, Leigh Eric. *Hearing Things: Religion, Illusion, and the American Enlightenment*. Cambridge: Harvard University Press, 2000.

Sehat, David. *The Myth of American Religious Freedom*. New York: Oxford University Press, 2011.

Sellers, Charles. *The Market Revolution: Jacksonian America, 1815–1846*. New York: Oxford University Press, 1991.

Sha'ban, Fuad. *Islam and Arabs in Early American Thought: The Roots of Orientalism in America*. Durham, N.C.: Acorn Press, in association with Duke University Islamic and Arabian Development Studies, 1991.

Sharpe, Eric J. *Comparative Religion: A History*. 2nd ed. La Salle, Ill.: Open Court, 1986.

Shipps, Jan. "Difference and Otherness: Mormonism and the American Religious Mainstream." In *Minority Faiths and the American Protestant Mainstream*, edited by Jonathan D. Sarna, 81–109. Urbana: University of Illinois Press, 1998.

———. "From Peoplehood to Church Membership: Mormonism's Trajectory since World War II." *Church History: Studies in Christianity and Culture* 76, no. 2 (June 2007): 241–61.

———. *Mormonism: The Story of a New Religious Tradition*. Urbana: University of Illinois Press, 1985.

———. *Sojourner in the Promised Land: Forty Years among the Mormons*. Urbana: University of Illinois Press, 2000.

Shipps, Jan, and Mark Silk, eds. *Religion and Public Life in the Mountain West: Sacred Landscapes in Transition*. Religion by Region. Walnut Creek, Calif.: AltaMira Press, 2004.

Simpson, Thomas W. "Mormons Study 'Abroad': Brigham Young's Romance with American Higher Education, 1867–77." *Church History: Studies in Christianity and Culture* 76, no. 4 (December 2007): 778–98.

Smith, Andrew F. Introduction to *The History of the Saints; or, An Exposé of Joe Smith and Mormonism by John C. Bennett*, vii–xliii. Urbana: University of Illinois Press, 2000.

———. *The Saintly Scoundrel: The Life and Times of Dr. John Cook Bennett*. Urbana: University of Illinois Press, 1997.

Smith, George D. *Nauvoo Polygamy: "But We Called It Celestial Marriage."* Salt Lake City: Signature Books, 2008.

Smith, Henry Nash. *Virgin Land: The American West as Symbol and Myth.* Cambridge: Harvard University Press, 1950.

Smith, Jonathan Z. *Imagining Religion: From Babylon to Jamestown.* Chicago Studies in the History of Judaism. Edited by Jacob Neusner, William Scott Green, and Calvin Goldsheider. Chicago: University of Chicago Press, 1982.

———. *Relating Religion: Essays in the Study of Religion.* Chicago: University of Chicago Press, 2004.

———. "Religion, Religions, Religious." In *Critical Terms for Religious Studies*, edited by Mark C. Taylor, 269–84. Chicago: University of Chicago Press, 1998.

Smith, Konden R. "Appropriating the Secular: Mormonism and the World's Columbian Exposition of 1893." *Journal of Mormon History* 34, no. 4 (Fall 2008): 153–80.

Smith, Timothy L. "The Ohio Valley: Testing Ground for America's Experiment in Religious Pluralism." *Church History* 60, no. 4 (December 1991): 461–79.

Stark, Rodney. *The Rise of Mormonism.* Edited by Reid L. Neilson. New York: Columbia University Press, 2005.

———. "The Rise of a New World Faith." *Review of Religious Research* 26, no. 1 (September 1984): 18–27.

Stein, Stephen J. *The Shaker Experience in America: A History of the United Society of Believers.* New Haven: Yale University Press, 1992.

Styers, Randall. *Making Magic: Religion, Magic, and Science in the Modern World.* New York: Oxford University Press, 2004.

Sullivan, Winnifred Fallers. *The Impossibility of Religious Freedom.* Princeton: Princeton University Press, 2005.

Talbot, Christine. "Mormonism and the Woman Question." Unpublished paper presented at the Joseph Fielding Smith Institute of Latter-day Saint History, Brigham Young University, Provo, September 2004, copy in author's possession.

———. "'Turkey Is in Our Midst': Orientalism and Contagion in Nineteenth Century Anti-Mormonism." *Journal of Law and Family Studies* 8, no. 2 (2006): 363–88.

Taves, Ann. *Fits, Trances, & Visions: Experiencing Religion and Explaining Experience from Wesley to James.* Princeton: Princeton University Press, 1999.

Taylor, Alan. "The Early Republic's Supernatural Economy: Treasure Seeking in the American Northeast, 1780–1830." *American Quarterly* 38, no. 1 (Spring 1986): 6–34.

———. "Rediscovering the Context of Joseph Smith's Treasure Seeking." *Dialogue: A Journal of Mormon Thought* 19, no. 4 (Winter 1986): 18–27.

Turner, James. *Without God, Without Creed: The Origins of Unbelief in America.* New Studies in American Intellectual and Cultural History. Baltimore: Johns Hopkins University Press, 1985.

Underwood, Grant. "Book of Mormon Usage in Early LDS Theology." *Dialogue: A Journal of Mormon Thought* 17, no. 3 (Autumn 1984): 35–74.

———. *The Millenarian World of Early Mormonism.* Urbana: University of Illinois Press, 1993.

———. "Re-visioning Mormon History." *Pacific Historical Review* 55, no. 3 (August 1986): 403–26.

Van Wagenen, Michael S. *The Texas Republic and the Mormon Kingdom of God.* No. 2, South Texas Regional Studies. College Station: Texas A&M University Press, 2002.

Van Wagoner, Richard S. *Mormon Polygamy: A History.* 2nd ed. Salt Lake City: Signature Books, 1989.

Vogel, Dan. *Joseph Smith: The Making of a Prophet.* Salt Lake City: Signature Books, 2004.

Vogel, Dan, and Scott C. Dunn. "'The Tongue of Angels': Glossolalia among Mormonism's Founders." *Journal of Mormon History* 19, no. 2 (Fall 1993): 1–34.

Wacker, Grant. *Heaven Below: Early Pentecostals and American Culture.* Cambridge: Harvard University Press, 2001.

Walker, Ronald W. "The Stenhouses and the Making of a Mormon Image." *Journal of Mormon History* 1 (1974): 51–72.

Walker, Ronald W., Richard E. Turley Jr., and Glen M. Leonard. *Massacre at Mountain Meadows.* New York: Oxford University Press, 2008.

Walker, Ronald W., David J. Whittaker, and James B. Allen. *Mormon History.* Urbana: University of Illinois Press, 2001.

Wenger, Beth S. *History Lessons: The Creation of American Jewish Heritage.* Princeton: Princeton University Press, 2010.

White, O. Kendall. *Mormon Neo-Orthodoxy: A Crisis Theology.* Salt Lake City: Signature Books, 1987.

Whittaker, David J. "The Book of Daniel in Early Mormon Thought." In *By Study and Also by Faith: Essays in Honor of Hugh W. Nibley on the Occasion of His Eightieth Birthday*, edited by John M. Lundquist and Stephen D. Ricks, 155–201. Salt Lake City and Provo: Deseret Book Co. and FARMS, 1990.

———. *Early Mormon Pamphleteering.* Dissertations in Latter-Day Saint History. Provo: Joseph Fielding Smith Institute for Latter-day Saint History and Brigham Young University Studies, 2003.

Winn, Kenneth H. *Exiles in a Land of Liberty: Mormons in America, 1830–1846.* Studies in Religion. Chapel Hill: University of North Carolina Press, 1989.

Wood, Gordon S. "Evangelical America and Early Mormonism." *New York History* 61, no. 4 (October 1980): 359–86.

Worster, Donald. *A River Running West: The Life of John Wesley Powell.* New York: Oxford University Press, 2001.

———. *Rivers of Empire: Water, Aridity, and the Growth of the American West.* New York: Pantheon Books, 1985.

Yorgason, Ethan R. *Transformation of the Mormon Culture Region.* Urbana: University of Illinois Press, 2003.

ACKNOWLEDGMENTS

I am grateful to the many talented people who have enriched this book. Three scholars have been particularly influential. Charles Cohen (University of Wisconsin–Madison), Grant Underwood (Brigham Young University [BYU]), and Kathryn Lofton (Yale University) have each given generously of their time and prodigious talents. Charles Cohen mentored the project in its early stage and has continued to be a valued conversation partner and critic. I have never known a more generous adviser or more committed teacher; each ink-drenched response to my work is now treasured evidence of his dedication to the craft. Grant Underwood has encouraged and shaped this project in hundreds of conversations. He blends a sharp mind with a gift for listening. Notorious talkers like me absolutely depend on friends like him. Kathryn Lofton's has become the scholarly voice in my head. Her intellectual gifts have the net effect of a tornado, and I have been happily caught in the storm for years. At one point, she picked me up intellectually, dusted me off, and politely willed this book into existence.

The members of the 2007–9 Young Scholars in American Religion program at the Center for the Study of Religion and American Culture (IUPUI) deserve special thanks, since their feedback and encouragement fundamentally shaped this book. Thanks to Philip Goff and Rebecca Vasko at the Center, to program leaders Paul Harvey and Amanda Porterfield, and to my cohorts Edward J. Blum, Darren Dochuk, Katherine Carté Engel, Rebecca Goetz, Charles F. Irons, Kathryn Lofton, Randall J. Stephens, Matthew A. Sutton, and Tisa J. Wenger. The time at the Center ranks as my career's unmatched highlight.

Several colleagues at Brigham Young University have left their mark on this project. Andrew Hedges was a skilled teacher and mentor who became a trusted colleague and valued friend. Former dean Robert Millet and I have spent unnumbered hours in conversation. My life has been greatly enriched by his experience and wisdom. Historian Brett Rushforth, now at the College of William and Mary, and I spent our commute together during a critical stretch of manuscript revisions; our carpool exchanges proved most helpful. College and department administrators Andrew Skinner, Kent Jackson, Raymond Wright, the late Paul Peterson, Arnold Garr, and Brent Top each offered support in various forms. Paul Peterson, especially, exemplified model leadership; I leaned on his experience and insight more than he knew. Brent Top arranged the leave that allowed me to complete the manuscript.

The University of Wisconsin–Madison history department provided exceptional training in history and religious studies. Many thanks to William Cronon, Ronald Numbers, the late Paul Boyer, Charles Hallisey, Stephen Kantrowitz, and Jean Lee. I count the late Jeanne Boydston's graduate seminars among my most significant intellectual experiences.

I twice benefited from Richard L. Bushman's expertise in American and Mormon history as a research fellow under his direction. There is no way to adequately express my gratitude for his influence on my life and career.

I am grateful to the manuscript's many readers. In addition to those already named, Lavina Fielding Anderson, Samuel Brown, Sarah Barringer Gordon, and David Holland read all or part of this work at one point or another. Sarah Gordon has been especially generous in her feedback and support. Over a period of several years, she has graciously blended expert criticism with warm encouragement. The second chapter benefited from critical readings by members of the BYU history department writing group. The fourth chapter was sharpened by members of Yale University's American religious history working group. Commentators and audience members at various scholarly meetings — the American Society of Church History, American Academy of Religion, and Mormon History Association — enhanced the text with their insightful responses. Critical conversations with Brian Birch, Kathleen Flake, Stephen Fleming, Terryl Givens, Steven Harper, Colleen McDannell, and Reid Neilson improved my thinking and interpretations.

At Brigham Young University, the staffs of the L. Tom Perry Special Collections, Harold B. Lee Library, Religious Education Faculty Support Center, Religious Studies Center, and Department of Church History and Doctrine deserve praise for their quiet excellence. At Special Collections, Larry Draper, Russ Taylor, and David Whittaker contributed expert assistance at critical junctures. The good people of the Historical Department, Church of Jesus Christ of Latter-day Saints, are worthy of similar thanks. I am grateful to Patty Smith of the Faculty Support Center for her help with manuscript preparation and for several episodes of tedious transcription. Stephen J. Greenberg and Crystal Smith at the History of Medicine Division of the National Library of Medicine offered generous assistance for some of the material appearing in the second chapter. A number of talented student assistants helped in various ways, including Megan Brimhall, Michael Taylor, Julie Stringer, Matthew Mangum, Stanley Thayne, David Golding, Nancy Madsen, Blake Behnke, Ashley Wright, Allan Davis, and Justin Haslem. Scott Marianno deserves special praise for taking on the massive source-checking duties. Grants from the University of Wisconsin–Madison Graduate School and history department made research trips possible. BYU's Religious Studies Center provided research funding. Many thanks to publications director Richard N. Holzapfel and to LDS history research directors Richard E. Bennett and Alexander Baugh.

Special thanks go to Elaine Maisner and those who work with her at the University of North Carolina Press. Elaine was supportive from the start and gave me wise feedback throughout the process. Two anonymous readers much improved the book. Together, they spent many hours on the manuscript, which I take as both a high compliment and a generous gift.

Steven K. Hatchett unstintingly contributed in the form of several rare documents. Ann E. Norton's generosity paved the way for my graduate career. My parents, Roger and Suzanne Fluhman, instilled in me what a fourth grade teacher called a "thirst for knowledge." They have ever been givers of good gifts to their children. My own children,

John, Savannah, Grace, and Sadie have been patient with some long days and distracted evenings. They are my favorite people. Finally, my wife Hollie shouldered the burden of this work with me. Her foresight prompted my entry into academia, and she has made the strains well worth the trouble. She put off a few of her own aspirations so I could write this book. I look forward to returning the favor.

INDEX

Brook Farm, 84

Brown, J. Newton, 26

Buchanan, James, 110, 117

Buck, Charles, 25–26

Buddhism (Buddhists), 16, 115, 138

Burris, John P., 129

Burton, Richard F., 120

Bush, George, 33

Bushman, Claudia L., 117

Bushman, Richard Lyman, 36

Bushnell, Horace, 106–7

Butler, Jon, 17

Calvin, John, 14, 44, 85

Campbell, Alexander, 28–29, 37, 56, 69, 73. *See also* Disciples of Christ

Campbellites. *See* Campbell, Alexander

Cannon, Martha Hughes, 122

Capitalism, 45, 84, 133–34, 141–42, 144–46

Carroll, Henry K., 138

Cartwright, Peter, 4

Carvalho, Solomon N., 119

Catholicism. *See* Roman Catholicism

Celestial marriage. *See* Polygamy

Chase, Willard, 41

Chidester, David, 119

China/Chinese, 114–15, 137

Church of England, 73, 117

Church of Jesus Christ of Latter-day Saints. *See* Mormonism

Clark, John A., 37

Clay, Henry, 100

Clayton, John M., 107

Cohen, Charles L., 81

Colas, Dominique, 85

Cole, Abner, 29, 36

Colfax, Schuyler, Jr., 124

Communitarianism, 7, 39, 45–46, 79–102 passim, 142, 144. *See also* Gathering, Mormon

Congregationalism (Congregationalists), 14, 106, 117

Consecration, law of, 45

Conyers, Josiah B., 100

Corrill, John, 88

Council of Fifty, 99, 172 (n. 122)

Counterfeiting, 9, 46–47

Cowdery, Oliver, 42–43, 70, 89

Cowdery, Warren A., 89

Cult(s), 3

Danites, 90–92

Davies, Douglas J., 3

Davis, David B., 140

Davis, George T. M., 79

Deism, 69–70, 73

DeLeon, Edwin, 31

Democracy, 16–17, 79, 92, 94–95, 113

Democratic Party (Democrats), 95–96, 109–10, 141–42

Denominationalism, 27, 69, 132

Deseret, proposed state of, 9, 106

Devil(s), 7, 56, 60

Disciples of Christ, 16, 28. *See also* Campbell, Alexander

Disestablishment, religious, 9–10, 16, 24–29, 52, 94–95

Dispensationalism, 28

Divination, 40, 42–43

Divinization, 4–5

Doctrine and Covenants, 4, 43–44, 92–94

Dodge, Augustus C., 108

Dorchester, Daniel, 137–38

Douglas, Stephen A., 100, 107, 109–10

Draper, John W., 113–15

Drew, Thomas S., 100

Dunklin, Daniel, 88

Eastern Orthodoxy, 33

Ecumenism, 2, 28

Edmunds Act (1882), 123

Edmunds-Tucker Act (1887), 142

Edwards, Jonathan, 65

Ellis, John, 74

Ely, Richard T., 140

England (Britain), 19, 25, 57, 115–17, 120–21
Enlightenment, 14, 27, 43–44, 55, 61, 69, 119, 130–31
Enoch, 83
Episcopalians, 73, 117
Ericksen, Ephraim, 140
Ethnicity, 113, 146
Evangelicalism (Evangelicals), 2, 5–6, 11, 16–17, 25, 29, 55, 58, 60–63, 65, 68–69, 75–76, 127, 133, 141. *See also* Protestantism
Evolution, theories of, 132–34

Faith healing. *See* Healing
Fanaticism, 25, 30–31, 53, 75, 83–86
Farmer, Jared, 28
Fitch, Thomas, 115
Flake, Kathleen, 18
Fleming, Stephen J., 44
Ford, Thomas, 47–48, 96–97, 100–101
Formalism, 54–55, 68, 76
Fourier, Charles, 84
Franchot, Jenny, 44
Frazer, James G., 133
Frémont, John C., 119
French Prophets, 25, 55, 57–58, 63

Gathering, Mormon, 38–39, 57, 79–102 passim. *See also* Communitarianism
Gibbon, Edward, 33
Givens, Terryl L., 18, 42, 118
Glossolalia. *See* Tongues speaking
Goetzmann, William H., 129
Gordon, Sarah Barringer, 17–18, 103, 115
Grant, Ulysses S., 124
Gregg, Thomas, 139
Guadalupe Hidalgo, Treaty of, 101
Gunnison, John W., 106, 144
Gypsies, 30

Hamburger, Philip, 17
Harmonists, 84

Harris, Martin, 35, 61, 66, 70
Harris, William, 38, 58, 71, 94
Hayes, Rutherford B., 142
Hayward, John, 73
Healing, 51, 53, 55–56, 58–60, 75
Heresy, 9–10, 18–19, 25–26, 54–55
Hermeticism, 46–47, 157 (n. 97). *See also* Magic
Heyrman, Christine Leigh, 60
Himes, Joshua V., 28, 154 (n. 34)
Hinckley, Gordon B., 1, 6
Hinduism (Hindus), 16, 116, 125
Holifield, E. Brooks, 69
Holst, Hermann Eduard von, 136
Hooper, William H., 116
Howe, Eber D., 37, 41, 44, 58, 61, 66–67, 73, 86, 88–89, 92–93
Huckabee, Mike, 7
Hume, David, 69
Hunt, James H., 74, 82
Hurlbut, D. Philastus, 37, 41
Hyde, Orson, 57, 90

Iconoclasm, 85
India, 114–17
Insanity, 49, 52, 54, 61–66, 75–76. *See also* Monomania
International Women's Year, 143
Irving, Edward, 57, 63
Irving, Washington, 36
Islam (Muslims), 3, 16, 24–25, 31–39, 98, 102, 106, 109–10, 114–15, 125

Jacobs, Ferris, Jr., 123
Japan/Japanese, 114
Jefferson, Thomas, 15, 103, 106
Jews. *See* Judaism
Johnson, Elsa, 59
Johnston, James F. W., 135
Jones, Megan Sanborn, 18
Judaism (Jews), 3, 29, 32, 34, 36–37, 81, 114–15, 125, 138–39, 145–46
Juster, Susan, 47, 84

Kane, Elizabeth W., 120
Kansas-Nebraska Act, 107
Kidder, Daniel P., 16, 52, 57
Kimball, Heber C., 112
Kirk, Thomas J., 51
Kirkbride, Thomas S., 63
Know-Nothing Party (American Party), 109

Land, Richard D., 2
Latter-day Saints. *See* Mormonism
Law, William, 99
Law of Consecration. *See* Communitarianism
Lee, Ann, 29. *See also* Shakerism
Lee, E. G., 30, 46, 61
Leiden, Jan van, 84–85
Liberalism, Protestant, 16, 62–63, 68, 133. *See also* Protestantism
Lincoln, Abraham, 110
Lucas, Samuel, 30, 87
Luther, Martin, 85, 116
Lyman, Francis M., 142
Lyon, Caleb, 108

Madness. *See* Insanity
Magic, 10–11, 15, 39–44, 46–47, 159 (n. 119). *See also* Astrology; Hermeticism; Witchcraft
Marks, David, 71, 73
Marsh, Eliza, 68
Marsh, Thomas B., 90
Masculinity, 122–24
Mason, Patrick Q., 18
Masuzawa, Tomoko, 114–15
Matthews, Margaret, 30
Matthews, Robert. *See* Matthias
Matthias (Robert Matthews), 21, 29–31, 75, 85
Matthys, Jan, 84
Mattison, Hiram, 29
Mazur, Eric M., 18
Mazzuchelli, Samuel, 28

M'Chesney, James, 30, 36, 38
Melanchthon, Philip, 85
Mesmerism, 49
Methodism (Methodists), 4, 16, 41, 59, 76, 125
Miles, George H., 34
Millennialism/Millennium, 28, 83–86, 99, 130, 134
Miller, William. *See* Millerism
Millerism (Millerites), 16, 63–64
Mining, 144–45
Miracles, 44–45, 52–61, 69–77. *See also* Healing; Spiritual gifts
Missouri, anti-Mormonism in, 53, 56–57, 82, 86–89, 111–12
Monomania, 49, 66, 76. *See also* Insanity
Moore, R. Laurence, 118
Mormonism (Mormons): classification of, 1–5, 14, 116, 127–32, 146–47; relationship to Protestantism, 2–5; and perceptions of history, 3–4, 6–7; and neo-orthodoxy, 5; in modern historiography, 6–7, 12, 16–17, 106, 134–40, 151 (n. 27); and authoritarianism, 11–12, 17, 28, 89, 111; organized resistance to, 12–13; early theology, 28–29; and cooperative economics/communitarianism, 44–46, 79–91; and tongues speaking, 56–57; and healing, 59–60; and biblical hermeneutics, 66–68; and revivalism, 76–77; and evangelism, 81–82, 111; statement on religious freedom, 82–83; and race, 111–12. *See also* Book of Mormon; Communitarianism; Gathering, Mormon; Nauvoo, Ill.; Polygamy; Smith, Joseph, Jr.
Morrill, Justin S., 109
Morrill Anti-Bigamy Act (1862), 110, 117, 142
Mountain Meadows massacre, 12
Muhammad, 24–25, 29–39, 47, 67, 90, 98, 102, 106, 110, 125. *See also* Islam

Stone, William L., 75, 85
Stowe, Harriet Beecher, 120
Stowell, Josiah, 41
Strong, Josiah, 141
Styers, Randall, 43
Sullivan, Winnifred Fallers, 18
Sunderland, La Roy, 59–60, 72–73, 92–93
Suttee, 116. *See also* India
Swartzell, William, 38, 58
Swedenborgianism (Swedenborgians), 125

Talbot, Christine, 118, 123
Tanner, Annie Clark, 143
Taves, Ann, 15, 54
Taylor, John, 124
Temple, 37, 97, 100, 106, 121, 145
Thatcher, Moses, 142
Theocracy, 9, 12, 91–101, 106–9, 119, 122, 125, 137–42
Theo-democracy. *See* Theocracy
Thugee, 116. *See also* India
Tongues speaking, 53, 55–58, 75
Towle, Nancy, 52–53, 68
Transcendentalism, 84
Transubstantiation, 45. *See also* Roman Catholicism
Tsvi, Shabbatai, 29. *See also* Judaism
Turner, Jonathan B., 30, 67, 74–75, 94

Unitarianism (Unitarians), 25, 55, 68, 139. *See also* Liberalism, Protestant
United Society of Believers in Christ's Second Appearing. *See* Shakerism
U.S. Constitution, 14, 17–18, 97, 100, 103, 106, 109, 115–16
U.S. Supreme Court, 103–5, 110–11, 115–16
Universalism (Universalists), 16, 28
Urim and Thummim, 42–43, 158 (n. 108). *See also* Seer stones
Utah statehood, 12–14, 140
Utah War, 109–10, 122

Van Buren, Martin, 35

Waite, Morrison R., 103, 110–11, 123
Wallace, Mike, 1
Ward, Austin N. (pseud.), 119
Ward, Maria N. (pseud.), 119
Wenger, Beth S., 146
Wetmore, Alphonso, 87
Whig Party (Whigs), 95–96
Whitefield, George, 65
Whitman, Jason, 55, 68
Whitmer, David, 70
Whitmer, John, 51
Whitney, Helen Mar Kimball, 121–22
Widtsoe, John A., 133
Wight, Lyman, 90
Wilkinson, Jemima, 29
Winn, Kenneth H., 18, 54
Witchcraft, 46, 52, 60. *See also* Magic
Wood, Gordon S., 38
Woodruff, Wilford, 1, 56
World religions, 3, 105, 114–15, 129–34. *See also* Buddhism; Hinduism; Islam; Judaism
World's Columbian Exposition (Chicago, 1893), 129–31

Xenoglossia. *See* Tongues speaking

Yorgason, Ethan R., 140, 143
Young, Ann Eliza Webb, 121
Young, Brigham, 12, 19, 51, 56, 84, 100, 107, 109, 111, 121, 143
Young, Joseph, 1

Zion, city of. *See* Communitarianism; Gathering, Mormon
Zion's Camp, 87–89, 92
Zwingli, Ulrich, 14, 44